DATE DUE

MY 24 '96			
NO 8 '96			
JA 2 '97			
MY 27 '99			
MR 29 '01			

DEMCO 38-296

ENDANGERED PEOPLES

ENDANGERED PEOPLES

Indigenous Rights and the Environment

**Colorado Journal of International
Environmental Law and Policy**

University Press of Colorado

Published by the University Press of Colorado
P.O. Box 849
Niwot, CO 80544

The University Press of Colorado is a cooperative publishing enterprise supported,
in part, by Adams State College, Colorado State University, Fort Lewis College,
Mesa State College, Metropolitan State College of Denver, University of Colorado,
University of Northern Colorado, University of Southern Colorado, and Western
State College of Colorado.

ISBN 0-87081-340-4

About the Contributors

JOY K. ASIEMA is a lecturer at the Kenya School of Law in Nairobi, Kenya, and is an attorney for the firm of Hamilton Harrison & Mathews, Advocates. She received her Bachelor of Laws at the University of Nairobi in 1987, and her LL.M. from Harvard Law School in 1992.

STANWOOD CURTIS FISH served as a legal extern from Vermont Law School in the Conservation Economics Department of Conservation International in the summer and fall of 1993. His studies and work have emphasized intellectual property and international resource law. Mr. Fish received his B.A. from Dartmouth College in 1990 and expects his J.D. and Masters in Environmental Law from Vermont Law School in May of 1994.

ROBERT K. HITCHCOCK is an Assistant Professor of Anthropology and the Coordinator of African Studies at the University of Nebraska, Lincoln, Nebraska. He has worked on rural development and human rights issues among indigenous peoples in southern and eastern Africa since 1975. In 1983–84 he was the Planning Advisor and Research Manager in the National Refugee Commission, Government of Somalia. In 1988 and 1990 he conducted evaluations of the Accelerated Remote Area Development Program for the Government of Botswana and the Norwegian Agency for International Development (NORAD). His work on the impacts of conservation policies and natural resource management projects among indigenous peoples in Zimbabwe was conducted in 1989 and 1992. He is the editor of *International Human Rights and Indigenous Peoples* with C. Patrick Morris and has written numerous articles on the status of indigenous peoples, especially those in Africa.

WINONA LADUKE, a member of the Mississippi Band Anishinabe, is Campaign Director of the White Earth Land Recovery Program, a reservation-based land and environmental advocacy and acquisition organization on the White Earth Reservation of Anishinabeg in northern Minnesota. She also serves as the Program Officer for the Seventh Generation Fund, a national native foundation providing grants to grassroots native environmental and social justice organizations. Ms. LaDuke has worked and written extensively on native environmental issues. She serves on the steering committee of the Indigenous Environmental Network and sits on the board of Greenpeace, USA. She was a visiting professor in International Affairs at the University of Oregon in 1993.

STEVEN M. RUBIN serves as the Director of the Conservation Economics Department of Conservation International in Washington, D.C. His Department provides technical assistance to Conservation International's field programs in countries throughout the world on issues in biodiversity prospecting, conservation finance, biodiversity product marketing, forestry economics, and ecotourism. Mr. Rubin worked as an attorney in private international law practice and as a consultant to international development agencies before joining Conservation International in 1989. He is the author of The Economist Publications' *Guide to Debt Equity Swaps in the 1990s* (Special Report No. 1203 & 1204). Mr. Rubin received his B.A. from Brown University in 1976 and his J.D. from the University of Southern California Law School in 1979.

FRANCIS D. P. SITUMA is a candidate for a Ph.D. at the Fletcher School of Law & Diplomacy at Tufts University in Medford, Mass., where he received his M.A. in Law and Diplomacy in 1992. He then was a teaching fellow at Harvard University. He has been appointed as an environmental law consultant to the United Nations Programe in Nairobi, Kenya. Mr. Situma received his Bachelor of Laws and LL.M. from the University of Nairobi.

MARIA STAVRAPOULOU is an assistant to the Representative of the UN Secretary General on Internally Displaced Persons. She also drafts reports for the General Assembly and the Commission on Human Rights as part of the mandate on Human Rights and Mass Exoduses in Geneva, Switzerland. She has worked for the UN High Commissioner for Refugees as an advocate for refugees and asylum seekers in Athens, Greece. Ms. Stavrapoulou received her LL.M. from both Harvard Law School and University College in London, England, after earning her Law Degree from the University of Athens School of Law.

CHRISTOPHER T. STEARNS is an associate with Hobbs, Straus, Dean & Wilder, a Washington, D.C., law firm specializing in the representation of American Indian and Alaska Native tribes and tribal organizations throughout the United States. Mr. Stearns received his J.D. from Cornell Law School and his B.A. from Williams College. Mr. Stearns represents Indian tribes and tribal organizations in matters involving tribal health issues, civil jurisdictional issues, educational issues, Indian Self-Determination Act contracts, and Self-Governance compacts. Mr. Stearns also has served as a board member of the Native American Bar Association (1992-1993) and taught a course in American Indian film stereotypes at the Maryland Institute College of Art (1993). Mr. Stearns is Navajo.

DEAN B. SUAGEE is of counsel to the Washington, D.C., law firm of Hobbs, Straus, Dean & Wilder, one of the nation's leading private law firms specializing in serving as legal counsel to American Indian and Alaska Native tribal governments and tribal organizations. Mr. Suagee received his J.D. from the University of North Carolina and his LL.M. in international legal studies from the American University. He specializes in environmental law and has worked with a number of tribal governments on environmental and cultural resource matters, including the establishment of tribal regulatory programs for environmental protection. His experience includes positions with the National Congress of American Indians and the Bureau of Indian Affairs. He is the author of several articles on environmental and cultural resources law in Indian country. He is a member of the Cherokee Nation.

ALBERT E. UTTON is a Professor of Law and the Director of the International Transboundary Resources Center at the University of New Mexico School of Law. Mr. Utton received his M.A. Jur. from Oxford University and his B.A. from the University of New Mexico. He is the editor-in-chief of the *Natural Resources Journal*. Mr. Utton serves on the Advisory Board of the *Colorado Journal of International Environmental Law and Policy*.

Table of Contents

ENDANGERED PEOPLES

Colorado Journal of International Environmental Law and Policy

International Human Rights, the Environment, and Indigenous Peoples

Robert K. Hitchcock[†]

The General Assembly of the United Nations, (UN), declared in December 1991 that the year beginning October 1, 1992, would be "The International Year for the World's Indigenous People." The goal of the International Year designation was to strengthen efforts to increase coordination, cooperation, and technical assistance "for the solution of problems faced by indigenous communities in such areas as human rights, the environment, development, education, and health."[1] The decision to acknowledge the importance of indigenous groups was made in part to pay homage to those peoples who, over the past 500 years since Columbus's arrival in the New World, have been affected so negatively by colonization and massive social change.

It has been suggested that a significant percentage of the world's people do not enjoy basic civil liberties and human rights today.[2] More than a billion people are poverty-stricken, and as many as a million people are enslaved. Indigenous peoples compose one segment of the world's population facing conditions that are especially stark.[3]

---

† Assistant Professor of Anthropology and the Coordinator of African Studies at the University of Nebraska, Lincoln, Nebraska, USA.
1. G.A. Res. 128, U.N. GAOR, 46th Sess., U.N. Doc. A/RES/46/128, 1991 U.N.Y.B. 540.
2. AMNESTY INT'L, AMNESTY INT'L REP. 1993, at 2 (1993).
3. For discussions of the status of indigenous peoples, see JULIAN BURGER, REPORT FROM THE FRONTIER: THE STATE OF THE WORLD'S INDIGENOUS PEOPLES (1987); STATE OF THE PEOPLES: A GLOBAL HUMAN RIGHTS REPORT ON SOCIETIES IN DANGER (Marc S. Miller, ed., 1993) [hereinafter STATE OF THE PEOPLES].

Sometimes called aboriginals, native peoples, tribal peoples, Fourth World peoples, or "first nations," indigenous peoples have suffered acts of genocide and discrimination and a lack of equal opportunity in employment for centuries. Despite widespread international concern over human rights, particularly since the end of the Second World War, indigenous peoples have suffered more serious abuses than those perpetrated upon most, if not all, other groups. Some analysts argue that indigenous peoples are probably the single most disadvantaged set of populations in the world today.[4]

I. DEFINING THE WORLD'S INDIGENOUS PEOPLES

The term "indigenous peoples" is usually used in reference to those individuals and groups who are descendants of the original populations residing in a country. It is estimated that there are 300,000,000 to 357,000,000 indigenous people residing in some 75 of the world's 184 countries, or about 6 percent of the world's population (see table 1). These peoples are quite diverse. They range from the highly urbanized Maaori of New Zealand to small, mobile groups of Aka foragers in the rain forests of central Africa, from sizable Indian peasant communities in South and Central America to pastoral nomads in the mountains of Pakistan and Afghanistan.

No single agreed-upon definition of the term "indigenous peoples" exists. According to the Independent Commission on International Humanitarian Issues, four elements are included in the definition of indigenous peoples: (1) pre-existence; (2) non-dominance; (3) cultural difference; and (4) self-identification as indigenous.[5] In some cases, the term indigenous applies to non-European groups residing in regions that were colonized by Europeans. The UN Special Rapporteur on the Problem of Discrimination Against Indigenous Populations notes that the term indigenous applies to those people who are isolated socially or to marginal groups that have managed to preserve their traditions in spite of being incorporated into states dominated by other societies.[6]

Analysts and researchers employ various approaches when defining indigenous peoples. The International Labour Organisation (ILO) and the nongovernmental organization Survival International use the term "tribal

---

4. Julian Burger, *An International Agenda, in* STATE OF THE PEOPLES, *supra* note 3, at 4.

5. INDEPENDENT COMMISSION ON INT'L HUMANITARIAN ISSUES, INDIGENOUS PEOPLES: A GLOBAL QUEST FOR JUSTICE 6 (1987).

6. JOSÉ R. MARTÍNEZ COBO, STUDY OF THE PROBLEM OF DISCRIMINATION AGAINST INDIGENOUS POPULATIONS, VOLUME V, CONCLUSIONS, PROPOSALS, AND RECOMMENDATIONS, U.N. Doc. E/CN.4/Sub.2/1986/7/Add.4 (1987).

TABLE 1. Estimated Numbers of the World's Indigenous Peoples[7]

Region	Number of Groups	Overall Population
North America	250	3,500,000
Indians (Canada) (633 bands)		1,500,000
Indians (United States) (515 tribes)		2,000,000
Latin America and	800	40,000,000
the Caribbean		
Ache (Paraguay)		400
Mapuche (Chile)		600,000
Miskito (Nicaragua)		75,000
Yanomami (Brazil, Venezuela)		15,000
Former Soviet Union	135	40,000,000
Saami (Russia)		65,000
China and Japan	56	67,000,000
Ainu (Hokkaido, Japan)		26,000
Shui (Guizhou, China)		280,000
The Pacific	750	2,000,000
Papuans (New Guinea)		1,300,000
South Asia	700	70,000,000
Adivasis (India)		63,000,000
Tribals (Bangladesh)		1,200,000
Southeast Asia	500	30,000,000
Orang Asli (Malaysia)		71,000
Penan (Borneo)		20,000
Thailand Hill Tribes		484,000
Australia and New	100	550,000
Zealand		
Aboriginals		300,000
Maaori (New Zealand)		250,000
Africa	2,000	50,000,000
Batwa (Pygmies) (7 countries, central)		200,000
Bushmen (San) (6 countries, southern)		95,000
Eyle (Somalia)		450
Hadza (Tanzania)		1,000
Maasai (Tanzania/Kenya)		500,000
Tuareg (Tamacheq) (5 countries, west)		3,000,000
GRAND TOTAL	5,290	357,000,000

7. The data contained in this table have been obtained from a wide variety of sources, including government censuses, reports of development agencies, and anthropological studies. Information was also drawn from BURGER, *supra* note 3; JULIAN BURGER, THE GAIA ATLAS OF FIRST PEOPLES: A FUTURE FOR THE INDIGENOUS WORLD (1990); ALAN THEIN DURNING, GUARDIANS OF THE LAND: INDIGENOUS PEOPLES AND THE HEALTH OF THE EARTH 8-14 (Worldwatch Paper 112, 1992); INTERNATIONAL WORK GROUP FOR INDIGENOUS AFFAIRS YEARBOOK 1991 (1992); *The Map: Earliest Residents*, WORLD MONITOR, March, 1993, at 11 (map insert).

and indigenous peoples" (and in the past also used "semi-tribal peoples").[8] The UN, the World Bank, and many indigenous groups prefer to use the term "indigenous peoples." The World Bank's Operational Directive on Indigenous Peoples stresses that no single definition is appropriate to cover the diversity of indigenous peoples. It then goes on to point out that these peoples can be identified by the following characteristics: (1) close attachment to ancestral territories and natural resources; (2) self-identification and identification by others as members of a distinct cultural group; (3) possession of an indigenous language, which is often distinct from a national language; (4) presence of customary social or political institutions; and (5) subsistence-oriented production systems.[9]

It is important to note that some indigenous peoples do not fit these criteria. Substantial numbers of indigenous peoples have been dispossessed so that they no longer retain their ancestral territories. They also have been denied access to natural resources in many of the countries in which they live. In Africa, for example, wildlife rights generally are restricted by the state, and indigenous people can be arrested and jailed for illegal hunting. Most African, Asian, and Native American indigenous peoples have market-oriented production systems. There are also indigenous peoples who do not have what many anthropologists would define as tribal sociopolitical systems (such as some Bushmen groups in southern Africa, Hadza in Tanzania, Penan in Sarawak, and Agta in the Philippines). Rather, they have relatively egalitarian systems and tend to lack sodalities (non–kin–based social units such as age grades and gender-based systems) and clan-type social institutions.

Indigenous peoples generally possess ethnic, religious, or linguistic characteristics that are different from the dominant groups in the societies where they exist. They also tend to have a sense of cultural identity or social solidarity that many members attempt to maintain. In some cases, members of indigenous groups try to hide their identity so as not to suffer racial prejudice or poor treatment at the hands of others. In other cases, they proclaim their ethnic affiliation proudly and openly.

II. SELF-GOVERNANCE AND SOVEREIGNTY AMONG INDIGENOUS PEOPLES

One of the most important issues facing indigenous peoples is that of sovereignty or, as many indigenous leaders put it, self-determination. An

---

8. INTERNATIONAL LABOUR OFFICE, INDIGENOUS PEOPLES: LIVING AND WORKING CONDITIONS OF ABORIGINAL POPULATIONS IN INDEPENDENT COUNTRIES 3-27 (1953) [hereinafter ILO, INDIGENOUS PEOPLES]; Virginia Luling, *Campaigning for Indigenous Peoples, in* INTERNATIONAL HUMAN RIGHTS AND INDIGENOUS PEOPLES (C. Patrick Morris & Robert K. Hitchcock, eds., forthcoming 1994) [hereinafter MORRIS & HITCHCOCK].
9. WORLD BANK, WORLD BANK OPERATIONAL MANUAL (1991) (Statement No. 2.34).

examination of the sociopolitical status of indigenous groups around the world reveals that very few of them are in control of the governments of the countries where they reside. The vast majority lack political power at the national or even the regional level.

A major reason for this situation is that many indigenous peoples were designated by colonial governments as "wards of the state," without legal rights to participate in political decisionmaking or to control their own futures.[10] This is true, for example, in Brazil, where Indians are designated in the Brazilian Civil Code as being under the tutelage of the state and thus legally are considered minors. As a result, they are neither allowed legally to own land, nor to undertake legal activities on their own behalf.[11]

Over the past 500 years literally millions of indigenous peoples have been either killed or dispossessed. Most indigenous peoples have also had to cope with state policies aimed at assimilating them into national societies through processes of forced acculturation. Penan in Malaysia and Amarakaeri Indians in Peru have been jailed for opposing the actions of logging companies. Mining activities in the Amazon have led to substantial numbers of deaths from disease and, in some cases, to the murders of local people, as was the case recently on the Venezuela-Brazil border.[12]

A large percentage of indigenous populations live below the poverty line. Infant mortality rates are high and health standards tend to be low. Some indigenous peoples live in remote areas, where they lack access to social services and markets. Others reside in urban slums with limited access to clean water and employment opportunities. The percentages of American Indians and Australian Aboriginals in prison are much higher than percentages for other groups, something that has been attributed in part to stiffer sentences.[13] Clearly, the situations faced by indigenous peoples merit significant international attention and remedy.

---

10. JOHN H. BODLEY, VICTIMS OF PROGRESS 12-14 (3d ed. 1990); C. Patrick Morris, *International Human Rights and Indigenous Peoples: The Failure of Guardianship*, in MORRIS & HITCHCOCK, *supra* note 8.

11. CODE CIVIL (Braz.) art. 6, III, art. 7 para. 2; For a discussion of this issue, *see* Lee Swepston, *The Indian in Latin America: Approaches to Administration, Integration, and Protection*, 27 BUFF. L. REV. 715 (1978).

12. James Brooke, *Miners Kill 20 Indians in the Amazon*, N.Y. TIMES, Aug. 20, 1993, at A10; Terrence Turner, *Brazil's Guilt in the Amazon Massacre*, N.Y. TIMES, Aug. 26, 1993, at A21; Survival Int'l, *Goldminers Massacre 19 Yanomami*, URGENT ACTION BULL. (Sept. 1993).

13. AMNESTY INTERNATIONAL, AUSTRALIA: A CRIMINAL JUSTICE SYSTEM WEIGHTED AGAINST ABORIGINAL PEOPLE (1993); AMNESTY INTERNATIONAL, UNITED STATES OF AMERICA: HUMAN RIGHTS AND AMERICAN INDIANS (1992); ELIZABETH S. GROBSMITH, INDIANS IN PRISON: INCARCERATED NATIVE AMERICANS IN NEBRASKA (forthcoming, 1994); Elizabeth S. Grobsmith, *The Relationship Between Substance Abuse and Crime Among Native American Inmates in the Nebraska Department of Corrections*, 48 HUM. ORGANIZATION 285 (1989); Frank Pommersheim & Steve Wise, *Going to the Penitentiary: A Study of Disparate Sentencing in South Dakota*, 16 CRIM. JUST. & BEHAV. 155 (1989).

III. INTERNATIONAL HUMAN RIGHTS EFFORTS ON BEHALF OF INDIGENOUS PEOPLES

In the past forty years there has been a dramatic upsurge in activity to promote human rights for indigenous peoples. A variety of organizations have been formed to enhance the well-being of these populations. Numerous meetings have been held to focus on the plight of indigenous peoples, particularly over the past twenty years. Investigations of human rights violations against specific groups of indigenous peoples have been conducted, as occurred in the 1970s, when Aché Indians in Paraguay were killed and enslaved,[14] and in the Chittagong Hill Tracts of Bangladesh, where genocidal actions have been carried out against tribal peoples.[15]

More and more calls have been heard from indigenous peoples themselves for protection of their basic rights. Yet even today there are only a few international human rights instruments that deal specifically with indigenous peoples, (For a list of the various declarations, statements, and charters relating to indigenous peoples' rights, see Appendix). For decades, the only international legal statement that dealt directly with indigenous peoples' rights was a convention (No. 107) passed in 1957 by the ILO and ratified by fewer than thirty countries.

The rights of indigenous peoples have emerged as a significant topic of discussion in international human rights forums primarily during the past decade. In 1982 the UN established a Working Group on Indigenous Populations under the auspices of the Sub-Commission on the Prevention of Discrimination and Protection of Minorities of the UN Human Rights Commission. One of the tasks of this working group was to produce a document on "The Universal Declaration on Rights of Indigenous Peoples," a draft of which was completed in July 1993 and submitted by the members of the Working Group for consideration by the Sub-Commission at its 46th session in August 1994.[16] Eventually, the declaration will be ratified by the General Assembly of the UN, although the exact wording of its various provisions may be altered somewhat.

---

14. Mark Münzell, *Manhunt, in* GENOCIDE IN PARAGUAY 19 (Richard Arens, ed., 1976).

15. Anti-Slavery Society, *The Chittagong Hill Tracts: Militarization, Oppression, and the Hill Tribes, in* GENOCIDE IN THE CHITTAGONG HILL TRACTS, BANGLADESH, INTERNATIONAL WORK GROUP FOR INDIGENOUS AFFAIRS DOC. 51 (Wolfgang Mey ed., 1984).

16. *Report of the Working Group on Indigenous Populations on its eleventh session,* U.N. Comm. on Human Rights, Sub-Comm. on Prevention of Discrimination and Protection of Minorities, 11th Sess., Annex I, Agenda Item 14, U.N. Doc. E/CN.4/Sub.2/1993/29 (1993) [hereinafter Draft Declaration]. For a discussion of the Draft Declaration, *see* Katja Kvaale, *The 11th Session of the UN Working Group on Indigenous Peoples (WGIP),* INT'L WORK GROUP FOR INDIGENOUS AFF. NEWSL., July-Sept. 1993; Anti-Slavery Int'l, *UN Drafts Rights for Indigenous Peoples,* ANTI-SLAVERY NEWSL., Oct. 1993, at 2.

A. Historical Protections Afforded Indigenous Peoples

Consideration of indigenous peoples' rights dates back to the early colonial period, when missionaries and interested individuals attempted to ensure that members of these groups were protected from the actions of settlers and individuals bent on gaining access to their lands, resources, and labor. The destruction of indigenous peoples and the alteration of their ways of life were issues addressed in parliamentary discussions in England in the eighteenth and nineteenth centuries, especially during debates over the question of slavery. The US government entered into treaties with indigenous peoples, something which indicated a tacit recognition of sovereignty. As a US representative to the Berlin Africa Conference in 1885 noted:

> Modern international law follows closely a line which leads to the recognition of the rights of native tribes to dispose freely of themselves and of their hereditary territory. In conformity with this principle my Government would gladly adhere to a more extended rule based on a principle which should aim at the voluntary consent of natives whose country is taken possession of in all cases where they have not provoked the aggression.[17]

In spite of these statements, the various representatives to the Berlin Conference refused to accept the notion that peoples considered "uncivilized" had sufficient rights to enable them to have a say in governance and land matters.[18] Settler states had legal instruments that considered land occupied by indigenous peoples as *terra nullius*, or land which was empty and thus open to occupation by colonial powers. This meant, in essence, that the colonizing agents were not required to pay compensation for the lands or resources over which they assumed control. They also had the option of removing the indigenous people residing there and relocating them.[19]

Aboriginal land rights and governance questions were addressed in detail in court cases and governmental decisions throughout the nineteenth and the early twentieth centuries and were the subject of a detailed assessment by a leading international lawyer, A. H. Snow who wrote a book on aboriginal rights for the US delegation to the Versailles Conference in 1919.[20] As Snow noted, some states had begun to accept the idea that they were obligated to carry out actions on behalf of indigenous peoples:

---

17. *Quoted in* ALPHEUS H. SNOW, THE QUESTION OF ABORIGINES IN THE LAW AND PRACTICE OF NATIONS (1919), *reprinted in* 20 THE INQUIRY HANDBOOKS 152 (1974).

18. GORDON BENNETT, ABORIGINAL RIGHTS IN INTERNATIONAL LAW 4 (Occasional Paper No. 37 of the Royal Anthropological Institute of Great Britain and Ireland, 1978).

19. *See e.g.*, KENT MCNEIL, COMMON LAW ABORIGINAL TITLE 193-306 (1989).

20. SNOW, *supra* note 17.

that guardianship of aboriginal tribes implies not merely protection, not merely a benevolence toward private missionary, charitable, and educational effort, but a positive duty of direct legislative, executive, and judicial domination of aborigines as minor wards of the nation and equally direct legislative, executive, and judicial tutorship of them for civilization, so that they may become in the shortest possible time civil and political adults participating on an equality in their own government under democratic and republican institutions.[21]

The "positive duty" of states to ensure that indigenous peoples in their areas received fair and just treatment was stated specifically in the Covenant of the League of Nations.[22] This covenant eventually was replaced by Chapter XI of the United Nations Charter, which requires member states responsible for overseeing "non–self–governing territories" to ensure that the welfare of people is promoted.[23]

A major strategy of the UN and other multilateral bodies concerned with indigenous peoples has been to conduct studies of their situations. The actual implementation of these studies, however, has not been easy. In May 1949, the UN General Assembly resolved that the Economic and Social Council should, with help from various specialized agencies and from the Inter-American Indian Institute, carry out investigations of the situations of indigenous peoples in the Americas. The United States resisted attempts to conduct such studies, in part because it did not wish to be held up for criticism by other UN member states. It was not until the 1970s and early 1980s that the UN was able to obtain detailed information on indigenous peoples' statuses.[24]

---

21. *Id.* at 108.

22. LEAGUE OF NATIONS COVENANT art. 23, para. b.

23. U.N. CHARTER art. 73; BENNETT, *supra* note 18, at 12.

24. For examples of the detailed data, *see Study of the Problem of Discrimination Against Indigenous Populations, Final Report (Supplementary Part)*, Comm. on Human Rights, Subcomm. on Prevention of Discrimination and Protection of Minorities, 35th Sess., Agenda Item 12, U.N. Doc. E/CN.4/Sub.2/1982/2/Add.1 (1982) (on action taken by UN agencies); *Study of the Problem of Discrimination Against Indigenous Populations, Final Report (Supplementary Part)*, Comm. on Human Rights, Subcomm. on Prevention of Discrimination and Protection of Minorities, 35th Sess., Agenda Item 12, U.N. Doc. E/CN.4/Sub.2/1982/2/Add.2 (1982) (on action taken by the Organization of American States); *Study of the Problem of Discrimination Against Indigenous Populations, Final Report (Supplementary Part)*, Comm. on Human Rights, Subcomm. on Prevention of Discrimination and Protection of Minorities, 35th Sess., Agenda Item 12, U.N. Doc. E/CN.4/Sub.2/1982/2/Add.3 (1982) (on employment and occupational training). *See also* Howard R. Berman, *The Development of International Recognition of the Rights of Indigenous Peoples, in* THE QUESTION OF INDIGENOUS PEOPLES IN AFRICA (Jens Dahl et al., eds., forthcoming 1994); Douglas Sanders, *The Re-Emergence of Indigenous Questions in International Law*, 1983 CAN. HUM. RTS. Y.B. 3; Douglas Sanders, *The UN Working Group on Indigenous Populations*, 11 HUM. RTS. Q. 406 (1989).

The ILO and other specialized UN agencies have been concerned with indigenous peoples' well-being since the early 1920s. These international bodies have examined the situations faced by indigenous workers, some of whom provided services at exploitative levels.[25] In 1926, the ILO Governing Body set up a Committee of Experts on Native Labour to frame international standards for indigenous workers. The primary objective of the ILO was to improve the living and working conditions of indigenous and tribal peoples and to adopt various instruments aimed at protecting vulnerable populations. In 1956, the International Labour Conference decided that greater attention should be paid to the rights of indigenous peoples, many of whom were non–wage earning in spite of their importance to the economies of the countries in which they lived.

After fairly extensive discussions and reviews of information on the working conditions of indigenous peoples in various parts of the world, the ILO adopted a convention (No. 107) concerning the Protection and Integration of Indigenous and Other Tribal and Semi-Tribal Populations in Independent Countries in 1957.[26] This convention—which contained articles on general policy, land, employment, training, education, rural industries, social security and health, and administration—was the only international human rights instrument covering the rights of indigenous peoples for a period of thirty years.

The articles of Convention 107 that dealt specifically with protection of the land and indigenous peoples resource access rights are Articles 11 through 14.[27] These articles hold that the rights of ownership, collective or individual, over lands of the members of indigenous and tribal populations are recognized and that populations concerned shall not be removed without their consent. In cases where removals are necessary, people are to be provided with lands of quality at least equal to that of the lands they occupied previously. Compensation is to be provided in kind, or in cash, or both for losses suffered.

Although the intentions of the ILO's Convention 107 designers were aimed at protecting and promoting indigenous and tribal peoples' political and economic rights, the instrument fell short in several areas. First, there was no mechanism for enforcement of the Convention's provisions. Second, the Convention was geared toward integrating indigenous and

---

25. ILO, INDIGENOUS PEOPLES, *supra* note 8; Lee Swepston, *International Protection of Indigenous and Tribal Peoples, in* MORRIS & HITCHCOCK, *supra* note 8.

26. International Labour Organisation Convention (No. 107) Concerning the Protection and Integration of Indigenous and Other Tribal and Semi-Tribal Populations in Independent Countries, June 26, 1957, 328 U.N.T.S. 247 [hereinafter ILO CONVENTION].

27. *Id.* arts. 11-14, 328 U.N.T.S. at 256-58.

tribal peoples into the national societies of the countries in which they lived, something that many indigenous groups felt was deleterious to their interests. Some leaders of indigenous groups called for revisions of Convention 107 because of what they perceived to be its paternalistic approach.[28]

Work began on a revision of Convention 107 at the ILO in Geneva in 1986.[29] Unlike the deliberations in Geneva in the 1950s, indigenous peoples played an active role in the discussions. It was argued at the ILO meetings that too little attention had been paid to the cultural rights of indigenous peoples in the previous convention, especially the rights of people to maintain their social and political integrity and their religious institutions. It was also noted that Convention 107 essentially permitted the non–consensual removal of peoples from their traditional territories "for reasons relating to national security, or in the interest of national economic development . . . ."[30] At the same time, there were no protections of indigenous lands from alienation through sale or mortgage to non–indigenous peoples.

The experience of indigenous populations from the mid-1940s through the mid-1980s was such that international development programs were seen as a means of depriving them of their lands and natural resources. This was particularly true of large-scale hydroelectric projects, agricultural programs, mining and petroleum extraction activities, and development programs aimed at assisting nonindigenous peoples to settle in the territories of indigenous peoples. (For a listing of some of the development projects that have had negative impacts on indigenous peoples, see Table 2). Many indigenous groups felt themselves to be essentially "victims of progress," because the majority of development projects appeared to be in the interests of governments, international agencies, and nonlocal people. It was for this reason that indigenous leaders began to press for greater recognition of their social, economic, and cultural rights and particularly for the right of self-determination. The debates over the revisions of Convention 107 underscored the fact that indigenous peoples wanted a greater say in political decisionmaking at an international level. These discussions led to the drawing up of a new convention (No. 169), which came into force on September 5, 1991.[31]

---

28. Russel L. Barsh, *Indigenous Peoples: An Emerging Object of International Law*, 80 AM. J. INT'L L. 369, 370 (1986).

29. Russel L. Barsh, *Revision of ILO Convention No. 107*, 81 AM. J. INT'L L. 756 (1987).

30. ILO CONVENTION, *supra* note 26, art. XII, para. 1, 328 U.N.T.S. at 256.

31. International Labour Organisation Convention (No. 169) Concerning Indigenous and Tribal Peoples in Independent Countries, June 27, 1989, 28 I.L.M. 1382.

Some of the principles of Convention No. 169 were incorporated into the draft "Universal Declaration of the Rights of Indigenous Peoples" which was drawn up by the various members of the Working Group on Indigenous Populations in the late 1980s and early 1990s.[32] This new document is a far-reaching statement of both the collective and individual rights of indigenous peoples. Self-determination is a key principle in the draft declaration, as is the right to full recognition of their own laws and customs, land tenure systems, and institutions for the management of land and natural resources. The Universal Declaration on the Rights of Indigenous Peoples underscores the importance of environmental protection, something that is considered a human right in the current draft. The document also stresses the significance of indigenous peoples' land rights and ownership and control of natural resources.

B. Current Efforts—Self Help

Today there are over a thousand different grassroots organizations among indigenous peoples in various parts of the world that are seeking to enhance their livelihoods and gain greater control over their areas.[33] Some of them are engaged in sustainable development, establishing agricultural projects, or improving water systems. A multipurpose development program has been implemented by a group of Ju/'hoansi Bushmen in Namibia, which is run by a cooperative consisting of representatives of more than thirty different communities.[34] Survival schools have been set up by Mohawks in Canada and Inuit in Alaska.[35] Australian Aborigines and Native Americans have established indigenous health facilities and child welfare projects.[36]

Indigenous peoples are protesting mistreatment at the hands of governments and multinational corporations, and they are effectively using

---

32. *See* Draft Declaration *supra* note 16.

33. *See* BODLEY, *supra* note 10, at 152-73; Jason W. Clay, *Organizing to Survive*, CULTURAL SURVIVAL Q., Dec. 1984, at 2; ALAN B. DURNING, ACTION AT THE GRASSROOTS: FIGHTING POVERTY AND ENVIRONMENTAL DECLINE (Worldwatch Paper 88, 1988); DURNING, GUARDIANS OF THE LAND, *supra* note 7; Robert K. Hitchcock, *Africa and Discovery: Human Rights, Environment, and Development*, 17 AM. INDIAN CULTURE & RES. J. 129 (1993).

34. Megan Biesele, *Land, Language, and Leadership*, CULTURAL SURVIVAL Q., Summer 1993, at 57; Dori Bixler et al., *Land Rights, Local Institutions, and Grassroots Development Among the Ju/'Hoansi of Northeastern Namibia*, IWGIA NEWSL. 23 (Apr.-June 1993).

35. BURGER, THE GAIA ATLAS, *supra* note 7, at 28-29, 145-47.

36. *Id.* at 144-45, 154-55; ALVIN M. JOSEPHY, JR., RED POWER: THE AMERICAN INDIANS' FIGHT FOR FREEDOM (1985); David Holstrom, *New Era for Reservation Education*, CHRISTIAN SCI. MONITOR, Sept. 30, 1991, at 12.

TABLE 2. *Development Projects that Have Had Negative Impacts on Indigenous Peoples*[37]

Project	Country	Impacts
Polonoroeste Project	Brazil	land invasion, deforestation, dispossession of Nambiquara and other Indians
Transmigration Program	Indonesia	environmental damage, local populations dispossessed forcibly, conflict expansion
National Land Management and Livestock Program	Botswana	Bushmen, Bakgalagadi, Herero populations dispossessed, expansion of overgrazing, land use conflicts
Narmada Valley Dams Project	India	dispossession, impoverishment, beatings, and intimidation of residents, loss of agricultural land, lack of appropriate resettlement and compensation
Chico Dams	Philippines	forced relocation, non-payment of compensation, oppression of local people
Chittagong Hills	Bangladesh	forced relocation, oppression, and intimidation of tribal peoples, genocidal actions
Manantali Dam	Senegal	dispossession, provision of land to outsiders resulting in warfare and conflict, malaria increase
Grande Carajas Project and Tucuri Dam	Brazil	disposession, loss of natural resources, expansion of land conflict and competition, local people impoverished
Tanzania Wheat Project	Tanzania	Barabaig agropastoralists removed from their lands, harrassed and jailed, denied access to winter grazing
Sarawak Logging	Malaysia	deforestation, dispossession, and oppression of Penan foragers

Project	Country	Impacts
Eduador Oil Developments	Ecuador	Waorani and other Indians forced off land, massive environmental problems with oil spills, poisoning of water, loss of biodiversity, lack of consultation and compensation
James Bay Hydroelectric Project	Canada	Cree and Inuit forced off land, loss of caribou and other wild animals and fish resources
Western Desert Uranium Mining	Australia	Aboriginals forced out of land and exposed to radiation from past nuclear tests
Kariba Dam	Zimbabwe and Zambia	flooding of lands, 50,000 Tonga dispossessed, social and economic disruptions, health problems
Kor Jor Gor (Land allocation project for the poor in degraded forest reserve areas)	Thailand	disposession of farmers, no compensation paid, no social infrastructure replacement, excessive cutting of trees by military-owned businesses, oppression of local populace
Bayano Dam	Panama	80% of Cuna Indians land flooded, loss of livelihood
Ethiopian Resettlement	Ethiopia	forcible resettlement, rising land and labor conflicts
Batang Ai Dam	Malaysia	Iban uprooted, deforestation and loss of wildlife resources

37. The information on development projects was obtained from a large number of sources, including the URGENT ACTION BULL. of Survival International; the bulletins and annual reports of the International Work Group for Indigenous Affairs; CULTURAL SURVIVAL Q. and the occasional publications of Cultural Survival; articles in THE ECOLOGIST; reports of the Minority Rights Group, Human Rights Watch, Amnesty International, the Institute for Development Anthropology, and Anti-Slavery International; and internal reports of international finance and development agencies such as the World Bank, the United States Agency for International Development, and the European Development Fund.

the media to further their interests. Indigenous leaders have emerged in many countries, and legal services have been established by indigenous groups to represent people in court. A number of groups have sought self-determination and protection of their civil and political rights. In the past two decades, however, greater attention has been paid to socioeconomic rights, especially everyone's right to: a decent standard of living; environmental conditions that are adequate to assure health and well-being; sufficient food, water, shelter, and income; and social security.

IV. HUMAN RIGHTS AND ENVIRONMENTAL PROTECTION: A SOUTHERN AFRICAN CASE STUDY

Concern about the loss of biological and cultural diversity has increased significantly over the past decade. There are several reasons for this concern, all of which are evident in areas where indigenous peoples reside. First, the rapidly expanding populations of developing countries and the diversification of their economies are having major impacts on the environment. Second, numerous scientific discoveries, some of them drawn from indigenous knowledge, have resulted in an expansion of the uses to which resources are put. Third, ecological diversity is diminishing as some species become extinct.

Governments and international environmental and development organizations have framed policies and put into place a variety of projects and programs aimed at conserving biodiversity.[38] The various biodiversity programs range from ecosystem protection to the enforcement of en-

---

In addition, specific information was found in the following publications: WADE DAVIS & THOM HENLEY, PENAN: VOICE FOR THE BORNEO RAINFOREST (1993); DURNING, GUARDIANS OF THE LAND, *supra* note 7; AN END TO LAUGHTER?: TRIBAL PEOPLES AND ECONOMIC DEVELOPMENT (Marcus Colchester, ed., 1985); HUMAN RIGHTS WATCH, INDIVISIBLE HUMAN RIGHTS: THE RELATIONSHIP OF POLITICAL AND CIVIL RIGHTS TO SURVIVAL, SUBSISTENCE, AND POVERTY (1992); HUMAN RIGHTS WATCH AND NATURAL RESOURCES DEFENSE COUNCIL, DEFENDING THE EARTH: ABUSES OF HUMAN RIGHTS AND THE ENVIRONMENT (1992); INDIGENOUS VIEWS OF LAND AND THE ENVIRONMENT (Shelton H. Davis, ed., 1991); MORRIS & HITCHCOCK, *supra* note 8; NATIVE POWER: THE QUEST FOR AUTONOMY AND NATIONHOOD OF INDIGENOUS PEOPLES (Jens Brøsted et al., eds., 1985); DAVID PRICE, BEFORE THE BULLDOZER: THE NAMBIGUARA INDIANS AND THE WORLD BANK (1989); BRUCE RICH, MORTGAGING THE EARTH: THE WORLD BANK, ENVIRONMENTAL IMPOVERISHMENT, AND THE CRISIS OF DEVELOPMENT (1994); CHRISTOPHER SIMPSON, THE SPLENDID BLOND BEAST: MONEY, LAW, AND GENOCIDE IN THE TWENTIETH CENTURY (1993); STATE OF THE PEOPLES, *supra* note 3; THE STRUGGLE FOR LAND AND THE FATE OF THE FORESTS (Marcus Colchester & Larry Lohmann, eds., 1993); TRIBAL PEOPLES AND DEVELOPMENT ISSUES: A GLOBAL OVERVIEW (John H. Bodley, ed., 1988); WHO PAYS THE PRICE?: EXAMINING THE SOCIOCULTURAL CONTEXT OF ENVIRONMENTAL CRISIS (Society for Applied Anthropology Report on Human Rights and the Environment, 1993).

38. *See, e.g.,* Steven M. Rubin & Stanwood C. Fish, *Biodiversity Prospecting: Using Innovative Contractual Provisions to Foster Ethnobotanical Knowledge, Technology, and Conservation,* 5 COLO. J. INT'L ENVTL. L. & POL'Y 23 (1994).

dangered species legislation and the establishment of germ plasm banks. These programs have important implications for the resource rights of indigenous populations. In many parts of southern Africa, for example, indigenous populations have been affected to a significant degree by the implementation of conservation and development projects by governments and nongovernmental organizations.

According to legal scholar Hurst Hannum, "[t]he history of indigenous peoples is, to a large extent, the chronicle of their unsuccessful attempts to defend their land against invaders."[39] In the past, these invaders included soldiers, companies like the Dutch East India Company or the British South Africa Company, or settlers who had little regard for the well-being of the people whose resources and lands they were encroaching upon.

In the past five years, there have been more and more cases in which development organizations have been responsible for carrying out programs that have had deleterious effects on rural populations, particularly those in the Third World. As some indigenous leaders have noted, "Governments want to control us, missionaries want our souls, and environmental organizations want our resources and our support."[40] Unfortunately, this support is often extremely costly to indigenous peoples and others living in areas with valuable wildlife and plant resources.

Nongovernmental organizations (NGOs) involved in environmental activities range from agencies running eco-tourism projects in the tropical rain forests of the Amazon to agencies overseeing biosphere reserves and national parks in central Africa. These programs have enabled a fairly sizable number of local people to expand their incomes while enhancing the conservation of wild species. They have also provided both employment and training opportunities for indigenous people.

Unfortunately, not all of these programs have had salutary effects. In many cases, local populations are excluded from the areas set aside as parks and reserves.[41] The benefits of tourism go to the NGOs or to tourism companies, not to local populations. In only a few instances, such as in Namibia, are local people allowed to collect limited amounts of resources such as firewood and medicinal plants. As one Ndebele man of

---

39. HURST HANNUM, AUTONOMY, SOVEREIGNTY, AND SELF-DETERMINATION: THE ACCOMMODATION OF CONFLICTING RIGHTS 92 (1990).

40. Interview with Gabalakani Tammae, peasant villager, in Huwana Ward, Bulalima-Mangwe District, western Zimbabwe (July 9, 1992).

41. See, e.g., Phyllis B. Jackson, Comment, National Parks and Indigenous Peoples, 4 COLO. J. INT'L ENVTL. L. & POL'Y 502 (1993).

Matabeleland Province in Zimbabwe put it: "We are being dispossessed in the name of conservation."[42]

A major human rights and environmental issue in the Republic of Botswana in southern Africa is the future of the Central Kalahari Game Reserve (CKGR). In 1986, after a fact-finding mission by the Botswana government, the Ministry of Commerce and Industry ruled that "[v]iable sites for economic and social development should be identified outside the Reserve and the residents of the Reserve encouraged—but not forced—to relocate at those sites."[43] There was pronounced local opposition to the proposed relocation, both on the part of reserve residents and in the Ghanzi District Council, which oversees the reserve. International human rights agencies (such as Survival International) vehemently protested the Botswana government's decision, as well. Efforts to find water and land for new settlements outside the reserve were unsuccessful, however, and no moves were made.

In March 1992, the Botswana government agreed to recognize !Xade, where substantial numbers of Basarwa and Bakgalagadi live in the reserve as a permanent settlement. The idea behind the decision was that an area of land within the reserve would be set aside, and people from other settlements inside the reserve would be relocated to !Xade and provided with land and development assistance. Resistance to this decision was overt among resident groups in the central Kalahari.

There were major problems with this decision. First, people did not want to be relocated to !Xade, because it was not part of their traditional territory. Second, the amount of land set aside for the residents of !Xade was insufficient to sustain hunting and gathering, which continued to make up a portion of many reserve residents' subsistence. Third, there were legal and constitutional questions as to whether eliminating the rights of the people in the reserve was appropriate.[44]

---

42. Interview with Joshua Ndlovu, Ndebele cattle owner, in Plumtree, Bulalima-Mangwe District, western Zimbabwe (July 10, 1992).

43. Report of the Central Kgalagadi Game Reserve Fact Finding Mission, Botswana Ministry of Commerce and Industry Circular No. 1, Ref. CI 4/8 II(II) (1986).

44. The Botswana Constitution and the various government land acts and white papers on government land policy maintain that all peoples, regardless of their ethnic background, have the right to sufficient amounts of land to meet their needs. Section 14(3)(c) of the Botswana Constitution deals specifically with Bushmen, while Section 15 contains provisions against discrimination. BOTS. CONST., arts. 14(3)(c), 15; Bots. Tribal Land Act, No. 54 (1968), *as amended by* Tribal Land (Amendment) Act, No. 48 (1969); *Rural Development in Botswana*, Government Paper No. 1 (1970); *National Policy on Tribal Grazing Land*, Government Paper No. 2 (1975); *National Policy on Land Tenure*, Government Paper No. 1 (1985); *National Policy on Agricultural Development*, Government Paper No. 1 (1991). For a discussion of the specific issue of Bushman land rights, *see* ELIZABETH A. WILY, OFFICIAL POLICY TOWARDS SAN (BUSHMEN) HUNTER-GATHERERS IN MODERN BOTSWANA, 1966-1978 (Nat'l Inst. Dev't & Cultural Res. Working Paper No. 23, 1979);

The CKGR was established as a game reserve in 1961 under the Fauna Conservation Proclamation as a place for both people and wildlife.[45] Local people were allowed to retain their residence and resource access rights in the reserve under this legislation. Outsiders were not allowed to hunt or gather, but an exemption was made for those people whose primary subsistence was derived from wild plants and animals.

Scientists and planners justified the group's removal from the reserve by saying that most of them had become pastoralists and therefore were no longer pursuing a "traditional" way of life. It was indeed the case that some people have obtained livestock under *mafisa* (long-term loan) arrangements. At the same time, an assessment of the livestock holdings of reserve residents revealed that few of them possess enough animals to be considered self-sufficient. Most people do not own cattle, and those who do keep them at cattle posts outside the reserve. About half a dozen people said that they had bought goats with money that they obtained from selling handicrafts to tourists. The majority of the people in the reserve pursue a mixed economic strategy, with foraging being supplemented by food and income obtained through participation in agropastoralism, wage labor, rural industries, and Botswana government drought relief programs.

It has been suggested that an underlying reason for the decision to remove people from the reserve was to respond to the interests of environmentalists who were pressuring the European Economic Community to withdraw financial support for Botswana unless greater efforts were made to conserve wildlife and other natural resources.[46] A second suggestion is

---

ELIZABETH A. WILY, LAND ALLOCATION AND HUNTER-GATHERER LAND RIGHTS IN BOTSWANA: THE IMPACT OF TRIBAL GRAZING LAND POLICY (1980); Robert K. Hitchcock, *Land Reform, Ethnicity, and Compensation in Botswana*, 14 CULTURAL SURVIVAL Q. 52 (No. 4, 1990); Robert K. Hitchcock, *Tradition, Social Justice, and Land Reform in Central Botswana*, 24 J. AFR. L. 1 (1980); Casey Kelso, *The Landless Bushmen*, 38 AFR. REP. 51 (1993); Alice Mogwe, *The Land Rights of the Basarwa (Bushmen) of Botswana*, 13 ANTI-SLAVERY REP. 99 (1992); Bathalefhi Moeletsi, The San of Botswana: Legal Status, Access to Land, Development, and Natural Resources, paper presented at the Second Regional Conference on Development Programs for Africa's San Populations, Gaborone, Botswana (Oct. 11-13, 1993).

45. Proclamation by the High Commissioner, Bechuanaland Protectorate, The Fauna Conservation Proclamation of 1961, HCN 33 §§ 4(3), 57(4); Central Kalahari Game Reserve (Control of Entry) Regulations, GN 38 (1963). For a discussion of the issues of Bushman hunting rights in the Central Kalahari Game Reserve, *see* ROBERT K. HITCHCOCK, U.S. AGENCY FOR INT'L DEV. MISSION TO BOTS., TRADITIONAL AND MODERN SYSTEMS OF LAND USE AND MANAGEMENT AND USER RIGHTS TO RESOURCES IN RURAL BOTSWANA, PART II: COMMUNITY-BASED RESOURCE MANAGEMENT 53-61 (1991); CLIVE SPINAGE, HISTORY AND EVOLUTION OF THE FAUNA CONSERVATION LAWS OF BOTSWANA 54-68 (1991).

46. Interviews with residents of the Central Kalahari Game Reserve and surrounding areas and of officials in the Gantsi District Council and the government of Botswana (1988, 1990, 1991); Robert K. Hitchcock, *Game Park vs. the San: Conservation and Sustainable Development in the Kalahari*, IWGIA NEWSL. July-Aug. 1991, at 7.

that some individuals in Botswana felt that it is important to "villagize" the Remote Area Dwellers (RADs) and thus bring them into the mainstream of life in the country.[47] There are also those who felt that DeBeers and other mining companies want complete access to the reserve for mineral exploitation purposes.[48] Finally, some have suggested that large-scale livestock owners wanted to see sizable portions of the reserve de-gazetted so that they could turn them into communal lands and set up cattle posts (*meraka*).[49]

According to central Kalahari residents, the decision to move people into !Xade could exacerbate existing problems of access to resources and environmental degradation. The relocation might also cause social conflicts with those people currently residing there. Clearly, the decision to remove people from their ancestral lands could serve to erode the social, economic, and political status of a sizable portion of the CKGR's population. It is also open to speculation whether the relocated people will have security of tenure over their new lands. It is clear that if Botswana is to achieve its goals of self-reliance and unity, careful thought will have to be given to the ways in which the Central Kalahari Game Reserve resettlement issue is handled.

V. CONCLUSION

The central question, therefore, is whether or not the various conservation and natural resource management programs being implemented in various parts of southern Africa and elsewhere are having the intended effect of improving the livelihoods of indigenous populations. Findings suggest that modifications of many of these programs are necessary if they are to enhance the standards of living and promote the socioeconomic rights of indigenous peoples. In the central Kalahari, for example, it would

---

47. Government of Botswana, Report of the Central Kgalagadi Game Reserve Fact Finding Mission (1985); Blaine Harden, *Farewell to the Kalahari: Bushmen Being Forced from Preserve*, WASH. POST, Mar. 27, 1988, at A1; Olekanye Paul, *Arrangements to Resettle RADs Outside Game Reserve Made*, BOTS. DAILY NEWS, Aug. 23, 1991, at 2; Johannes Pilane, *Government, Reserve Residents Are Consulting—Nwako*, BOTS. DAILY NEWS, Aug. 16, 1988, at 4; Sheila Rule, *For the Fleet-Footed of the Bush, a Last Foothold*, N.Y. TIMES, June 20, 1988, at A4; Molotsi Sekgoma, *Ministers Ask RADs to Leave Game Reserve*, BOTS. DAILY NEWS, June 7, 1988, at 3.

48. Robert K. Hitchcock, *Foragers on the Move: San Survival Strategies in Botswana Parks and Reserves*, CULTURAL SURVIVAL Q., Feb. 1985, at 31; Survival International, *Botswana: Kalahari Peoples Threatened with Expulsion from Game Reserve*, URGENT ACTION BULL. (Apr. 1989); Peter Warren, *Kalahari Bushmen, Civilization in Conflict*, SAN ANTONIO EXPRESS NEWS, Dec. 21, 1992, at 1D.

49. Robert K. Hitchcock, *Appendix 4: The Central Kalahari Game Reserve: A Case Study in Remote Area Research and Development*, in MONITORING, RESEARCH, AND DEVELOPMENT IN THE REMOTE AREAS OF BOTSWANA (Robert K. Hitchcock, ed., 1988).

behoove the government of Botswana to allow people to retain their residence and resource use rights and to facilitate their involvement in wildlife management and eco–tourism programs.

There is an even more insidious side to some of the actions of conservation organizations. In southern and eastern Africa, US government funds and financial assistance from environmental organizations are sometimes being used to support antipoaching efforts.[50] In Kenya, Tanzania, Uganda, and Zambia, sizable numbers of suspected poachers have been shot.[51] These actions have served, it has been argued, to reduce the losses of such endangered or threatened species as rhinoceros and elephant. There is a major question, however, as to whether or not the killing of people is really the most effective way to promote conservation.

Data gathered in the course of evaluating natural resource management projects in Zimbabwe, Zambia, Namibia, and Botswana suggest that innocent people, many of them women and children, have been killed and tortured at the hands of wildlife department personnel.[52] In most cases, the people affected were members of indigenous minority groups, some of

---

50. AFRICA'S CONSERVATION FOR DEVELOPMENT (BOTSWANA, KENYA, TANZANIA, AND ZIMBABWE) (Rodger Yeager, ed., 1987); CONSERVATION IN AFRICA: PEOPLE, POLICIES AND PRACTICE (David Anderson & Richard Grove, eds., 1987); CONSERVATION OF NEOTROPICAL FORESTS: WORKING FROM TRADITIONAL RESOURCE USE (Kent H. Redford & Christine Padoch, eds., 1992); FINN LYNGE, ARCTIC WARS (1991); STUART A. MARKS, THE IMPERIAL LION: HUMAN DIMENSIONS OF WILDLIFE MANAGEMENT IN CENTRAL AFRICA (1984); RESIDENT PEOPLES AND NATIONAL PARKS: SOCIAL DILEMMAS AND STRATEGIES IN INTERNATIONAL CONSERVATION (Patrick C. West & Steven R. Brechin, eds., 1991); SUSTAINABLE HARVEST AND MARKETING OF RAIN FOREST PRODUCTS (Mark Plotkin & Lisa Famolare, eds., 1992).

51. See JONATHAN S. ADAMS & THOMAS O. MCSHANE, THE MYTH OF WILD AFRICA: CONSERVATION WITHOUT ILLUSION (1992); JONATHAN M. BLACKWELL ET AL., ENVIRONMENT AND DEVELOPMENT IN AFRICA: SELECTED CASE STUDIES (1991); GEORGE LEDEC & ROBERT GOODLAND, WILDLANDS: THEIR PROTECTION AND MANAGEMENT IN ECONOMIC DEVELOPMENT (1988); LIVING WITH WILDLIFE: WILDLIFE RESOURCE MANAGEMENT WITH LOCAL PARTICIPATION IN AFRICA (Agnes S. Kiss, ed., 1990); NON-GOVERNMENTAL ORGANIZATIONS AND NATURAL RESOURCES MANAGEMENT: AN ASSESSMENT OF EIGHTEEN AFRICAN COUNTRIES (Michael Brown, ed., 1993).

52. Casey Kelso, *Hungry Hunter-Gatherers Tortured*, WEEKLY MAIL, July 24-30, 1992, at 12; Casey Kelso, *The Inconvenient Nomads Deep Inside the Deep*, WEEKLY MAIL, July 24-30, 1992, at 12; *Wildlife Atrocities Exposed: Basarwa Speak Out*, MOKAEDI (Gaborone, Botswana), Sept. 1992; Alice Mogwe, WHO WAS (T)HERE FIRST?: AN ASSESSMENT OF THE HUMAN RIGHTS SITUATION OF BASARWA IN SELECTED COMMUNITIES IN THE GANTSI DISTRICT, BOTSWANA (Bots. Christian Couns. Occasional Paper No. 10, 1992); *Human Rights Abuses Against Basarwa*, MMEGI: THE REPORTER, May 29-June 4, 1992, at 5.

whom claim that they are the victims of genocidal actions designed to remove them from the land so it may be used for other purposes.[53]

The question that a number of indigenous groups are asking today is whether or not it is appropriate for environmental organizations and foreign donor agencies to be involved in promoting activities that have such negative effects on their lives.[54] As one Tyua woman in Bulalima-Mangwe District in western Zimbabwe put it, "Just because these people say that they are helping preserve the environment does not mean that they should be able to violate our human rights."[55]

Clearly, it is not only governments and multilateral development banks that should be required to follow international human rights standards. Conservation and development agencies need to be made aware that they must carry out detailed environmental and social impact assessments both prior to and during the course of project implementation. They, too, must take the rights of the people with whom they deal into careful consideration. Finally, greater efforts must be made to ensure that the benefits of environmental programs flow to the communities that are bearing the bulk of the costs.

---

53. Unpublished interview notes of Robert Hitchcock & Stuart Marks, northern Botswana (1991); unpublished interview notes of Robert Hitchcock & Fanuel M. Nangati, western Zimbabwe (1992).

54. RAYMOND BONNER, AT THE HAND OF MAN: PERIL AND HOPE FOR AFRICA'S WILDLIFE (1993); PAUL ANDRE DEGEORGES, ADMADE: AN EVALUATION TODAY AND THE FUTURE POLICY ISSUES AND DIRECTION (1992); H. HEDLUND ET AL., A FEASIBILITY STUDY TO ADVISE ON THE INSTITUTIONAL STRUCTURE OF THE LUANGWA INTEGRATED RESOURCE DEVELOPMENT PROJECT (1991); ROBERT K. HITCHCOCK, COMMUNITIES AND CONSENSUS: AN EVALUATION OF THE ACTIVITIES OF THE NYAE NYAE FARMERS COOPERATIVE AND NYAE NYAE DEVELOPMENT FOUNDATION IN NORTHEASTERN NAMIBIA (1992); ROBERT HITCHCOCK & STUART A. MARKS, U.S. AGENCY FOR INT'L DEV. MISSION TO BOTS., TRADITIONAL AND MODERN SYSTEMS OF LAND USE AND MANAGEMENT AND USER RIGHTS TO RESOURCES IN RURAL BOTSWANA, PART I: FIELD DATA AND ANALYSIS (1991); ROBERT HITCHCOCK & FANUEL M. NANGATI, ASSESSMENT OF THE COMMUNITY-BASED RESOURCE UTILIZATION COMPONENT OF THE ZIMBABWE NATURAL RESOURCES MANAGEMENT PROJECT (690-0251) (1992); ULLA KANN ET AL., LET THEM TALK: A REVIEW OF THE ACCELERATED REMOTE AREA DEVELOPMENT PROGRAM (1990); MOGWE, *supra* note 52; DELIA OWENS & MARK OWENS, AMONG THE ELEPHANTS (1992).

55. Interview with Leohang Kemotohetse (pseudonym), in western Bulalima-Mangwe District, Zimbabwe (July 1992).

APPENDIX I—DECLARATIONS, STATEMENTS, AND CHARTERS RELATING TO INDIGENOUS PEOPLES' RIGHTS[56]

1. The United Nations Charter (1945).

2. The Universal Declaration of Human Rights (1948).

3. The United Nations Convention on the Prevention and Punishment of the Crime of Genocide (1951).

4. Convention 107: Convention Concerning the Protection and Integration of Indigenous and Other Tribal and Semi-Tribal Populations In Independent Countries (1957), International Labour Organisation (ILO).

5. Recommendation 104: ILO Recommendation Concerning the Protection and Integration of Indigenous and Other Tribal and Semi-Tribal Populations in Independent Countries (1957).

6. The International Convention on the Elimination of All Forms of Racial Discrimination (1966).

7. The International Covenant on Civil and Political Rights (1966).

8. The International Covenant on Economic, Social, and Cultural Rights (1966).

---

56. The full citations for the materials in this table are:

1. U.N. CHARTER.

2. Universal Declaration of Human Rights, G.A. Res. 217 (III), U.N. Doc. A/810 at 71 (1948).

3. The 1948 United Nations Convention on the Prevention and Punishment of the Crime of Genocide, Dec. 9, 1948, 78 U.N.T.S. 277 (Jan. 12, 1951).

4. ILO Convention (No. 107) Concerning the Protection and Integration of Indigenous and Other Tribal and Semi-Tribal Populations in Independent Countries, June 26, 1957, 328 U.N.T.S. 247.

5. *Recommendation 104: ILO Recommendation Concerning the Protection and Integration of Indigenous and Other Tribal and Semi-Tribal Populations in Independent Countries* (1957).

6. International Convention on the Elimination of All Forms of Racial Discrimination, *opened for signature* Mar. 7, 1966, 660 U.N.T.S. 195 (entered into force Jan. 4, 1969).

7. International Covenant on Civil and Political Rights, *opened for signature* Dec. 19, 1966, G.A. Res. 2200, U.N. GAOR, 21st Sess., U.N. Doc. A/6316 (1966), *reprinted in* 6 I.L.M. 368 (1967).

8. International Covenant on Economic, Social and Cultural Rights, *opened for signature* Dec. 19, 1966, G.A. Res. 2200, U.N. GAOR, 21st Sess., U.N. Doc. A/6316 (1966) (entered into force Jan. 3, 1976) *reprinted in* 6 I.L.M. 360 (1967).

9. "Declaration of Barbados" (Passed at the Symposium on Inter- Ethnic Conflict in South America, Barbados, Jan. 25-30, 1971), Programme to Combat Racism, World Council of Churches.

10. "Declaration on Human Rights" (Passed at the Second General Assembly of the World Council of Indigenous Peoples, Kiruna, Sweden, Aug. 24-27, 1977).

11. "Declaration of Principles for the Defense of the Indigenous Nations and Peoples of the Western Hemisphere" (Statement passed at the International Non-Government Organization Conference on Discrimination Against Indigenous Populations in the Americas, Geneva, Switzerland, Sept. 20-23, 1977).

12. United Nations Declaration and Programme of Action to Combat Racism and Racial Discrimination (1978).

13. The Indigenous and Tribal Peoples Convention No. 169 of 1989, International Labour Organization (brought into force on September 5, 1991).

14. "Recognizing and Strengthening the Role of Indigenous People and Their Communities" (Chapter 26, United Nations Conference on Environment and Development, Agenda 21) (adopted on June 14, 1992, Rio de Janeiro, Brazil).

15. "The Draft Universal Declaration on the Rights of Indigenous Peoples" (United Nations Working Group on Indigenous Populations) (1993).

---

9. *Declaration of Barbados: For the Liberation of the Indians*, Programme to Combat Racism and the Commission of the Churches on International Affairs of the World Council of Churches, PCR 1/71(E) (passed at the Symposium on Inter-Ethnic Conflict in South America, Bridgetown, Barbados, Jan. 25-30, 1971) *reprinted in* THE SITUATION OF THE INDIAN IN SOUTH AMERICA 376 (W. Dostal ed., 1972).

10. *Declaration on Human Rights* (Passed at the Second General Assembly of the World Council of Indigenous Peoples, Kiruna, Sweden, Aug. 24-27, 1977).

11. *Declaration of Principles for the Defense of the Indigenous Nations and Peoples of the Western Hemisphere* (Statement passed at the International Non-Government Organization Conference on Discrimination Against Indigenous Populations in the Americas, Geneva, Switzerland, Sept. 20-23, 1977).

12. *U.N. Declaration and Programme of Action to Combat Racism and Racial Discrimination* (1978), *reprinted in* BODLEY, *supra* note 10, at 217.

13. International Labour Organisation Convention (No. 169) Concerning Indigenous and Tribal Peoples in Independent Countries, June 27, 1989, 28 I.L.M. 1382.

14. *Agenda 21*, United Nations Conference on Environment and Development, ch. 26, U.N. Doc. A/CONF.151/4 (Part III) (1992).

15. Draft Declaration, *supra* note 16.

Biodiversity Prospecting: Using Innovative Contractual Provisions to Foster Ethnobotanical Knowledge, Technology, and Conservation

Steven M. Rubin[†]
Stanwood C. Fish[††]

I. INTRODUCTION

Biodiversity around the world is under assault from a variety of forces. From tropical forests, to arid plains, to marine ecosystems, human activities endanger hundreds of thousands of species.[1] While the habitat of so many species is disappearing,[2] so too is our knowledge of those species

---

† Steven M. Rubin is Director of the Conservation Economics Department of Conservation International Foundation, Washington, D.C.

†† Stanwood C. Fish will graduate from Vermont Law School in May 1994 and has been serving as a legal extern with Conservation International during the summer and fall semesters of 1993.

The authors wish to express their appreciation to Conservation International, particularly to Peter Seligmann, Russ Mittermeier, and Mark Plotkin whose distinguished careers in conservation have made this article possible. The authors also wish to thank Lindsey Lambert whose corporate experience and sound business judgement were of profound importance to this undertaking. Of course, these people are not responsible for any errors, opinions, or conclusions set forth in this article, which remain solely the responsibilities of the authors.

1. *See generally*, Convention on Biological Diversity, *opened for signature* at United Nations Conference on Evironment and Development, June 5, 1992, Preamble, 31 I.L.M. 818, 822-23 [hereinafter Biodiversity Convention]; JOHN C. RYAN, LIFE SUPPORT : CONSERVING BIOLOGICAL DIVERSITY 7-24 (Worldwatch Paper 108, 1992). *See also*, Paul R. Ehrlich, *The Loss of Biodiversity: Causes and Consequences, in* BIODIVERSITY 21 (E.O. Wilson, ed. 1988).

2. At current deforestation rates, the Caribbean and Central and South America will lose an estimated 15% of all currently identified plant species and 2% of all of tropical America's plant families, increasing to 66 and 14% respectfully by the end of the twenty-first century. BOARD ON AGRICULTURE, NATIONAL RESEARCH COUNCIL, MANAGING GLOBAL GENETIC RESOURCES: FOREST TREES 23 (1991) (*citing* Daniel Simberloff, *Are We On the Verge of a Mass Extinction in Tropical Rain Forests?, in* DYNAMICS OF EXTINCTION 165 (David K. Elliott, ed., 1986)).

and the ecosystems of which they are a part.[3] Cultures and traditions that have preserved essential resources benefitting local communities as well as the larger global community face mounting pressure from destructive clearcutting for agricultural crops, fuel, livestock, and timber. Increasingly, large timber and other resource concessions are being granted in an effort to earn foreign exchange and service burdensome loans.[4] In this article the authors examine natural product drug development, or biodiversity prospecting,[5] as a means to conserve tropical biodiversity and sustainably develop tropical country economies in manners that directly validate the knowledge of indigenous and other forest peoples while also providing benefits to their communities.

Part II of this article discusses the history of genetic trade, illustrating the lack of conservation incentives within the commercialization of genetic resources. The authors provide a review of developments in the biodiversity prospecting field and explore the nature of various participants, intermediaries, and collaborators. Following this background discussion, the article discusses selected principles and objectives advanced in the 1992 Biodiversity Convention and illustrates how biodiversity prospecting agreements among private parties and governments may be used to help realize these objectives. The article specifically discusses private agreements in light of the Convention's interest in preserving biological diversity, promoting sustainable use, and recognizing the sovereign rights of states over their genetic resources.

Part III evaluates the role of private agreements in the biodiversity prospecting industry, specifically their ability to function as a tool for the conservation of biological and cultural diversity. Here the authors discuss innovative approaches to conservation and development explored in the process of negotiating a contract funded by the National Institutes of Health's International Cooperative Biodiversity Group initiative.[6] The

---

3. Robert K. Hitchcock, *International Human Rights, the Environment, and Indigenous Peoples*, 5 COLO. J. INT'L ENVTL. L. & POL'Y 1, 12-13 (1994).

4. SUSAN GEORGE, THE DEBT BOOMERANG: HOW THIRD WORLD DEBT HARMS US ALL 2 (1992); Anthony B. Anderson, *Deforestation in Amazonia: Dynamics, Causes, and Alternatives, in* ALTERNATIVES TO DEFORESTATION 3, 9 (Anthony B. Anderson, ed. 1990).

5. Here and throughout the paper, natural product development, biodiversity prospecting, and bioprospecting refer to the process of collecting, extracting, and screening samples of biological specimens for potential commercial value in the pharmaceutical area. Except where specified, the authors do not intend to include other commercial values for biodiversity, though many exist.

6. The authors are currently finalizing a contract for the NIH/ICBG program which Conservation International and four other partners have been awarded. The partners include a South American country and its national pharmaceutical, a major US pharmaceutical, a botanical garden, and a state university. *See* Warren E. Leary, *U.S. Aids Program to Produce Drugs in Developing Nations*, N.Y. TIMES, Dec. 8, 1993, at A20.

agreement between Conservation International and a major US pharmaceutical company, a botanical garden, a university, and a South American pharmaceutical company highlights the interdependence of research institutions, commercial pharmaceutical companies, in situ and ex situ conservationists, and developing countries high in biological diversity. In the first section of Part III the authors illuminate a number of legal issues that arise in the commercialization of genetic resources and discuss key provisions to be included in a prospecting contract in the sequence in which they would generally appear in such an agreement. These provisions include the access to and collection of biological samples, as well as related local knowledge, and consent agreements under which such knowledge may be acquired. This section also develops recommendations for the encoding of biological and ethnobotanical information relating to samples as a manner of ensuring accurate reporting of research activity.

The second section of Part III presents scenarios for screening plant and other biological resources and provides a legal framework for less industrialized countries to participate in the fractionation and development of biologically active samples. From the standpoint of optimizing benefits to the source country, the third section discusses pioneering contract provisions pertaining to rights in inventorship, ownership of inventions, licensing, and the protection of the intellectual property of local plant users and indigenous peoples. This section also describes state–of–the–art methods by which the exclusivity that commercial partners typically seek may be reasonably limited, thereby maximizing the present and future values of resources investigated under the agreement.

The fourth section of Part III considers compensation due to a source country in consideration for the extension of rights to private parties to evaluate resources for potential commercial use. Here, mechanisms described include concession fees, extended use fees, royalties, transfers of appropriate technology, and opportunities for source countries to participate in research and development and to provide sustainable future supplies of commercial quantities of raw and/or improved material.

Part IV describes selected conservation and development issues, such as challenges involved in allocating and distributing financial benefits as well as encouraging national legislation for the sustainable management of biodiversity.

Although bioprospecting represents only one among many conservation tools, the article concludes that it is an especially valuable tool in the effort to stem current tropical deforestation trends and the resulting loss of species. Because the bioprospecting industry is dependent on conservation advances, it provides an effective means of bringing critical conservation concerns to the attention of industrial and governmental leaders. They represent one of the most comprehensive conservation approaches to date—providing short– and long–term benefits for both indigenous peoples and national industries.

II. INCENTIVES FOR CONSERVATION, THE UNCED[7] CONVENTION, AND THE EVOLUTION OF PRIVATE CONTRACTS AND NATIONAL REGULATIONS GOVERNING BIODIVERSITY PROSPECTING

A. The Problem: A Lack of Compensation and Incentives for Conservation

In and around the remaining centers of high biodiversity are also the poorest communities in the world. These communities—especially those of tribal peoples—have never shared in the bounties of the land . . . . The best way to liberate these communities from the vicious cycle of poverty is through empowerment—the control of their own natural resources, and access to information and technology. To support the advocacy of these issues is to support the cause of biodiversity conservation.[8]

The international conservation movement has begun to recognize the importance of economic development to the conservation of biodiversity. Biodiversity conservation is increasingly seen to take the form of "an offensive effort seeking to meet peoples' needs from biological resources while ensuring the long-term sustainability of Earth's biotic wealth."[9] With the support of the Biodiversity Convention[10] and other multilateral agreements,[11] indigenous peoples and developing countries enjoy a stronger position with respect to the management of and remuneration for their natural chemical and genetic resources, their "biological wealth." The process of commercializing these resources, referred to as natural product development, has immense potential to contribute to biodiversity conservation and economic development. Over the last quarter century, one-fourth of all dispensed prescriptions in the United States used active ingredients

---

7. For a discussion of the United Nations Conference on Environment and Development, *see* Special Issue, *United Nations Conference on Environment and Development*, 4 COLO. J. INT'L ENVTL. L. & POL'Y 1 (1993).

8. WORLD RESOURCES INSTITUTE ET AL., GLOBAL BIODIVERSITY STRATEGY: GUIDELINES FOR ACTION TO SAVE, STUDY, AND USE EARTH'S BIOTIC WEALTH SUSTAINABLY AND EQUITABLY 79 (1992) [hereinafter WRI, GLOBAL BIODIVERSITY STRATEGY] (quoting Celso Roque, Department of Environment and Natural Resources, Philippines).

9. *Id.* at 5.

10. Biodiversity Convention, *supra* note 1, 31 I.L.M. 818.

11. *See* Hitchcock, *supra* note 3, at 21-22, for a list of international declarations, statements, and charters relating to indigenous rights.

extracted from plants under natural product development.[12] In 1990 the market sales for these plant-derived drugs totalled $15.5 billion.[13] Medicines derived from plants originally used by indigenous peoples have an annual world market of $43 billion, while other natural product markets—such as the seed industry, insecticides, herbicides, and industrial biotechnological applications—may well reach or exceed the value of the medicinal market.[14] The late Alwyn Gentry, senior curator with the Missouri Botanical Garden, once estimated that tropical medicines, once fully developed, will add $900 billion to Third World economies.[15]

Despite these sizable markets, natural products often provide very little incentive or capacity for conservation. Pharmaceutical products based on traditional medicine have returned less than .0001% of their profits to the local plant users who assisted research and discovery efforts.[16] This lack of compensation endangers valuable traditional plant knowledge. As modern drugs based on traditional knowledge appear in forest communities, they supplant the indigenous traditions to which they owe their existence. Today, about seventy-four percent of plant-derived pharmaceutical drugs have the same or related use as they first did in traditional medical applications.[17] Even so, the unregulated history of natural chemical and genetic trade has proceeded at the expense of gene-rich countries. Recent examples of this inequitable development of natural chemical resources include the Rosy Periwinkle, found in Madagascar, and the Endod berry, found in Somalia. The country of Madagascar has realized no financial benefit from Eli Lilly's use of the Rosy Periwinkle, *Vinca rosea*, a plant long used by local people which has provided a treatment for childhood leukemia. Treated as a "global commons," the Periwinkle, found in a highly threatened ecosystem, has not provided any of the valuable incentives for conservation that it might have.[18] One observer has asked:

---

12. Walter V. Reid et al., *A New Lease on Life, in* BIODIVERSITY PROSPECTING: USING GENETIC RESOURCES FOR SUSTAINABLE DEVELOPMENT 1, 7 (Walter V. Reid et al., eds., 1993) [hereinafter BIODIVERSITY PROSPECTING].

13. *Id.* at 7. For an introduction to the growing uses and markets for biological resources *see id.* at 6-15.

14. Darrell Posey, *Intellectual Property Rights: Just Compensation for Indigenous Knowledge,* ANTHROPOLOGY TODAY, August 1990, at 13, 15.

15. Kevin Krajick, *Sorcerer's Apprentices,* NEWSWEEK FOCUS, Jan. 18, 1993, at 2.

16. Posey, *supra* note 14, at 15.

17. Norman R. Farnsworth, *Screening Plants For New Medicines, in* BIODIVERSITY, *supra* note 1, at 83, 95.

18. In 1985 the sales of vincristine and vinblastine (used for treatment of childhood leukemia and Hodgkins' disease respectively) amounted to approximately US$ 100 million, 88% of which was profit. *Id.* at 94-95.

But why should Madagascar preserve the Rosy Periwinkle? The world
community reaps benefits from this plant, but what are the benefits to
the local people or to the Madagascan government? The answer is:
None at all. No money flows back to Madagascar for the drugs
produced, and it is even unlikely that the drug itself is available to the
poor peasants of Madagascar, should they need it. There is on the face
of it no reason whatsoever for Madagascar to preserve the Rosy
Periwinkle.[19]

Similarly, the Endod berry, *Phytolacca dodecoandra*, was found to be
effective as a natural molluscicide by scientists at the University of Toledo.
The Endod may offer a solution to the zebra mussel invasion in the Great
Lakes, an environmental disaster that has crippled water supplies and
threatens marine ecosystems. The berry has been cultivated for centuries in
Africa, where indigenous peoples of Ethiopia have been using it as a
detergent and fish intoxicant.[20] A recent patent application by the University of Toledo and three individual scientists threatens to circumvent
Ethiopia's control of the Endod and the rights to intellectual property and
royalties related to the plant's use as a molluscicide. Without capturing the
financial benefits of products derived from their biodiversity and traditional knowledge, gene-rich countries are left without essential financial incentives to conserve their wildlands.

Although both of these examples illustrate the need for reform in the
way that natural chemical and genetic material is collected and commer-
cialized, it is important to first understand the collection agreements most
commonly used by researchers and collection agencies today. More equitable private prospecting and collecting agreements between a number of
different partners have appeared only recently. These partners include
industries using genetic information and natural chemical compounds
either in recombinant DNA processes, chemical analog synthesis, or bioas-
say screening and isolation. In the past, such industries have collected and
used tropical plant, animal, marine, microbial, and soil samples either
themselves or via a private collector without requesting permission for the
right of access or providing remuneration in consideration for the use and
commercialization of such resources.[21] This circumvention of a country's

---

19. Arne Schiøtz, *Conserving Biological Diversity: Who is Responsible?* 18 AMBIO
454, 454 (1989), *cited in* A. B. Cunningham, *Indigenous Knowledge and Biodiversity:
Global Commons or Regional Heritage?* CULTURAL SURVIVAL Q., Summer 1991, at 4, 5.

20. Chakravarthi Raghaven, *Patent Application Highlights "Stealing" of South's
Genetic Resources,* Third World Network Features (1993).

21. Richard Stone, *The Biodiversity Treaty: Pandora's Box or Fair Deal?,* 256
SCIENCE 1624 (1992). *See also,* Raghaven, *supra* note 20.

right to control the use of its own genetic resources has become all too common in today's genetic marketplace.[22]

A number of developments in the nascent field of biodiversity prospecting, however, foreshadow a new era in the commercialization and conservation of biodiversity. Public research institutions such as the National Institutes of Health and Mexico's National Biodiversity Commission, as well as private and semiprivate institutions (such as INBio in Costa Rica and others in Japan and Indonesia) have all begun to inventory biological species and to explore the conservation and development potential of biodiversity prospecting.[23] Collection agencies such as Biotics[24] and ex situ conservationists such as the Missouri Botanical Garden have begun to explore more equitable intermediary roles between countries of collection and commercial prospectors. Because the agreements that these intermediaries strike with pharmaceutical and biotechnological companies are confidential, they are difficult to analyze. Nevertheless, policies that direct royalties to in-country collaborators have begun to appear, although some collectors and intermediaries withdraw from royalty income altogether in an attempt to maintain their research orientation.[25]

Shaman Pharmaceuticals, a unique combination of collector, ethnobotanist, and pharmaceutical company, appears intent on making ethnobotany a potent drug discovery technique. An exclusive concentration on ethnobotanically used plants distinguishes Shaman from other pharmaceuticals. Shaman claims that this yields an estimated fifty to seventy percent hit rate in their lab.[26] Shaman currently has at least two drugs under clinical evaluation, one treating respiratory viruses and another for her-

---

22. *See generally*, Jack R. Kloppenburg, Jr. & Daniel Lee Kleinman, *Plant Genetic Resources: The Common Bowl, in* SEEDS AND SOVEREIGNTY: THE USE AND CONTROL OF PLANT GENETIC RESOURCES 1 (Jack R. Kloppenburg, Jr. ed., 1988).

23. Reid et al., *supra* note 12, at 25-26.

24. Biotics, Ltd. is a private collection agency which supplies research groups and companies with biological samples of plants and other resources. Biotics purchases samples from countries and contracts to share any royalties it earns with the country of collection. *See, id.* at 25.

25. Sarah A. Laird, *Contracts for Biodiversity Prospecting, in* BIODIVERSITY PROSPECTING, *supra* note 12, at 99, 113-14.

26. Gary Stix, *Back to Roots: Drug Comanies Forage for New Treatments*, SCI. AM., Jan. 1993, at 143, 143; Interview with Mark J. Plotkin, Ph.D., Vice President, Guianas and Plant Conservation Regional Program, Conservation International, Washington, DC (Aug. 23, 1993); Mark Plotkin, announcement at ICBG press conference (Dec. 7, 1993). "Hit rate" refers to that percentage of samples which show biological activity in a given series of chemical screens.

pes.[27] Shaman has pledged to donate a portion of its sales to its nonprofit arm, the Healing Forest Conservancy.[28]

Publicly recognizing the importance of issues related to biodiversity prospecting, Glaxo Group Research recently stated that it "understands the impact unauthorized and/or unrestrained removal of plant materials from their indigenous habitats can have on the environment and economy of a country and that third world sources may be particularly vulnerable."[29] This statement reflects the heightened awareness of some commercial prospectors and suggests that a new era linking natural chemical and genetic resource use and conservation may be underway. Implementing such policies into collection contracts for commercial product development marks the beginning of a new era in equitable biodiversity resource use.

A promising step into this new era is the Merck & Co., Ltd. agreement with INBio, Costa Rica's private, nonprofit organization charged with assessing biodiversity and integrating nondestructive use of such diversity.[30] The Merck-INBio agreement was received as a "pioneering agreement" that might serve as a model for future accords.[31] The Costa Rican agreement partially funds the collection, inventory, extraction, and documentation required to produce reliable and replicable extracts for screening. In addition, the agreement supports the training of local taxonomists and researchers and establishes in-country capacity for fractionation of active chemical compounds.[32] Merck has agreed to pay a royalty to INBio on the net sales of products derived under the agreement in exchange for the right to evaluate parts of Costa Rica's biodiversity.[33] Although the details of the Merck-INBio agreement have yet to be scrutinized by the legal community, this first-generation biodiversity prospecting and conservation agreement shows bioprospecting's potential to further the objectives of the Biodiversity Convention, discussed below.[34]

---

27. *Eli Lilly & Co. Investing in Rain-forest Research*, WALL ST. J., Oct. 23, 1992, at B3.

28. David Riggle, *Pharmaceuticals From the Rainforest*, IN BUSINESS, Feb. 1992, at 26.

29. Laird, *supra* note 25, at 105.

30. Reid et al., *supra* note 12, at 1.

31. Jim Detjen, *Company's Accord on Rain Forests Could Be Model for Preservation*, PHILADELPHIA INQUIRER, Sept. 20, 1991, at A1.

32. INBio of Costa Rica and Merck Enter Into Innovative Agreement to Collect Biological Samples While Protecting Rainforest, Sept. 19, 1991 (press release by Merck & Co., Inc.) (on file with the COLO. J. INT'L ENVTL. L & POL'Y).

33. Neil D. Hamilton, *Feeding Our Future: Six Philosophical Issues Shaping Agricultural Law*, 72 NEB. L. REV. 210, 253 n.196 (1993).

34. For reviews of the Merck/INBio agreement *see* Kristen Peterson, *Recent Intellectual Property Trends in Development*, 33 HARV. INT'L L. J. 277 (1992); Shayana Kadidal, *Plants, Property, and Pharmaceutical Patents*, 103 YALE L. J. 223 (1993).

B. The Biodiversity Convention[35] and Biodiversity Prospecting Agreements

In June of 1992, the United Nations Conference on Environment and Development (UNCED) met in Rio de Janeiro to consider a landmark international treaty responding to the social, economic, and environmental concerns of ecosystems that have been threatened as a result of post–World War II development and "certain human activities."[36] Originally signed by 150 UN member states present at UNCED,[37] the Convention on Biological Diversity asserts, among other things, that developed and less-developed nations will strive jointly to establish measures promoting ecosystem conservation, technology transfer, and the survival of indigenous peoples.[38] In June 1993 the United States signed the Biodiversity Convention.[39]

Although the Convention fails to set forth any specific standards for the promotion or regulation of biodiversity prospecting, it does articulate several over-arching principles that encourage and empower developing countries to create their own standards within the contexts of private international contractual agreements among prospecting parties and local groups.[40] In this article we discuss these principles and the use of private international biodiversity prospecting agreements as a means to achieve the goals put forward by the Convention. Recent direct experience working on such an international agreement suggests that prospecting ventures can effectively promote conservation and sustainable development, two principal objectives of the Convention.[41]

In addition, in many instances some form of regulatory legislation may very well be a desirable and necessary context for negotiated agreements. However, in this area, as in others, sound legislation may well derive from appropriate case-by-case contract experience. Furthermore, when it does appear, national legislation and regulation of biodiversity prospecting will provide additional guidance for the terms and conditions of private contracts but will not supplant the need for them. Accordingly, the type of information and analysis provided here will be of interest both

---

35. Biodiversity Convention, *supra* note 1.

36. *Rio Declaration on Environment and Development,* United Nations Conference on Environment and Development, U.N. Doc. A/CONF.151/5/Rev.1 (1992), *reprinted in* 31 I.L.M. 874.

37. Reid et al., *supra* note 12, at 2.

38. *Id. See, e.g.,* Biodiversity Convention, *supra* note 1, preamble, art. 1, 31 I.L.M. at 822-23.

39. *See U.S. Signs Biodiversity Treaty, Urges Global Patent Protection for Biotech,* 16 Int'l Envtl. Rep. (BNA) No. 12, at 432 (June 16, 1993).

40. Biodiversity Convention, *supra* note 1, 31 I.L.M. at 822.

41. *Id.* at art. 1, 31 I.L.M. at 823.

in contexts where legislation already exists as well as in those where it does not. The following section discusses conservation-based development policies given expression in the Biodiversity Convention and illustrates the manner in which biodiversity agreements may function to promote such policies, paving the way for more far-reaching national legislation and/or regulation.

Article 1 expresses the Convention's three main objectives: the conservation of biological diversity, the sustainable use of biological resources, and the fair and equitable sharing of resulting benefits.[42] Article 1 implicitly acknowledges the interdependent relationship of those countries controlling genetic resources and those possessing the technology and resources to enhance and commercialize those materials.

Article 2 defines key terms that appear throughout the Convention. "Biological diversity" is defined as "variability among living organisms . . . includ[ing] diversity within species, between species and of ecosystems."[43] "Sustainable use" is defined as "the use of components of biological diversity in a way and at a rate that does not lead to the long-term decline of biological diversity, thereby maintaining its potential to meet the needs and aspirations of present and future generations."[44] "Biological resources" appears in both the Preamble and Article 2 and is defined as including genetic resources with "actual or potential" use to humanity.[45]

Private prospecting agreements can be used as instruments to create incentives for sustainable use and conservation of biodiversity and to equitably allocate benefits to contracting parties commensurate with their contributions.[46] Biodiversity prospecting efforts exemplify the Convention's concern for biodiversity and sustainable use by promoting in situ conservation of the potentially valuable information found in threatened ecosystems.[47] Biodiversity prospecting may also be used to promote measures to conserve rare and endangered species and to ensure the availability of such genetic information for future generations by way of in situ conservation efforts. Perhaps most importantly, biodiversity prospecting agreements may also provide a means by which the global community can turn local governments and peoples into biodiversity stakeholders, thus creating a viable economic alternative to competing ecologically destructive sources of income.

---

42. *Id.*
43. *Id.* at art. 2, 31 I.L.M. at 823.
44. *Id.* at art. 2, 31 I.L.M. at 824.
45. *Id.* at art. 2, 31 I.L.M. at 823.
46. *Id.* at arts. 11, 19, 31 I.L.M. at 827, 830.
47. *Id.* at art. 8, 31 I.L.M. at 825-26. *See also,* Leary, *supra* note 6.

Article 5 encourages Parties to the Convention to "cooperate . . . through competent international organizations [CIOs] . . . for the conservation and sustainable use of biological diversity."[48] Under prospecting agreements, this facilitating role of CIOs may be fulfilled by international conservation organizations. In this capacity, conservation organizations may ensure, among other things, that the "sustainable use" is in fact sustainable and that the incentives for conservation are optimized.

Article 7 recommends the identification, sampling, monitoring, and organization of data relating to species and habitats.[49] Agreements between international conservation organizations, tropical countries, and private prospectors typically provide for the collection and identification of genetic resources. The accords may also provide for the use of geographic information systems that record and monitor the locations of sampled species in geographic databases.[50]

Article 8, sections (i) and (j) encourage Parties to "preserve and maintain [the] knowledge, innovations and practices of indigenous and local communities embodying traditional lifestyles relevant for the conservation and sustainable use of biological diversity and promote their wider application . . . ."[51] Prospecting contracts may be used to promote this policy through the creation of ethnobotanical databases and the establishment of trust funds to reimburse communities for contributions to product development.[52] Private contracts may also be used to encourage prospectors to use local knowledge by implementing royalty structures that place premiums on products derived from ethnobotanical knowledge.[53]

In addition, prospecting agreements may include measures relative to the collection process to protect endangered species and populations, as encouraged in Article 8(k). Prospecting agreements may also "provid[e] financial and other support for *in situ* conservation," as called for in Article 8(m). Likewise, ex situ conservation, as envisioned by Article 9, may occur as an extension of the collection and extraction process.

---

48. Biodiversity Convention, *supra* note 1, at art. 5, 31 I.L.M. at 825.
49. *Id.* at art. 7, 31 I.L.M. at 825.
50. Conservation International's ICBG program will benefit from the use of CI's Global Information System (CI/GIS). The Merck–INBio agreement utilized a database provided by Intergraph. *See,* Rodrigo Gámez et al., *Costa Rica's Conservation Program and National Biodiversity Institute (INBio), in* BIODIVERSITY PROSPECTING, *supra* note 12, at 53, 63-65.
51. Biodiversity Convention, *supra* note 1, art. 8(j), 31 I.L.M. at 826.
52. *See infra,* sections II(E)(iv), III(B).
53. *See infra,* section II(E)(iii).

Article 12(a) provides that contracting parties shall establish, maintain, and promote research facilities and educational resources that promote and ensure the sustainable use of biological diversity, in part through the use of advanced scientific methods.[54] Facilities and training may naturally be provided for in the consideration package of a prospecting agreement.[55] As explained in Part III of this article, in-kind consideration serves many tangible conservation and development goals that outright financial consideration may not accomplish as easily.

Together, articles 15 and 16 assert the interdependence of countries controlling genetic resources and those creating technologies that make use of those resources. Article 15(1) recognizes "the sovereign rights of states over their natural resources" and establishes that "the authority to determine access to genetic resources rests with the national governments . . . ."[56] Article 15 serves to refute the notion that genetic resources are part of humanity's global heritage. It suggests that naturally occurring chemicals and genetic sequences have the potential to be as tangible an asset as undiscovered petroleum reserves. Consequently, monitoring biological resources and conserving fragile ecosystems have become essential components of many states' national security efforts.[57] With respect to commercialization, Article 15 encourages Parties to "facilitate access to genetic resources" on "mutually agree[able] terms . . . subject to prior informed consent."[58] In addition, biodiversity research should involve the participation of source country scientists and, where possible, take place within such countries.[59]

Prospecting agreements may provide a case example of the regulated access envisioned in articles 15 and 16. By including informed consent provisions and by stipulating that all national regulations be complied with, such agreements put into practice the grounding tenets of the Biodiversity Convention. Hence, countries contracting with individual prospectors will regulate the scope of access (for example, flowering plants only) and use (such as specific therapeutic applications only) in accordance with the level of the remuneration and likelihood of success.[60] Article 15(7) also states that Parties to the Convention shall seek "fair and equitable" means of sharing profits arising from the research and marketing of biodiversity

---

54. Biodiversity Convention, *supra* note 1, art. 12, 31 I.L.M. at 827.
55. *See, e.g.,* Leary, *supra* note 6.
56. Biodiversity Convention, *supra* note 1, art. 15(1), 31 I.L.M. at 828.
57. *See* WRI, GLOBAL BIODIVERSITY STRATEGY, *supra* note 8, at 5.
58. Biodiversity Convention, *supra* note 1, art. 15(2), (4), (5), 31 I.L.M. at 828.
59. *Id.* at art. 15(6), 31 I.L.M. at 828.
60. *See infra,* section II(B)(ii).

resources.[61] By creating reliable databases and assisting in professional collection, extraction, and fractionation, tropical countries may enhance the value that they add to the commercial process and improve their bargaining position vis-à-vis patents, licensing, and royalties.

Under Article 16, contracting parties shall "provide and/or facilitate access for and transfer to other Contracting Parties of technologies that are relevant to the conservation and sustainable use of biological diversity or make use of genetic resources . . . ."[62] In addition, access to and transfers of technology "shall be provided on terms which recognize and are consistent with the adequate and effective protection of intellectual property rights."[63] In effect, this Article reinforces the intellectual property rights of industrialized nations, without mention of those belonging to indigenous peoples.[64] Elsewhere, Article 16(5) maintains that contracting parties shall cooperate in order to ensure that national and international laws are supportive of and do not run counter to the Convention's intentions. Intellectual property attorney Michael Gollin aptly notes that Article 16 addresses governments, not private institutions. He states that "there is merit in requiring countries to promote voluntary biodiversity prospecting agreements, to 'prime the pump' of the biodiversity prospecting trade."[65]

In other words, by using private prospecting agreements to recognize, protect, and reward local and indigenous intellectual property rights under the more stringent intellectual property rights of commercial partners in industrialized nations, the governments of developing nations can enhance the flow of revenue and technology transfer to their countries. As mentioned before, private contracts may act as an impetus for national legislation envisioned in Article 16, functioning as a proving ground of sorts. Although it may be meritorious, the prospecting trade cannot succeed in any of its goals without compensating indigenous and local peoples, stewards of the biodiversity information so crucial to both industry and global conservation. All prospecting agreements must establish terms protecting and compensating indigenous intellectual property while also encouraging the exchange of appropriate technology through novel consideration packages.[66]

---

61. Biodiversity Convention, *supra* note 1, art. 15(7), 31 I.L.M. at 828.

62. *Id.* at art. 16(1), 31 I.L.M. at 829.

63. *Id.* at art. 16(2), 31 I.L.M. at 829.

64. Article 18(4) encourages but fails to stipulate to protection of indigenous intellectual property equivalent to that accorded industrial property in Article 16(5). *See, Id.* at art. 16(5), 18(4), 31 I.L.M. at 829-30.

65. Michael A. Gollin, *The Convention on Biological Diversity and Intellectual Property Rights, in* BIODIVERSITY PROSPECTING, *supra* note 12, at 289, 295.

66. *See infra,* section II(E)(iv).

Article 18(2) outlines how technical and scientific cooperation should "be given to the development and strengthening of national capabilities, by means of human resources development and institution building."[67] In essence, this provision promotes the establishment of agreements that administer, foster, and provide for the proper allocation of profits, royalties, and fees. As expressed in Article 18(5), "Contracting Parties shall, subject to mutual agreement, promote the establishment of joint research programmes and joint ventures for the development of technologies . . . ."[68]

Finally, the promulgation of national legislation implementing the Biodiversity Convention is encouraged in Article 11, which binds contracting parties to adopt "as far as possible and appropriate, . . . economically and socially sound measures that act as incentives for the conservation and sustainable use of components of biological diversity."[69] Prospecting ventures provide practical experience and a potentially useful framework for any future legislative action.

III. CONTRACTUAL PROVISIONS PROMOTING CONSERVATION, SUSTAINABLE DEVELOPMENT, AND THE PROTECTION OF INDIGENOUS INTELLECTUAL PROPERTY IN THE CONTEXT OF PRIVATE BIODIVERSITY PROSPECTING AGREEMENTS

In June 1992, recognizing the urgent need to assist developing countries in the conservation of their biodiversity, the NIH and the United States Agency for International Development, in conjunction with other US Agencies, issued Request For Applications #TW-92-01.[70] The request for the International Cooperative Biodiversity Group (ICBG) explicitly states that its intent is to "promote the conservation of biological diversity through the discovery of bio-active agents from natural products, and to ensure [that] the equitable economic benefits from these discoveries accrue to the country of origin."[71]

Initially, the NIH received more than thirty applications to the ICBG program. Of these initial applications, five have been selected for funding.[72] After several months of preparation, the authors submitted several draft agreements to the NIH for comment and approval. A final contract in its eighth draft has finally been agreed upon by the parties to the ICBG

---

67. Biodiversity Convention, *supra* note 1, art. 18(2), 31 I.L.M. at 830.

68. *Id.* at art. 18(5), 31 I.L.M. at 830.

69. *Id.* at art. 11, 31 I.L.M. at 827.

70. National Institutes of Health et al., Request for Applications No. TW-92-01 (June 12, 1992).

71. *Id.* at 4.

72. Leary, *supra* note 6.

application. As collaborators in such a unique and challenging project, we have sought to develop novel legal approaches intended to promote policies expressed in the Biodiversity Convention, to protect the rights of our partners in developing countries, and to satisfy NIH guidelines. This must all be done while still retaining the participation of the major pharmaceutical companies and university researchers.

A. Innovative Contractual Provisions for Promoting Tropical Country Rights in Genetic Resources

This section explains the major provisions that should appear in a bioprospecting contract in the sequence in which the issues generally arise, namely: access, sample supply, screening, inventions, licensing, compensation, and conservation. Obviously, this discussion is intended as a general survey of such provisions. The actual provisions of a contract will necessarily depend upon all the facts and circumstances under which it is negotiated.

1. Natural Chemical and Genetic Resource Access: General Understandings

Prospecting agreements are fast becoming one of the most influential tools in promoting conservation of and stewardship over biodiversity resources. Proper stewardship over genetic resources maximizes the number of species conserved in situ.[73] Regulating access to these species and the information they contain is increasingly accepted by governments, industries, and nongovernmental organizations (NGOs) as a method of proper stewardship.[74]

Parties may use several means to regulate access to plant and other genetic material. Currently, government regulation of access to genetic resources is incomplete. For example, countries often require permits for exploring and exporting biological samples, although these measures are not required for sample extracts.[75] Where government legislation is lax or absent, the provisions of a contract can function to increase the source country's regulation of naturally occurring chemicals and genetic information by requiring permits or approval.

---

73. Biodiversity Convention, *supra* note 1, at preamble, art. 8, 31 I.L.M. at 822-23, 825-26.

74. Daniel H. Janzen et al., *Research Management Policies: Permits for Collecting and Research in the Tropics, in* BIODIVERSITY PROSPECTING, *supra* note 12, at 131, 131-33. Article 15 of the Biodiversity Convention, *supra* note 1, art. 15, 31 I.L.M. at 828, grants sovereigns control over genetic resource access, recognizing it as a fundamental requisite for achieving the objectives of the Convention. The establishment of the Mexican Biodiversity Commission, described in Reid et al., *supra* note 12, at 25-26, reflects Mexico's desire to replicate an INBio-like institution.

75. *See, generally*, Janzen et al., *supra* note 74, at 131-35.

More generally, it is a good idea for agreements to state that "the Parties acknowledge that the source country regulates the access to and maintains sovereignty over its natural chemical and genetic resources." A broad recital such as this one, indicating early in the contract the understanding of the parties on this issue, is likely to strengthen the host country's position in the course of negotiating licensing and royalty clauses as well as in executing other obligations.

It is also advisable for prospecting contracts to specifically refer to the permits required for in-country collection and to assert that the acquisition of such national and subnational approval is a condition precedent to collection.[76] Further, the agreements themselves may stipulate several conditions by which such access, once granted, may be used. Important considerations regarding access include methods of collection, use of encoding systems, and access to traditional knowledge.

a. Methods of Collection

Agreements governing the collection of biological material will need to provide for the collection methods to be used, the material to be collected, and the amount of biological data to be supplied. Because collectors are often independent collaborators subcontracted for their performance, who have no financial stake in the success or failure in the prospecting efforts, they will, under most circumstances, perform collection as requested. It is extremely important, therefore, to select a collector with a demonstrated commitment to conservation, and a successful track-record and work history to implement conservation measures. Indeed, as agreements should specify precautions relating to endangered species, private land, and large scale recollection, the collector must exercise flexibility to adhere to such agreements.

A contract between a source country and a prospector may use random (comprehensive) and/or ethnobotanically-guided methods of collection. Ethnobotanical knowledge not only identifies the plants, insects, or other materials of practical use (for example, as a traditional medicine), it can also show how the material is used and which specific illnesses or conditions it is intended to treat.[77] Other prospectors might desire to use a comprehensive collection method, collecting and screening for its potential biological activity each biological sample in the category available to them.

Comprehensive, ethnobotanical, and combined collection methods all provide different degrees of access to the resource. Contracts using a

---

76. *See* David Downes, et al., *Biodiversity Prospecting Contract, in* BIODIVERSITY PROSPECTING, *supra* note 12, at 255, 259. *See generally id.* at 268-72; Janzen et al., *supra* note 74.

77. *See* Farnsworth, *supra* note 17, at 84-90.

comprehensive method of collection provide a high degree of access to the type of biota for which access is provided. Generally, under the comprehensive approach, all organisms within the category of biota under study are collected for testing; for example, all flowering plants or all insects may be eligible for collection. This ensures prospectors that screening efforts will encompass a complete number of samples in a given geographic or biological area. This method provides prospectors with biological material without, however, any information on previous ethnobotanical uses which might exist.

Ethnobotanically based collection of specimens is directed by the knowledge of indigenous and local peoples. Recently, ethnobotanical research has piqued the interest of commercial prospectors and collectors. In one study where randomly collected plants tested by National Cancer Institute (NCI) for anti–HIV activity showed only six percent activity, ethnobotanically collected plants illustrated twenty-five percent activity.[78] Another research project has found that eighty-six percent of the traditionally used plant species in Samoa demonstrated pharmacological activity in the laboratory.[79]

The potential contribution of this knowledge has been validated in numerous other ways. For example, the start-up Shaman Pharmaceuticals made an initial public offering of stock in excess of $40 million based on its initial success using traditional knowledge as part of its discovery process. Major pharmaceuticals like Merck and Eli Lilly, as well as public researchers like the NCI, receive information regarding ethnobotanical uses of plants.[80] The value of this collection technique to prospectors is also evident in the reduction of product lead time. Whereas most drugs do not proceed to human trials for at least five to fifteen years, Shaman has brought a drug into clinical trials in sixteen months.[81] Cutting the time to market by such a great margin has obvious competitive advantages. In terms of sheer volume, the access provided by ethnobotanical collections is likely to be narrower than that of comprehensive collections, yet the access to traditional knowledge may be increasingly accepted as of greater value than comprehensive access.[82]

---

78. Michael Balick, *Ethnobotany and the Identification of Therapeutic Agents from the Rainforest, in* BIOACTIVE COMPOUNDS FROM PLANTS 22 (Derek J. Chadwick & Joan Marsh, eds., 1990), *cited in* Laird, *supra* note 25, at 119.

79. Paul Alan Cox, *Ethnopharmacology and the Search for New Drugs, in* BIOACTIVE COMPOUNDS FROM PLANTS, *supra* note 78, at 40, *cited in* Laird, *supra* note 25, at 120.

80. Laird, *supra* note 25, at 121.

81. Riggle, *supra* note 28, at 27.

82. Plotkin Interview, *supra* note 26 (hit rates of ethnobotanical samples thought to be as high as 60-80% at Shaman). The contract being negotiated by the authors will provide an unusual comparison between the two in one country with the same set of screens.

A third approach to collection uses both random and ethnobotanically guided methods. This approach provides prospectors with both the opportunity for high-throughput screening and ethnobotanically guided screening. Such dual collections may also provide indigenous groups and gene-rich countries with data to validate traditional knowledge and to establish the importance of its protection and conservation as one of the many facets of biodiversity. At the same time, dual collections present challenges regarding the manner in which samples are given preference in the laboratory and are assigned royalty rates in licensing negotiations. Consideration is given to these two challenges in the later sections.

Aside from carefully selecting and specifying an optimal method of collection, source countries should seek to limit collection within appropriately defined biological borders.[83] For instance, countries might divide their biodiversity resource into individual concessions, allocating flowering plant, animal, insect, marine, and soil samples to the most appropriate prospecting industries. Using a concession-type approach to genetic resources may generate greater conservation efforts while optimizing commercial potential within each biological and/or industrial sector. Although the structure and implementation of a regulatory concession over biodiversity is beyond the scope of this discussion regarding individual private agreements, it is important to note the possible applications of such a system.[84]

---

83. Countries may also choose to limit collections geographically, avoiding conflicts over land tenure and private property rights.

84. A biodiversity concession system might follow the general outlines of mineral leasing laws in the United States. Five general principles, originally found in GEORGE CAMERON COGGINS ET AL., FEDERAL PUBLIC LAND AND RESOURCES LAW 511 (3d ed. 1993), are presented here, adapted by the authors for present purposes:

> 1. Permission to access, prospect, or develop biodiversity must be secured from the government, whether via competitive bidding, permitting, or other schemes.

> 2. Government and non-governmental entities shall receive financial consideration in the form of filing fees, royalties, rents, and bonus payments.

> 3. The government may, at its discretion, lease the resource or components of the resource in the manner it finds most beneficial. Concessions may be limited in time, geographical area, biota, or end use and/or product application.

> 4. The government may utilize measures to ensure the lessor develops the resource diligently and in good faith.

> 5. The government may also design lease agreements to address issues concerning competing resources, lessors, local interests, communities, and the environment.

Concession regulations might also require that individual agreements concerning lessors implement a variety of development and conservation goals. Additionally, while some agreements might utilize a joint venture approach where risk and capital are shared, others might be limited to a fee and royalty basis. Other possibilities include production sharing arrangements and various service contracts.

b. Use of Encoding Systems

Access to biological material may or may not include access to the botanical or biological information identifying the item. As the chemical information contained in any given material may also be found in identical or similar material in other countries, a contract should ensure that a country providing the materials that contain the relevant chemical and genetic information also receives corresponding remuneration. Because source countries have become suppliers not of plants, microbes, or soil samples, but of valuable natural chemical structures, controlling access to this material may, especially in cases involving nonendemic species, require controlling access to information identifying the biological background and geographic location of the biological material.

Although a country may consider securing an agreement with a prospector not to collect in countries with similar flora, it may, in addition to or in lieu of such an agreement, simply use an encoding system that tags each sample with a bar code. Such a code should correspond to a data bank containing all of the information pertaining to the sample, including the date, time, and location of collection as well as other information providing biological identification.[85] This type of coding system ensures that the prospector contacts the source country upon discovering biological activity in a sample. In order to acquire the identity of an active plant or any additional sample material—both of which may be required for additional research, isolation, or fractionation—the source country must be contacted. At this point the source country should have contractual authority to request information on the positive result and potential therapeutic uses involved.

c. Access to Traditional Knowledge

Regulating access to the indigenous and traditional knowledge of shamans and others raises disclosure and intent issues. A prospecting agreement should contain provisions to ensure that ethnobotanical information is collected only with full disclosure of the purposes and intentions of the collector and the prospector. The agreement should set forth the procedures to be used to ensure the informed consent of shamans and others concerned. Informed consent provisions serve to apprise local plant users and the communities in which they work of the potential results of sharing such knowledge. The prospectors' intentions to patent, license, and market products should be fully disclosed. If a royalty structure exists in a

---

85. Downes, et al., *supra* note 76, at 259.

prospecting agreement, the agreement should make reference to such a structure and indicate the likely applications of the proceeds. Contributors of traditional knowledge should also be introduced to the patent system and be familiarized with the operation of secured intellectual property rights. The possibility of unprecedented amounts of foreign currency entering an economy that makes little or no regular use of cash requires that all of these issues be addressed in the informed consent agreement.

2. Screening and the Scope of Resource Use

A prospecting agreement can be used to carefully define and delimit a prospector's screening rights. These rights relate to ownership of inventions, intellectual property, licensing, and exclusivity as described below. A prospector's screening rights may also be defined by limits on periods and imposition of fees for sample use, and through limits in the range of therapeutic areas screened, as set forth in this section in the paragraphs below.

a. Time Limits and Fees for Sample Use

One way to regulate use of an extract under the terms of a prospecting agreement is to limit the time period during which a prospector may examine and test the extract. For example, a prospecting agreement might specify a six-month trial period during which the prospector would enjoy screening rights. Such a provision might read that the prospector shall declare, within six months of receipt of an Extract, whether or not it has a continuing interest in such Extract. If the prospector does not declare a continuing interest in an Extract, the remaining provisions of this agreement cease to apply to that Extract and such Extract shall be destroyed by the prospector.

By limiting testing to an initial six-month period in the absence of a declaration of continued interest, the future value of biological material is preserved, because it can be made available to other prospectors within a reasonable time after its being collected and extracted. This period also encourages diligent research by laboratory and development partners, avoiding a situation where the samples are "tied-up" with a single prospector. In an effort to avoid having a prospector declare continued interest in those samples that are not entering actual development, source countries may employ remunerated extended use provisions.

Extended use provisions govern the retention of an extract beyond the initial experimental period and offer an excellent opportunity for a country commercializing its genetic resources to demonstrate immediate financial returns. By instituting a permit or rental scheme, parties may stipulate to appropriate fees for continued exclusive use of samples of continuing interest to the prospector. Many commercial prospectors will insist on research and development periods of up to four to six years beyond the initial six-month test period. This exclusive use of a sample after it has shown biological activity in one or more screens may be worth over $10,000 per year, depending on the activity, market potential, and other factors.[86] While extended use fees may vary in value, they should share some common attributes. Permits may be granted for limited periods, such as six months or two years. In addition, the fee for continued exclusivity may rise with each additional period, but should be agreed upon at the initiation of the agreement. The increase would correspond to the rise in value to the developer of the retained sample. Permitting schemes may also require the prospector to submit screening data of extracts when entering the extended-use period, thus enhancing the source country's bargaining position.

Extended use fee structures should be agreed upon in advance. Fees and extended use time periods should be clearly specified. Although prospectors may argue that fees inhibit their operations, the research and development advantages that they enjoy as a result of prolonged exclusivity justify the cost. These advance payments of consideration also create goodwill among host country collectors and institutions, and therefore facilitate the collection process.

Most importantly, fees and royalties compensate participating countries for developing the collection infrastructure, databases, legislation, and taxonomies needed to assure future commercial-scale re-collections, in situ conservation, and conservation of indigenous knowledge regarding biological material. Moreover, a significant investment is necessary to assure collaborators that identical biological material from identical sources will be available for repeat testing against newly developed screens and future diseases. The extended use fees help to cover these advance costs incurred by source country institutions.

By discouraging a prospector from monopolizing samples and by promoting the early flow of consideration in the contract, extended use provisions encourage greater conservation efforts on behalf of contracting countries. They also serve to assure prospectors security and exclusivity in any increased research efforts. The negotiation position of seeking advance fees for extended use is reasonably strong. Indeed, from the standpoint of a prospector, the fees forestall the prospect of having only six months to

---

86. Interview with Neil Belson, attorney in private practice in Washington, DC (August, 1993).

develop a new AIDS vaccine, or of losing a multimillion dollar investment, due to an inability to re-collect a sample, or because a competitor has gained access to the same resource. In the event that such provisions prove unworkable or inappropriate, parties may agree to a maximum number of extracts to be held by the prospector:

> during any given contract year, the number of Extracts declared to be of continuing interest shall not exceed a percent of the total number of Extracts provided by the source country during such contract year, unless mutually agreed upon by the parties.

b. Therapeutic Limits of Screening

Countries may also limit the scope of extract use by stipulating to specific therapeutic or industrial areas in which the extracts may be tested. For instance, research within the pharmaceutical area may be limited to cardiovascular diseases, AIDS, or cancer. On the other hand, a country that has an opportunity to screen its biodiversity may prefer a pan-therapeutic testing program, running extracts through as many screens as are available at the time. Although both the specific and the pan-therapeutic scopes have their advantages, the point is negotiable and remains one in which a country may assert control and sovereignty over its genetic resources.[87] In any event, a contract should contain a list of all therapeutic or other areas in which material will be tested for activity. By maintaining a record of what screens have been applied to its genetic resources, a country may greatly preserve the market value of its resources with future prospectors.

3. Inventions and the Protection of Intellectual Property Rights

Following the UNCED and the Biodiversity Convention, protection of indigenous and traditional ethnobotanical knowledge became identified with the commercialization of plants and the genetic information they contain.[88] Prospecting agreements may present an ideal opportunity for the preservation and protection of indigenous and local knowledge if they attempt to use such knowledge in the collection of plants and other biological material.

---

87. While pan-therapeutic research might maximize the chances of commercial discoveries within one collection effort, research with a more limited scope offers a country the opportunity to enter into various contracts with numerous collaborators screening for different activities. This multitude of contracts might stimulate greater competition for the resource, raising the market value of biodiversity access. It also might stifle interest in the genetic resources altogether due to a lack of exclusivity.

88. Lee P. Breckenridge, *Protection of Biological and Cultural Diversity: Emerging Recognition of Local Community Rights in Ecosystems Under International Environmental Law*, 59 TENN. L. REV. 735, 767, 772-73 (1992).

Providing patent protection for indigenous knowledge has become an issue of great importance as the number of industries seeking to use biodiversity and the indigenous knowledge related to it have grown.[89] Additionally, the imminent threats to biodiversity conservation, cultural survival, and ecological balance have focused attention on the value of indigenous knowledge to conservation and the rate at which it is being lost to economic and social forces.[90] Although it is not a solution in and of itself, recognizing indigenous knowledge as a form of intellectual property may—by providing cultural, economic, and scientific incentives—stem the loss of this varied knowledge and the resources it has managed and used for hundreds of years.[91] At the very least, what is needed is "a mechanism linking the recognition of the origin and value of these resources *and* a mechanism for 'capturing' a portion of the profits arising from the use of these resources for local communities and habitat conservation in the tropical zone."[92] Bioprospecting contracts provide both of these mechanisms while also overcoming some of the difficulties in patenting indigenous knowledge.

a. Existing Obstacles to Patent Protection of Indigenous Ethnobotanical Knowledge

The obstacles to protecting indigenous knowledge under an industrialized intellectual property regime are numerous. First, there is a lack of uniformity in international patent law. For instance, many countries do not protect pharmaceutical products and inventions, while others have ventured so far as to protect living organisms and gene sequences from human DNA.[93] Due to the lack of international standards for many substantive areas of patent law, the debate over intellectual property rights for indigenous knowledge has made little headway.[94] However, the UN Working Group on Indigenous Populations has created a Draft Declaration on In-

---

89. Trade secret law presents one manner of protecting such knowledge if it has been an object of efforts to preserve its secrecy and satisfies other criteria. Trade secrets are a creature of state law, however, and do not afford the assurance and protection required for commercial partners' research and development expenditures. Michael A. Gollin, *An Intellectual Property Rights Framework for Biodiversity Prospecting, in* BIODIVERSITY PROSPECTING, *supra* note 12, at 159, 172-73. *See also* JOSEPHINE R. AXT ET AL., CONGRESSIONAL RESEARCH SERVICE, BIOTECHNOLOGY, INDIGENOUS PEOPLES, AND INTELLECTUAL PROPERTY RIGHTS 61-63 (1993) [hereinafter CRS REPORT].

90. Donald Dale Jackson, *Searching For Medicinal Wealth in Amazonia,* SMITH-SONIAN, Feb. 1989, at 94, 94-95, *cited in* CRS REPORT, *supra* note 89, at 34.

91. CRS REPORT, *supra* note 89, at 20.

92. Cunningham, *supra,* note 19, at 5.

93. J.W. BAXTER & JOHN P. SINNOT, WORLD PATENT LAW AND PRACTICE (1992), *cited in,* Gollin, *supra* note 89, at 169; Gollin, *supra* note 89, at 168.

94. CRS REPORT, *supra* note 89, at 21.

digenous Rights, which shows some advance on this issue.[95] The report expressly states that "[i]ndigenous peoples have the right to special measures for protection, as intellectual property, of their traditional cultural manifestations, such as . . . seeds, genetic resources, medicine and knowledge of the useful properties of fauna and flora."[96] In addition to this report, the chair of the working group, Erica-Irene A. Daes, issued a working paper entitled Intellectual Property of Indigenous Peoples: A Concise Report of the Secretary-General.[97] This paper stressed the need to provide legal and technical support to protect such intellectual property rights upon the consent of indigenous groups.[98]

Still obstacles remain, including the collective and folkloric nature of some indigenous knowledge, the "product of nature doctrine," and other standard requirements of patentability. Indigenous knowledge, generally, is held collectively—handed down through generations, passed on through the exchange of knowledge for goods, and/or contributed to by many within a community.[99] The novelty requirement of US patent law prohibits the patenting of an invention that has been known, used, or published in the United States more than one year previous to the patent application.[100] Inventors must also swear to an oath that they are the first inventor.[101] Because much indigenous knowledge regarding plants and their medicinal uses has been published, it is likely unpatentable without significant alteration or nonobvious improvement.[102] Furthermore, it would likely be difficult for indigenous plant users to claim that they are the first to have invented a plant use, due to the knowledge having been part of their community for decades, if not centuries. The novelty of indigenous knowledge, therefore, may not be sufficient for patent law. This would not be as significant an impediment if patent law could accept the collective knowledge of an indigenous group as novel, at least when it is unknown outside of the community sharing the knowledge.

---

95. *Id.* at 31 (*citing Discrimination Against Indigenous Peoples, Report of the Working Group on Indigenous Populations on its Tenth Session,* Comm. on Human Rights, Subcomm. on Prevention of Discrimination and Protection of Minorities, 44th Sess., Agenda Item 15, at Annex I, U.N. Doc. E/CN.4/Sub.2/1992/33 (1992) [hereinafter WGIP Report]).

96. WGIP Report, *supra* note 95, at 49, para. 19.

97. *Discrimination Against Indigenous Peoples, Intellectual Property of Indigenous Peoples: Concise Report of the Secretary General,* Comm. on Human Rights, Subcomm. on Prevention of Discrimination and Protection of Minorities, 44th Sess., Agenda Item 15, U.N. Doc. E/CN.4/Sub.2/1992/30 (1992).

98. CRS REPORT, *supra* note 89, at 32.

99. *Id.* at 35.

100. *See* 35 U.S.C. § 102 (1988).

101. *Id.*

102. CRS REPORT, *supra* note 89, at 58.

The "product of nature" doctrine represents another obstacle to patenting indigenous intellectual property. The subject matter test of 35 U.S.C § 101 prohibits the patenting of the laws and products of nature; the substance of a patent may not merely be the discovery of some natural phenomenon.[103] Instead, the US Supreme Court has ruled that a "modified natural product does not become statutory subject matter until its essential nature has been substantially altered."[104] In essence, the success of an indigenous intellectual property claim under patent law would require that the knowledge involved be something beyond the use of a product of nature. It is possible that the preparations of plant remedies may satisfy this subject matter test. In this case the inventor would have produced a "non obvious composition of matter derived from a product of nature by using their knowledge . . . ."[105] Even where indigenous knowledge appears to be a product of nature, there should be some improvement in existing patent law to protect such knowledge that contributes to other useful, novel, and nonobvious products.

b. Facilitating Patent Protection of Indigenous Knowledge

There are techniques that private contracts may use to facilitate patent protection for indigenous knowledge, whether it is currently patentable subject matter or not. Parties to a contract should stipulate to the protection of indigenous knowledge in any sections dealing with the collecting, patenting, and licensing of local knowledge that leads to patentable inventions. The extent of contribution by indigenous or local people will likely vary in degree and substance. Therefore, to optimize the ability of local and indigenous plant users to secure patent protection, a bioprospecting contract should ensure that all indigenous knowledge collected is well-documented regarding its origin, processes, and applications. Careful documentation, kept confidentially, will assist in later patent application and filing. Agreements should state that nothing stated within them will abridge the intellectual property rights of nationals and local people under the laws governing the contract. Parties may also stipulate that "shamans" or "local or indigenous peoples" may be inventors under the agreement. This is particularly important in anticipating a situation where a shaman and a prospector are both responsible for an invention or where the contributions of local plant users are, by themselves, insufficient for patent requirements. An ideal position for this assertion of the rights of indigenous people would

---

103. Funk Bros. Seed Co. v. Kalo Innoculant Co., 333 U.S. 127, 130 (1948).
104. American Fruit Growers, Inc. v. Brogdex Co., 283 U.S. 1 (1931).
105. CRS REPORT, *supra* note 89, at 54.

be in a provision regarding the ownership of inventions or patent rights of the contracting parties. It might read:

> All inventions made by employees or agents of a single party including the shamans or traditional plant users of the source country shall be owned solely by that party or shaman. All jointly made inventions shall be held jointly between such parties or shamans.

Providing for such general and specific protection is not enough to guarantee that the intellectual property rights of shamans and others will enjoy protection. Patents are costly and require great expertise to initiate, maintain, defend, and license. Agreements may facilitate better access to intellectual property protection by stipulating that prospectors will bear the costs involved in the application, appeals, and prosecution of infringements. Not only does it make sense for commercial partners, such as pharmaceuticals, to bear these costs, but it has also become accepted practice.[106] Without this formal assistance, a mere assertion of intellectual property rights promises little protection and even less potential for compensation and conservation.

4. Licensing of Inventions

To ensure that all joint inventions of local plant users, shamans, or other individuals in the country of collection and foreign researchers are jointly controlled, contracts controlling a prospecting agreement must allocate licensing rights to inventions derived from samples provided under the agreement. Where a prospector is not the sole inventor of a patented product, licensing rights should be allocated to all inventors. Rights to commercialize an invention may be limited in time such that if joint inventors cannot negotiate a mutually agreeable royalty rate within a year or less, such rights revert to the inventor or joint inventors. In the event that a shaman holds a patent jointly with a commercial company, both parties negotiate the licensing provisions and control the use of the invention. This partnership requires that any invention jointly held by a shaman or other national be used under their supervision and authority. Such a provision avoids subjecting local or indigenous knowledge to unauthorized use.

Provisions regarding exclusivity represent perhaps the most powerful controls over the scope of use in prospecting agreements. A highly exclusive contract, it may be argued, is more likely to succeed in the development of a commercial product due to the security provided to the commercial partner. Such is not necessarily the case in prospecting agreements where exclusivity may be limited without compromising the likelihood of

---

106. Downes et al., *supra* note 76, at 263.

discovery. As argued later, limits on exclusivity may in fact stimulate research efforts, preserve the market value of national biological resources, and promote more immediate flows of consideration for the contract itself.

One of the more powerful tools for circumscribing the scope of use is a limited exclusive licensing provision. By restricting the right to exclusive licenses to a year or less (with the option to license out to other companies if mutually agreeable terms cannot be reached), countries improve their leverage over a commercial company during royalty negotiations. This added pressure to negotiate an equitable license fee assures less affluent countries that their resources will not fall hostage to the delaying tactics of a commercial prospector possessing the time and resources to postpone negotiations.

5. Compensation for the Use of Genetic Material

The third cornerstone of such an agreement is the compensation and legal consideration offered for the use of such genetic material. The issue of compensation may present several difficulties, even in the simplest sales royalty agreement. This section highlights the interdependence of research institutions, commercial pharmaceutical companies, in situ conservationists, ex situ conservationists, and countries high in species diversity—though perhaps low in industrial technology.

A contract may provide for royalties, advance payments, contract fees, sample fees, technology transfer, any combination of all of these, and more. The appropriate combination may vary greatly, depending on the country involved and its state of industrialization. Generally, consideration reflects the degree of value added by the parties and the potential or actual market value of a final commercial product.[107] However, biodiversity prospecting in tropical countries and many other geographic areas requires additional consideration to ensure the conservation of biodiversity. This additional consideration might best be referred to as the "value needed." This value needed would reflect those resources necessary to preserve genetic information in situ, where it may be continuously observed, used, and made available for future collections. This value needed concept appears to a have been implicitly acknowledged by the NIH in their ICBG program and by a few international pharmaceutical companies in their growing commitments to conservation of biodiversity. The value needed concept represents an internalization of one of the largest externalities in the world—the preservation of genetic wealth.

---

107. Laird, *supra* note 25, at 111-12.

a. Contract or Sample Fees

Beginning with the most basic compensation, the contract or sample fee, parties should note several important factors. First, the idea of a contract fee or an up–front payment based on the size and unique qualities of the material offered for use is completely nonrisk bearing. In other words, the country seeking to minimize its role in risk–dependent benefits should concentrate on front–loading benefits like these or technology transfer, both of which may be provided independent of drug discovery. Second, an up–front payment gives the government an assurance that the contract is not just another example of business as usual; the early flow of consideration provides a platform from which government agencies and nongovernmental organizations may advocate new or improved legislation and resource regulation, promoting continued commercialization of national biodiversity resources. In a process where many years may pass before financial return is realized, an up–front contract fee provides essential conservation incentives and may enable the development of chemical and genetic resource technologies.

b. Royalties from Net Sales of Natural Product Development

Consideration should also include royalties from net sales, a risk–bearing form of remuneration. Such remuneration has been cited as a "rallying point" for those concerned with the equity of prospecting agreements.[108]

Royalty provisions in a prospecting contract may or may not be fixed. Parties may agree to several different royalty ranges according to the level of value added by the parties. Under this scheme, a direct isolate might earn two or three times the amount of royalties earned by a synthesized analog. Where royalty ranges are agreed upon in an initial agreement, parties must negotiate final royalty rates upon the licensing of a patent or the discovery of a product. When determining these final rates, consideration must be given to the level of intellectual property protection secured, the potential sales, competitive impact of related products, and the extent of contribution of ethnobotanical knowledge or uses, as well as other concerns. Parties to a prospecting contract should attempt to establish minimums for royalty ranges, though not at the expense of up–front consideration. It should be noted that royalty provisions and upfront consideration may have an inverse relationship. Parties should design their own consideration packages,

---

108. Royalties are generally dependent on "the parties' relative risks and contributions to the development of the final product. Generally, the larger the advance and up-front payments a party receives, the smaller its share in the royalty." *Id.* at 111.

combining an appropriate level of risk-based, long-term consideration with upfront compensation independent of drug discovery.

Royalty schemes within prospecting agreements also present an opportunity for the remuneration of indigenous knowledge, the conservation of biodiversity, and the support of educational, commercial, and research efforts. The various techniques that will help ensure royalty returns serve these ends follow in the remainder of this section. Some take form in the royalty structure itself and others in a Memorandum of Understanding or similar agreement between in-country beneficiaries.[109]

c. Compensating Indigenous Knowledge

Within the royalty structure there is an opportunity to recognize and compensate the value of indigenous knowledge both where it has and has not played an actual role in drug discovery and development. When negotiating royalty rates, parties should establish added premiums for situations where local knowledge has contributed to the collection, preparation, testing, development, or other processing of a sample. The options for drafting such provisions can vary greatly as parties to an agreement decide whether and how to use local knowledge. The considerations vary, depending on the degree to which local knowledge is used. For instance, some prospectors may wish to benefit from local knowledge only at the collection stage, thereafter relying solely on high throughput screening. Other prospectors may choose to continue using local knowledge throughout their research.

Where prospectors choose not to use traditional knowledge, whether due to concerns about compensation or a lack of confidence in the value of such information, they still should stipulate to compensating local knowledge. In cases where prospectors develop products derived from plants or other materials that have been used and conserved by local people, remuneration is due. Without such recognition of the value of traditional plant use and stewardship of these plants and the forest ecosystem as a whole, the role of indigenous and semi-indigenous peoples in the management of natural resources goes unremunerated, and unnoticed as well. A royalty system that posts a premium on products derived from plants with a record of indigenous use, regardless of whether that knowledge is used or the plant was collected randomly, provides incentives to the very people whose management practices must be encouraged. These incentives then exist for local as well as national governments, including forest and wildlife managers and others who take part in land tenure and land rights

---

109. *See infra*, section III(B).

decisions affecting local and indigenous peoples. Providing such incentives also encourages the perpetuation of such knowledge in local and indigenous communities where traditional practices are losing their stature and community value.[110]

In the event that prospectors seek to "jump start" a screening operation by using traditional knowledge in the collection and research stages of product development, they may also institute a royalty premium to the rate accorded samples without any indigenous use. The difference in this premium structure would be that a higher "second tier" premium would apply. This would replace the one mentioned earlier wherever the final commercial use has any reasonable nexus to the previous indigenous use. The term "reasonable nexus" leaves room for both parties to negotiate the final royalty rate without feeling bound to the second tier premium in all cases of previous indigenous use. The inherent difficulty with such language is that the "nexus" itself may take one or more of several different forms. For instance, a similarity may exist between the systemic, therapeutic, or other use of the local product and the prospector's commercial product. A similarity may also exist between the active chemical constituents or the function of such constituents in previous indigenous medicines and commercial products.

Where this reasonable nexus exists, compensation for traditional knowledge may seem undeserved to some, due in part to heavy overhead costs. This argument may garner more merit where such a nexus exists, but without the benefit of any actual input from local people or their knowledge; in other words, where a prospector develops a product from a randomly collected sample and that product bears some reasonable nexus to a traditional use, the knowledge has not made a direct contribution to the discovery. Although such a plant under traditional use may have been preserved by such use, it may not always be the case. Still, the application of such a premium, even in the event that local knowledge is not used, provides the incentive to conserve and continue to expand such knowledge. In the event that a contract provides such a premium, an incentive also exists for prospectors to maximize their use of local knowledge. As many ethnobotanists have illustrated, and as the ICBG program should confirm, such knowledge greatly enhances the prospector's chances of valuable discoveries.[111]

---

110. Darcy Ribeiro, *Os Indios e a Civilizacao*, RIO DE JANEIRO: EDITORA CIVILIZACAO BRASILEIRA (1970), *cited in* POSEY, *supra* note 14, at 15.
    111. Farnsworth, *supra* note 17, at 95.

Many other aspects of the royalty structure should receive important scrutiny, including the reporting of sales and accounting procedures. Parties should also stipulate to a royalty structure that provides for royalties on products that do not involve a patent, anticipating a situation where a prospector chooses to go forward with commercial sales either before a patent is issued or in the event that one is refused.[112] Although other concerns exist regarding the royalty scheme in prospecting or collection contracts, these are some of the major concerns relative to local knowledge and conservation incentives.[113]

d. Technology Transfer and Training

Other forms of consideration exist for the parties of a prospecting contracts beyond traditional financial remuneration. One such important form is the transfer of appropriate technology and training. This is an essential component of a sustainable conservation/development consideration package, as necessary for conservation as it is for development. Although several elements of the consideration package may be fungible, building local human and technological capacity is not. Further, providing in-kind transfers of technology and training not only represents slighter financial costs to commercial prospectors, it also increases sample quality and dependability of later recollection and fractionation of active samples.

Parties to genetic resource agreements should compose consideration packages designed as much around conservation as around sustainable development and local capacity building. As noted repeatedly by Calestous Juma, Executive Director of the African Centre for Technology Studies, "[e]fforts that do not build such capacity will only perpetuate the traditional export of raw materials from developing countries, which has left their human capital and technological capacity underdeveloped."[114] As Juma notes, the development of national capacity in this arena is "knowledge intensive"; massive transfer of high-technology equipment is not appropriate in and of itself. This and other observations relevant to technology transfer should be taken into account when assessing the best mix of technology and training.

---

112. This scenario may easily be envisioned, especially where the local knowledge in a particular country has been public for more than a year. Where a commercial product is dependent on this information, its patent applications may be refused. Congress might reconsider the applicability of this requirement de novo in the case where conservation and sustainable development are dependent on ownership rights to knowledge which has been "public" only in a closed community in the rainforest.

113. For an excellent compilation of advance payment and royalty issues *see* Laird, *supra* note 25, at 108-14.

114. Calestous Juma, *Policy Options for Scientific and Technological Capacity-Building, in* BIODIVERSITY PROSPECTING, *supra* note 12, at 199, 199.

The consideration package in an agreement commercializing genetic resources should ensure that the maximum degree of downstream processing occurs in-country by providing technical assistance to develop collection, database, and fractionation capabilities. In addition, the contract should stipulate to specific transfers and research training. If a university or other institute, such as a botanical garden, is involved, research exchange programs should be agreed upon. These provide a foundation upon which further human capacity may grow. Stipulations within prospecting agreements such as these have very unique abilities to direct the formulation of technology development policies in less-industrialized countries. These abilities are explored along with others in Part IV of this article. For the purposes of developing a consideration package, technology transfer, with the appropriate education and training assistance, represents one of the most important aspects of the parties' agreement, assuring long-term capacity and institution building.

e. Right of First Refusal of Supply

In an effort to promote both conservation incentives and economic alternatives within forest communities, the agreement should also provide the country of collection with a first right of refusal to sustainably supply future biological material necessary for development and production.[115] Although right of first refusal may seem to some a right that follows from participation in a prospecting collaboration, it may best figure into a contract as a component of consideration. As such, a country secures the right to supply future raw material, as opposed to relying on unspoken assumptions of good faith. Regardless, countries should negotiate for the right of first refusal, contracting to provide the prospector with all that they are able to on a sustainable basis. Contracts stipulating such rights must also provide that environmental assessments be completed before commercial recollection begins, ensuring that any harvesting, cultivation, and/or processing does not jeopardize environmental quality or human health. In all events, a contract that does not address this issue may drive into extinction the very species it seeks to preserve. Contracts may consider stipulating to a combination of sustainable harvesting and cultivation, thereby providing harvest employment in local communities while also developing the capacity to supply biological material without disturbing in situ stocks.

---

115. Laird, *supra* note 25, at 117-19.

IV. ENSURING CONSERVATION, EQUITY, AND ECONOMIC DEVELOPMENT

A. A Permanent Financial Stake in Conserving Biodiversity

With so many methods of consideration available to the parties, it is important that each is scrutinized for its impact on conservation as well as social and economic development. Some argue that biodiversity prospecting contracts fail to directly link the benefits of biodiversity commercialization with the conservation of biodiversity.[116] In other words, once the biological material of a nation has been screened, there is no longer an incentive to maintain the diversity of species. Additionally, the identification of some species as valuable, and the subsequent cultivation of those species, may result in the acceleration of loss of essential crop diversity. This impression may be dispelled in several ways. First, the possibility of future re–collection and the resulting income provide a relatively direct incentive for conservation.[117] Second, as new screens are developed and new diseases arise, there will likely be a rise in demand to reevaluate or re-screen material. Therefore, the evolving nature of natural products screening and biotechnology (and its rapidly growing capabilities) provides an ongoing incentive to conserve species within their ecosystems, where they may be explored for specific applications, whether or not they have been previously screened.

B. Equity and Resource Stewardship

Bioprospecting projects that fail to return benefits and provide consideration to local peoples for their contributions may be subject to harsh criticism. As stewards of biodiversity, it is essential that communities receive incentives for conservation. Although incentives may be provided through the distribution of royalties, prospectors may wish to avoid becoming involved in the allocation process. In some cases, it may be appropriate to settle the issue of allocation and distribution in a separate agreement such as a Memorandum of Understanding (MOU). Such a memo need only

---

116. Vandana Shiva, Biotechnology and the Environment, published by the Third World Network, 28-29 ISBN: 983-9747-06-01

117. *Cf.* R. David Simpson et al., *Marginal Values and Conservation Incentives in the Commercialization of Indigenous Genetic Resources*, paper presented to the Ass'n of Envt'l & Resource Economists in Boston, MA (Jan. 5, 1994). This recent paper argues that "the conservation incentives generated by bioprospecting cannot be large enough to make any appreciable impact on land conversion decisions." The authors regret that they received the paper just as this article was going to press and cannot address directly the arguments made and therein espoused. It is worth noting, however, that five governments have committed to the objectives of the NIH ICBG, embracing bioprospecting as an alternative to unsustainable development.

involve the in-country beneficiaries of disbursed royalties and might not involve any of the original parties to the prospecting agreement.

Within the group of beneficiaries there should be groups capable of applying financial resources toward national and community conservation and development goals. An MOU or similar agreement allocating royalties might therefore include as beneficiaries governmental agencies responsible for natural resources, indigenous affairs, and national parks and conservation. The agreement might also include nongovernmental organizations such as conservation and environmental advocacy groups as well as indigenous coalitions or communities. Universities and national herbariums might receive a portion of the benefits, because they frequently play pivotal roles in increasing local industrial capacity and ex situ conservation, respectively. Finally, national pharmaceutical or agricultural industries may benefit in accordance with their contributions to the collaboration and their requirements for creating in-country screening and development capacities.

Recognizing the difficulties inherent in infusing millions of dollars into a developing economy, parties to the MOU (if not to the contract as well) should develop an agreement as to how the proceeds from the contract shall be allocated and disbursed. Allocation may follow from contributions and requirements; as mentioned earlier. Generally, this is an issue for groups within the source country to deliberate. It is not, however, an issue that parties to the contract should abandon. Parties should monitor the manner in which funds are to be disbursed to ensure that their allocation and impact are favorable.[118]

Trust funds or segregated accounts would function well as a tool for ensuring that funds promote conservation and do not destroy the cultural fabric of indigenous communities. Such a fund (or a foundation established to manage such a fund) can facilitate the creation of conservation incentives within indigenous communities, provide resources for the creation of sustainable development and natural resource management projects and support research and the exchange of specialists and scholars. To effectively promote these objectives, a foundation should provide information and assistance relating to the operation, objectives, and resources of the fund. Additionally, the trustees of such a fund might subject all of the applications for funding to the scrutiny necessary to promote long-term conservation priorities. Offshore trusts or funds held in hard currency may also

---

118. *See, e.g.,* Tim Bristol, *James Bay,* TURTLE Q., Fall/Winter 1991, at 18 (discussing impacts of hydropower development on Cree and Inuit peoples in Canada).

hedge against inflation and devaluation, allowing greater protection for funds than if held in-country.

Because conservation is a crucial element in a successful prospecting effort, industrial partners also have a vested interest in assuring that proceeds directly benefit conservation and conservation-dependent development, such as screening and fractionation. The involvement of collectors and prospectors should continue, assuring that funds are used in a manner consistent with their objectives.

Finally, parties to an international agreement should explore alternative dispute resolution methods that may save the parties time and other resources compared to judicial remedies. Prospecting contracts involving royalties and other fees which must be finalized upon the discovery of a product or the licensing of a patent present a particularly strong need for arbitration. Since industrial partners will have access to in-house legal expertise and greater financial resources, arbitration may balance the parties disputes in a more equitable fashion. The United Nations Commission on International Trade Laws (UNCITRAL) is one useful model of arbitration that the parties may adopt for their purposes.[119]

V. CONCLUSION

The Biodiversity Convention provides a basis to change the rules of the game with respect to plant collections and forms of biodiversity prospecting. Countries rich in biodiversity are now encouraged to begin regulating the access to and use of their genetic resources to ensure long-term economic development and sound natural resource management. Private biodiversity prospecting agreements are one effective way to begin this process, while also increasing local incentives and capacities for conservation and sustainable development. Such contracts may include provisions which ensure that access to and collection of both natural chemical and genetic material and traditional knowledge are regulated and that compensation is provided, whether in the form of intellectual property protection, royalties, or technology transfer and training. Further, the development of private prospecting agreements, under the aegis of the Biodiversity Convention, provides experience for countries to improve their laws and regulations regarding genetic resource development.

In sum, bioprospecting is an important tool that can be used to foster the conservation of biodiversity through the creation of a natural products

---

119. *Report of the U.N. Commission on International Trade Law*, U.N. GAOR, 31st Sess., Supp. No. 17, at 32-35, U.N. Doc. A/31/17 (1976).

industry in developing countries. Contracts between gene-rich developing countries and industrial prospectors can be used to advance many of the best objectives put forward in the Biodiversity Convention, providing benefits to all parties. Ironically, as genetic resources come under increasingly imminent destructive threats, they increase in importance in the struggle to improve the global human condition.

Indigenous Self-Government, Environmental Protection, and the Consent of the Governed: A Tribal Environmental Review Process

Dean B. Suagee[†]
Christopher T. Stearns[††]

I. INTRODUCTION

Indigenous peoples seek recognition under international law of their collective human rights to govern themselves within their traditional homelands. They seek assistance in defending their homelands against environmentally destructive and culturally devastating so-called "development." The Draft Declaration of the Rights of Indigenous Peoples (Draft Declaration),[1] which is under consideration in the United Nations (UN), declares that indigenous peoples are entitled to certain enumerated human rights, including the right of self-determination,[2] and that they are entitled to assistance from national governments and the international community in exercising these rights.[3]

If we can assume that the Draft Declaration eventually will be adopted by the United Nations General Assembly with substantive provisions acceptable to indigenous peoples, that adoption will constitute the formal reversal, as a matter of international law, of hundreds of years of practice by the world's states. Achieving widespread reversal in nations' actual practice will be much more difficult. Established patterns of dominance over indigenous peoples, and exploitation and expropriation of their homelands by nations with more powerful technologies and domineering

---

† Member of the Cherokee Nation and of counsel to Hobbs, Straus, Dean & Wilder, a Washington, D.C., law firm.

†† Member of the Navajo Nation and an associate with Hobbs, Straus, Dean & Wilder, a Washington, D.C., law firm.

1. *Report of the Working Group on Indigenous Populations on its eleventh session,* U.N. Comm. on Human Rights, Sub-Comm. on Prevention of Discrimination and Protection of Minorities, 11th Sess., Annex I, Agenda Item 14, U.N. Doc. No. E/CN.4/Sub.2/1993/29 (1993) [hereinafter Draft Declaration].

2. *Id.* at art. 3.

3. *Id.* at arts. 13, 14, 15, 16, 28, 29, 35, 37, 38, 40.

worldviews, will take time and effort to change. The recognition in international law of the human rights of indigenous peoples will be an important step in the right direction, but it certainly will not be the end of the struggle. Rather, it will only begin a new era of the struggle.

In this new era in which human rights of indigenous people are recognized, a major theater of action will be the reform of national laws.[4] Some indigenous peoples can expect to seek recognition as fully independent states, but most will seek recognition of some form of autonomous self-government within existing states. The experiences of the American Indian tribes and nations within the United States of America hold many lessons, both positive and negative, relevant to the fashioning of workable arrangements for indigenous autonomy. This article examines the US model for self-government by Indian tribes in the field of environmental protection.

In the United States, as in many other countries, national policies have encouraged or forced indigenous individuals to assimilate into the dominant society. These policies have been abandoned in the United States, but their legacy remains. One aspect of this legacy is the fact that on many reservations a large percentage of residents are not tribal members, either Indians of other tribes or non-Indians, and many of these people are landowners within reservation boundaries. Tribal governments now face the difficult issue of how to accommodate the legitimate interests of nonmembers, including their human rights, while still carrying on *tribal* self-government. Although it is difficult, we think that this issue can be resolved.

This article explores this issue and suggests a general approach that tribal governments might take in the field of environmental protection. Although we focus on the rights and interests of nonmember reservation residents, we think the suggested approach also would be useful in providing some structure in which non-Indians who are not reservation residents, such as neighboring landowners and public interest organizations, can interact with reservation Indians on environmental issues that cross jurisdictional boundaries. If tribes in the United States can fashion ways of accommodating the interests of nonmembers, we think that indigenous peoples in other parts of the world would be interested in the approaches taken by US tribes.

---

4. Many of the articles in the Draft Declaration call on states to take "effective measures to ensure that the rights of indigenous peoples are respected." *E.g., id.* at arts. 13, 14, 15, 16, 17, 28, 35, 37.

Part II frames the issue in the context of international law, focusing on the emerging law of the rights of indigenous peoples and on some of the relevant existing human rights norms. To simplify this framework, we focus on one of the most essential aspects of human rights law: the idea that governments are vested with sovereignty as part of a social compact and that the just exercise of sovereign powers must reflect the consent of the governed. In Part III we offer some observations on Indian experiences with the US model of the social compact. Throughout much of US history, the federal government has asserted power over Indian tribes with very little regard for niceties such as the consent of the governed. We believe that efforts to bring nonmembers into a present-day tribal social compact must be built upon an appreciation of the historical pattern of disregard for consent on the part of Indian people. This part also critiques recent US Supreme Court decisions that severely undercut the doctrine of tribal sovereignty. The Court majority appears to be quite concerned about hypothetical infringements on the rights of nonmembers, especially non-Indians. At the same time it routinely disregards, denies, or flippantly acknowledges the lack of tribal consent to the historical imposition of federal laws, the very laws that set the stage for the current situation in which the rights of nonmembers figure so prominently in the Court's analysis.

Part III includes an overview of the law of environmental protection in Indian country in the United States. It discusses the approach taken in recent amendments to the major federal environmental laws, amendments that authorize tribes to assume roles in carrying out these federal laws similar to the roles performed by state governments. We see this as a manifestation of the US social compact that presents tribal governments with an historic opportunity and an enormous challenge.

Part IV proposes a framework in which tribal governments could provide nonmembers with meaningful opportunities to participate in tribal environmental protection programs. We suggest that tribes go well beyond the minimal requirements of the Environmental Protection Agency's (EPA) regulations and enact tribal legislation that would give nonmembers a real sense of enfranchisement. Mainstream environmental groups could help tribes to build effective environmental protection programs. By building effective tribal programs, tribes will also be cultivating public support for their programs because the tribes will be serving a broad range of public interests. Public support will help tribal programs to withstand the challenges that are sure to arise, and public support will be especially important when those challenges are resolved in the legislative arena.

II. EMERGING INTERNATIONAL LAW OF INDIGENOUS SELF-GOVERNMENT

Over the past decade, the UN has taken the lead in formulating international standards for the recognition and protection of the rights of indigenous peoples. Within the UN, the lead role has been performed by the Working Group on Indigenous Populations, which was established in 1982.[5] At its eleventh session, held in 1993, the Working Group completed drafting a Declaration of the Rights of Indigenous Peoples. The Draft Declaration is now beginning to work its way up the UN hierarchy, with initial consideration being given by the Subcommission on the Prevention of Discrimination and the Protection of Minorities at its forty-sixth session in 1994.[6]

Although the formulation and adoption of the Draft Declaration is only a part of the emerging international law of indigenous rights, it is an essential part. Extensive literature exists on the Draft Declaration[7] and other aspects of the emerging international law of indigenous rights.[8] Most of this subject area is beyond the scope of this article. We have chosen to focus on those principles expressed in the Draft Declaration that are specifically concerned with environmental protection.

---

5. The formation of the Working Group on Indigenous Populations was proposed by the Sub-Commission on Prevention of Discrimination and Protection of Minorities in its resolution 2 (XXXIV) of September 8, 1981, was endorsed by the Commission on Human Rights in its resolution 1982/19 of March 10, 1982, and was authorized by the Economic and Social Council in its resolution 1982/34 of May 7, 1982. *See* Res. 1982/19 U.N. GAOR, Hum. Rts. Comm. (1982); *Report of the Working Group on Indigenous Populations on its eleventh session*, U.N. Commission on Human Rights, Sub-Comm. on Prevention of Discrimination and Protection of Minorities, 11th Sess., Agenda Item 14, U.N. Doc. E/CN.4/Sub.2/1993/29 paras. 62–67 (1993) [hereinafter *Working Group 1993 Report*] at 4.

6. *Id.* at 44.

7. *See generally* S. James Anaya, *Indigenous Rights Norms in Contemporary International Law*, ARIZ. J. INT'L & COMP. L. Vol. 8, No. 2 at 1 (1991); Robert N. Clinton, *The Rights of Indigenous Peoples as Collective Group Rights*, 32 ARIZ. L. REV. 739 (1990); Hurst Hannum, *New Developments in Indigenous Rights*, 28 VA. J. INT'L L. 649 (1988); Dean B. Suagee, *Self-Determination for Indigenous Peoples at the Dawn of the Solar Age*, 25 U. MICH. J. L. REV. 671 (1992); Robert A. Williams, Jr., *Encounters on the Frontiers of International Human Rights Law: Redefining the Terms of Indigenous Peoples' Survival in the World*, 4 DUKE L.J. 660 (1991).

8. For example, another aspect of the emerging international law of the rights of indigenous peoples has been the adoption by the International Labour Organisation of a revised convention on the rights of indigenous peoples, I.L.O. Convention No. 169. Convention Concerning Indigenous and Tribal Peoples in Independent Countries, *adopted* June 27, 1989, 28 I.L.M. 1382 [hereinafter Convention 169]. *See generally* Anaya, *supra* note 7, at 10–15; Russel L. Barsh, *An Advocate's Guide to the Convention on Indigenous and Tribal Peoples*, 15 OKLA. CITY U. L. REV. 209 (1990); Lee Swepston, *A New Step in the International Law on Indigenous and Tribal Peoples: ILO Convention No. 169 of 1989*, 15 OKLA. CITY U. L. REV. 677 (1990).

A. *Principles in the Draft Declaration*

The Draft Declaration consists of some forty-five articles, many of which concern the relationships of indigenous peoples to the natural environment of their traditional homelands. Some of these articles emphasize the rights of indigenous peoples to the possession and use of their traditional territories, some emphasize the importance of the natural world in indigenous cultural practices, and others emphasize the rights of indigenous peoples to exercise self-government within their territories. Articles 25 and 26, which are particularly relevant to environmental protection, read as follows:

Article 25

> Indigenous peoples have the right to maintain and strengthen their distinctive spiritual and material relationship with the lands, territories, waters and coastal seas and other resources which they have traditionally owned or otherwise occupied or used, and to uphold their responsibilities to future generations in this regard.[9]

Article 26

> Indigenous peoples have the right to own, develop, control and use the lands and territories, including the total environment of the lands, air, waters, coastal seas, sea-ice, flora and fauna and other resources which they have traditionally owned or otherwise occupied or used. This includes the right to the full recognition of their laws, traditions and customs, land-tenure systems and institutions for the development and management of resources, and the right to effective measures by states to prevent any interference with, alienation of or encroachment upon these rights.[10]

Article 25 acknowledges both the spiritual nature of the relationship that indigenous peoples have to their territories and their widely shared belief in responsibility to future generations. Article 26 makes it clear that indigenous peoples have human rights to make use of wildlife, plant life, and other aspects of the natural world for the good of human communities. These two articles taken together reflect a basic value held by most indigenous peoples: the natural world is sacred, and indigenous communities are part of the natural world.[11]

Several other articles in the Draft Declaration elaborate on the rights of indigenous peoples to govern human uses of the resources and human

---

9. Draft Declaration, *supra* note 1, at art. 25.

10. *Id.* at art. 26.

11. *See generally* DAVID SUZUKI & PETER KNUDTSON, WISDOM OF THE ELDERS: HONORING SACRED NATIVE VISIONS OF NATURE (1992); J. Baird Calicott, *American Indian Land Wisdom, in* THE STRUGGLE FOR THE LAND: INDIGENOUS INSIGHT AND INDUSTRIAL EMPIRE IN THE SEMIARID WORLD 255 (Paul A. Olson, ed., 1990).

effects on the environment of their traditional territories.[12] Article 33 sets some important limits on the ways in which indigenous peoples may carry out their governmental powers. This articles reads:

Article 33

> Indigenous peoples have the right to promote, develop and maintain their institutional structures and their distinctive juridical customs, traditions, procedures and practices, *in accordance with internationally recognized human rights standards.*[13]

In other words, indigenous peoples are expected to respect the human rights of all individuals within their jurisdiction, whether or not such individuals are members of indigenous communities or citizens of indigenous nations.

The next section takes note of a few key internationally recognized human rights standards. These include both those that support affirmative actions by indigenous governments to promote the human rights of indigenous individuals and those that place some limits on the prerogatives of indigenous governments, just as they limit the prerogatives of all sovereign governments.

B. Existing Human Rights Norms

Most of the body of international human rights law has emerged since the founding of the UN following the end of the Second World War.[14] In addition to including human rights in the statement of purposes and principles in the UN Charter,[15] the UN General Assembly adopted both the Universal Declaration of Human Rights[16] and the Convention on the Prevention and Punishment of the Crime of Genocide[17] in its early years.

In 1966, the UN General Assembly adopted and opened for ratification by member states the two principal multilateral treaties for the protection of human rights: the International Covenant on Civil and Political Rights[18] and the International Covenant on Economic, Social and Cultural

---

12. *See* Draft Declaration, *supra* note 1 at arts. 21, 23, 24, 28, 29, 30 and 31.

13. *Id.* at art. 33 (emphasis added).

14. Richard B. Bilder, *An Overview of International Human Rights Law, in* GUIDE TO INTERNATIONAL HUMAN RIGHTS PRACTICE 5 (Hurst Hannum ed., 1984).

15. U.N. CHARTER, art. 1, ¶ 3 (purposes include "promoting and encouraging respect for human rights and fundamental freedoms for all").

16. G.A. Res. 217, U.N. GAOR, 3rd Sess., 183rd plen. mtg., at 71, U.N. Doc. A/810 (1948).

17. G.A. Res. 260, U.N. GAOR, 3rd Sess., 179th plen. mtg., at 174, U.N. Doc. A/810 (1948).

18. G.A. Res. 2200, U.N. GAOR, 21st Sess., Supp. No. 16, at 52, U.N. Doc. A/6316 (1966).

Rights.[19] Scholars and activists sometimes refer collectively to these two international covenants, along with the Universal Declaration and the Optional Protocol to the International Covenant on Civil and Political Rights,[20] as the International Bill of Human Rights.[21] In proclaiming the rights of individuals against states, these instruments constitute significant limits on the basic principle of international law that a state's sovereignty over matters within its domestic jurisdiction is not subject to intervention by other states or by international organizations.[22]

An analysis of the norms proclaimed in the International Bill of Human Rights could be carried out in great detail. We have chosen to focus on three articles of the Civil and Political Rights Covenant that go to the heart of this article's subject matter. First, Article 27 proclaims:

> In those States in which ethnic, religious or linguistic minorities exist, persons belonging to such minorities shall not be denied the right, in community with the other members of their group, to enjoy their own culture, to profess and practice their own religion, or to use their own language.[23]

Indigenous peoples all over the world have been deprived of this human right. It is largely because of this widespread deprivation that in its Draft Declaration the UN Working Group on Indigenous Populations has emphasized the collective right of indigenous peoples to exercise autonomous self-government within their traditional territories. This amounts to a recognition that autonomous self-government is a prerequisite to protect the rights of indigenous peoples to carry on their own cultures, religions, and languages. Article 33 of the Draft Declaration suggests that if an indigenous people were to become an independent state, and if such a state were to include ethnic, religious, or linguistic minorities most likely including individuals belonging to the previously dominant nonindigenous culture, the newly constituted indigenous state would be bound to honor the human rights of such nonindigenous individuals to carry on their culture, religion, and language.

---

19. G.A. Res. 2200, U.N. GAOR, 21st Sess., Supp. No. 16, at 49, U.N. Doc. A/6316 (1966).

20. International Covenant on Civil and Political Rights, *supra* note 18, at 59.

21. Kathryn J. Burke, *Introduction* NEW DIRECTIONS IN HUMAN RIGHTS xi (Ellen L. Lutz et al. eds., 1989). In addition to these instruments, the UN and other international organizations, including regional international organizations, have adopted numerous other instruments relating to human rights. *See generally* GUIDE TO INTERNATIONAL HUMAN RIGHTS PRACTICE, *supra* note 14.

22. *See, e.g., Declaration on Principles of International Law Concerning Friendly Relations and Co-operation Among States in Accordance with the Charter of the United Nations,* G.A. Res. 2625, U.N. GAOR, 25th Sess., at 1, U.N. Doc. A/2625 (1970).

23. International Covenant on Civil and Political Rights, *supra* note 18, at art. 27.

In addition, Articles 25 and 26 of the Civil and Political Rights Covenant proclaim human rights that should be taken into account by indigenous peoples that choose to exercise autonomous self-government within an existing state rather than to become an independent state. These two articles read:

Article 25

Every citizen shall have the right and the opportunity, without any of the distinctions mentioned in article 2 and without unreasonable restrictions:

(a) To take part in the conduct of public affairs, directly or through freely chosen representatives;

(b) To vote and to be elected at genuine periodic elections which shall be by universal and equal suffrage and shall be held by secret ballot, guaranteeing the free expression of the will of the electors;

(c) To have access, on general terms of equality, to public service in his country;[24]

Article 26

All persons are equal before the law and are entitled without any discrimination to the equal protection of the law. In this respect, the law shall prohibit any discrimination and guarantee to all persons equal and effective protection against discrimination on any ground such as race, colour, sex, language, religion, political or other opinion, national or social origin, property, birth or other status.[25]

We have chosen to focus on these principles in the Civil and Political Rights Covenant because they go to the heart of the concept of sovereignty in the modern world. These principles reflect one of the "self-evident" truths proclaimed in the US Declaration of Independence, that governments derive "their just powers from the consent of the governed."[26] Sovereignty *is* a social compact. Although this statement describes the real world in some countries much more than in others, in the United States people believe that governments exist to serve the public good; therefore if a government fails to faithfully carry out its responsibilities to the public, the citizens have the right to change the government, usually by throwing out the individuals and/or parties in charge. In this context, it will be a real challenge for tribal governments in the United States to fashion effective

---

24. *Id.* at art. 25.
25. *Id.* at art. 26.
26. THE DECLARATION OF INDEPENDENCE para. 2 (U.S. 1776).

environmental regulatory programs that non-Indians subject to tribal jurisdiction will accept rather than resist. If Indian tribal governments can
succeed in this effort, the models that they develop could prove very useful
for other indigenous peoples around the world.

III. INDIAN EXPERIENCES IN THE AMERICAN SOCIAL COMPACT

Western civilization generally regards itself as having given the rest
of the world the idea that governments derive their powers from the
collective will of their citizens and that individuals have rights that governments cannot take away. A number of scholars have shown that the social
philosophers who are credited with having developed these ideas, and the
founding fathers of the American republic who incorporated these ideas
into a system of government, drew upon their knowledge of how the Indian
nations of eastern North America governed themselves[27] (especially the
nations of the Haudenosaunee or Iroquois Confederacy). Some writers
have noted that the framers of the Constitution overlooked certain key
aspects of the Iroquois Great Law of Peace, such as the role of women.[28]
Similarly, if Indian leaders had been participants in the American constitutional convention, the Constitution might include specific provisions to
reflect Indian values, such as responsibilities to future generations and the
natural world and respect for the wisdom of the elders.

Some principles that have become central to the American social
compact might have less importance or might not fit at all in an Indian
social compact. For example, the principle of "one person-one vote" would
conflict with the Iroquois tradition of the clanmothers selecting the chiefs
based on their abilities rather than by popular vote.[29] Because people have
responsibilities toward the natural world and toward future generations, an

---

27. *See generally* Oren R. Lyons, *The American Indian in the Past, in* EXILED IN THE
LAND OF THE FREE: DEMOCRACY, INDIAN NATIONS, AND THE U.S. CONSTITUTION 13 (Oren
R. Lyons & John C. Mohawk, eds. 1992) (hereinafter "EXILED IN THE LAND OF THE FREE");
John C. Mohawk, *Indians and Democracy: No one Ever Told Us, in* EXILED IN THE LAND
OF THE FREE, *supra* at 43; Robert W. Venables, *American Indian Influences on the America
of the Founding Fathers, in* EXILED IN THE LAND OF THE FREE, *supra* at 73; Donald A. Grinde,
Jr., *Iroquois Political Theory and the Roots of American Democracy, in* EXILED IN THE LAND
OF THE FREE, *supra* at 227; Robert J. Miller, *American Indian Influence on the United States
Constitution and Its Framers,* 18 AM. INDIAN L. REV. 133 (1993); Gregory Schaaf, *From
the Great Law of Peace to the Constitution of the United States: A Revision of America's
Democratic Roots,* 14 AM. INDIAN L. REV. 323 (1989); *contra* Erik M. Jensen, *The Imaginary
Connection Between the Great Law of Peace and the United States Constitution: A Reply
to Professor Schaaf,* 15 AM. INDIAN L. REV. 295 (1990).

28. Renée Jacobs, *Iroquois Great Law of Peace and the United States Constitution:
How the Founding Fathers Ignored the Clan Mothers,* 16 AM. INDIAN L. REV. 497 (1991).

29. *Id.* at 508.

Indian social compact might give greater weight to the votes of those who try to faithfully carry out these responsibilities.

We leave it to others to debate the extent to which American Indian political thought and social organization influenced the development of social compact theory and the belief that individuals have certain inalienable rights, but we think it is clear that the larger American society and the world owe at least some kind of a debt of gratitude to North American Indians. This debt should be at least acknowledged. To the extent that it makes sense to speak of repayment of this debt, the repayment should take the form of supporting the surviving Indian tribes and nations of United States in their efforts to exercise their collective human right of self-government.

A. The Changing Terms of Relations Between the United States and Indian Tribes

This article makes no pretense of offering either a detailed analysis of the field of federal Indian law or a detailed discussion of the history of relations between the federal government and the Indian tribes and nations.[30] But some knowledge of history is necessary if one is to make any sense of much of the body of federal Indian law, and although there are broad patterns and common themes, the history of each tribe's relations with the federal government is unique.

Throughout most of the history of the United States, Congress exercised sweeping powers over Indian peoples with little regard for consent on the part of Indians, either as tribes or individuals. Federal policymakers, including the judges whose decisions often have professed to discern congressional intent from scant indicia,[31] generally have acted on the basis of one of two fundamentally different attitudes toward Indian tribes. One paradigm regards the tribes as separate peoples for whom the federal government is obliged to provide a measure of protection; the other regards the tribes as primitive forms of social organization that should be abolished as individual Indians become assimilated into the larger society.[32]

---

30. *See generally* FELIX S. COHEN, HANDBOOK OF FEDERAL INDIAN LAW (Rennard Strickland et al. eds. 1982); ROBERT N. CLINTON ET AL., AMERICAN INDIAN LAW (3rd. ed. 1991); DAVID H. GETCHES ET AL., FEDERAL INDIAN LAW (3rd. ed. 1993); *see also* Vine Deloria, Jr., *Laws Founded in Justice and Humanity: Reflections on the Content and Character of Federal Indian Law*, 31 ARIZ. L. REV. 203, 210–213 (1989) (arguing the Cohen's HANDBOOK should be used as a source of information and criticizing the elevation of the HANDBOOK to the status of a treatise).

31. *See* Deloria, *supra* note 30, at 204.

32. *See* CHARLES F. WILKINSON, AMERICAN INDIANS, TIME, AND THE LAW 23–31 (1987). *See also* COHEN, *supra* note 30, at 49, 128–132, 139–41, 152, 180–88.

During the early period of treaty making between the United States and the most powerful of the eastern Indian nations, the treaties that were made were genuine bilateral agreements between parties of comparable power. Therefore, those tribes and nations that accepted the superior sovereignty of the United States "relatively freely" consented to become subject to the sovereignty of the federal government in accordance with the terms of their treaties.[33] A similar point could be made regarding some of the early treaties with the tribes of the Great Plains.

After the early treaty period, however, the relationship between the United States and the tribes became much more one-sided. In many cases the United States unilaterally changed the terms of relations agreed to in treaties or ignored treaty promises altogether. Even as the treaties became one-sided and the tribes were pressed to give up more and more of their lands, the treaties were still founded on the premise that tribes would remain separate peoples and on the understanding that tribal homelands or "reservations" were essential if tribes were to maintain their separateness.[34] This premise was understood by both the tribes and by the federal government and, although the tribes did not want to give up most of their lands, they did want to remain separate.

As the balance of power became increasingly one-sided during the course of the nineteenth century, the belief that Indian tribes should be treated as separate peoples gave way to the belief that Indians should be assimilated into larger society. This occurred over the span of several decades, but the watershed event was the enactment of the General Allotment Act of 1887, also known as the Dawes Act.[35] Under the policy of allotment, Congress attacked the basic tribal value and cultural practice of holding land in common.[36] The allotment era of federal Indian policy saw numerous separate legislative acts directed toward specific reservations, although other tribes escaped altogether. For those tribes whose reservations were allotted, the basic approach was to take land out of tribal ownership and divide it into parcels for allotment to individuals.

---

33. Richard B. Collins, *Indian Consent to American Government*, 31 ARIZ. L. REV., 365, 374–75 (1989).

34. *See* WILKINSON, *supra* note 32, at 18.

35. Act of February 8, 1887, ch. 119, 24 Stat. 388 (codified as amended at 25 U.S.C. §§ 331–34, 339, 341–42, 348–49, 354, 381 (1988)). *See also* WILKINSON, *supra* note 32, at 19–20.

36. Theodore Roosevelt is said to have described the General Allotment Act as "a mighty pulverizing engine to break up the tribal mass." *Quoted in* WILKINSON, *supra* note 32, at 19.

Congress ultimately repudiated this policy when it enacted the Indian Reorganization Act of 1934,[37] but by the end of the allotment era Indian tribes and individuals held only about a third of the land that the tribes had held in 1887.[38] Some of these lands passed out of Indian possession when the trust restrictions were lifted and the lands became subject to state property taxes. Other lands were declared "surplus" and were sold to non-Indians or opened for homesteading. This is the historical explanation for the presence of substantial populations of non-Indian landowners within the boundaries of many reservations that, according to treaties, were set aside for the exclusive use of Indians forever.

Viewed from the perspective of the late twentieth century, the General Allotment Act can be seen for what it was—an attempt to carry out cultural genocide against Indian tribes and nations.[39] If the federal government were to carry out such a policy in the modern era, tribal leaders could oppose it on many grounds, including calling attention to the violations of international human rights law inherent in such a policy.[40] But it happened and, as a result, many tribes now have many non-Indians living within their reservation boundaries.

---

37. Act of June 18, 1934, ch. 576, § 1, 48 Stat. 984 (codified at 25 U.S.C. § 461 (1988)).

38. Of approximately 138 million acres of Indian lands in 1887, only 48 million acres remained in 1934. COHEN, *supra* note 30, at 138.

39. *See* Draft Declaration, *supra* note 1, at art. 7. The allotment policy fits four of the kinds of actions listed in Article 7 as examples of cultural genocide, including:

> (a) Any action which has the aim or effect of depriving [indigenous peoples] of their integrity as distinct peoples, or of their cultural values or ethnic identities;

> (b) Any action which has the aim or effect of dispossessing them of their lands, territories or resources;

> (c) Any form of population transfer which has the aim or effect of violating or undermining any of their rights;

> (d) Any form of assimilation or integration by other cultures or ways of life imposed on them by legislative, administrative or other measures.

See also Suagee, *supra* note 7, at 695–97 (discussing genocide and cultural genocide); Anaya, *supra* note 7, at 16 (human rights norm inherent in the Genocide Convention that all cultural groupings have the right to exist); Rennard Strickland, *Genocide-at-Law: An Historic and Contemporary View of the Native American Experience*, 34 KAN. L. REV. 713 (1986).

40. For example, one could argue that the allotment policy violates Article 27 of the International Covenant on Civil and Political Rights, quoted in the text accompanying note 23, *supra*, and that it violates several articles of the Draft Declaration, *supra* note 1, including Article 7. Although the Supreme Court has recognized that Congress subsequently repudiated the policy of allotment and sale of so-called "surplus" reservation land, the Court nevertheless has decided modern cases by looking to the congressional intent of the allotment policy. Rosebud Sioux Tribe v. Kneip, 430 U.S. 584 (1977); Solem v. Bartlett, 465 U.S. 463, 468–72 (1984); Brendale v. Confederated Tribes and Bands of the Yakima Nation, 492 U.S. 408, 422–23 (1989). Persons on whom we bestow the title "Justice" should be able to find a way to make repudiated congressional policy yield to contemporary international human rights standards.

In recent decades the belief that tribes are entitled to a measured separatism from the larger American society has regained prominence in federal law and policy. Congress has enacted a substantial body of legislation in support of tribal self-government, including the Indian Self-Determination and Education Assistance Act of 1975.[41] During this modern era of federal Indian policy, sometimes referred to as the "self-determination" era,[42] tribal governments have become increasingly involved in carrying out a wide range of governmental functions.

On many reservations the expanding sphere of tribal governmental functions has included taxing and regulating the activities of non-Indians within reservation boundaries. In many cases, however, non-Indians or state governments have challenged tribal authority in federal courts. In addition to challenging tribal authority, many of these cases also have raised issues regarding whether state laws can be applied within reservation boundaries. Since the early years of the United States, the supremacy of federal authority in Indian affairs has served to protect tribes against the imposition of state laws within reservations.[43]

In the modern era, decisions by the US Supreme Court have employed principles which are neither clearly articulated nor consistently applied, thus making it hard to predict whether tribal or state authority, or both, will be sustained in a given case. Many commentators have criticized the reasoning of the Supreme Court's recent Indian law decisions,[44] which have had the effect of eroding tribal sovereignty in an era when Congress and the Executive have been generally supportive of tribal sovereignty. In a particularly damaging blow to tribal sovereignty, the Court in a 1978

---

41. 25 U.S.C. §§ 13a, 450–450n, 455–458e (1988), 42 U.S.C. § 2004b (1988).

42. *See generally* COHEN, *supra* note 30, at 180–206 (discussing the self-determination era). The self-determination era followed the assimilationist "termination" era, during which the federal government abruptly and unilaterally ended the special status under federal law of many tribes. *Id.* at 152–80.

43. *See generally* COHEN, *supra* note 30, at 275–79. Of course, in some cases the plenary authority of Congress also has been used to render Indians expressly subject to state laws without regard for tribal consent, e.g., Public Law 280 imposing state criminal law and civil adjudicatory jurisdiction on reservation Indians in certain states. *See* COHEN, *supra* note 30, at 362–70.

44. *See generally* Mary Beth West, *Natural Resources Development on Indian Reservations: Overview of Tribal, State, and Federal Jurisdiction,* 17 AM. INDIAN L. REV. 71, 76–88 (1992) (describing the erosion of the infringement test, the shift from an emphasis on tribal sovereignty to an emphasis on federal preemption, the rise of the implicit divestiture test, and the rise of the balancing og governmental interests analysis); *see also* Judith v. Royster & Rory SnowArrow Fausett, *Control of the Reservation Environment: Tribal Primacy, Federal Delegation, and the Limits of State Intrusion,* 64 WASH. L. REV. 581, 600–07 (1989); Curtis G. Berkey, *International Law and Domestic Courts: Enhancing Self-Determination for Indigenous Peoples,* 5 HARV. HUM. RTS. J. 65, 70–75 (1992); Comment, *Toward Consent and Cooperation: Reconsidering the Political Status of Indian Nations,* 22 HARV. C.R.-C.L. L. REV. 507, 556–83 (1987) (hereinafter *Toward Consent*).

decision fashioned a new rule that tribes can lose aspects of their sovereignty by implication as a result of their dependent status.[45] Prior to the announcement of the "implicit divestiture" rule, tribes were assumed to have retained all those aspects of their original sovereignty that had not been given up or were expressly taken away or limited by an act of Congress.[46] The practical effect has been to invite challenges to tribal sovereignty. Even in cases in which tribal governmental powers have been held not to have been implicitly divested, and in which federal law and policy have been held to preempt state authority, the Court has suggested that the interests advanced by a state must still be considered. A strong enough state interest might tip the balance in favor of sustaining state regulatory authority.[47]

B. Supreme Court Confusion Over Tribal Regulatory Authority and the Power to Exclude

Regulatory power is a fundamental attribute of sovereignty, through which the sovereign exercises control over the conduct of individuals and land use within its territory. Although the power of tribes to regulate the conduct of members on tribal lands is settled,[48] the extent to which tribes may regulate the conduct of nonmembers is less certain. In recent cases, such as *South Dakota v. Bourland,*[49] the Supreme Court has created considerable confusion about the extent to which a tribe may regulate the conduct of nonmembers on fee lands within reservation boundaries.

1. Sources of Tribal Regulatory Authority

The Supreme Court's decisions defining the scope of tribal regulatory power demonstrate a fundamental uncertainty over the extent to which tribes retain regulatory authority as an aspect of their original sovereignty.[50]

---

45. Oliphant v. Suquamish Indian Tribe, 435 U.S. 191 (1978).

46. *See* Berkey, *supra* note 44, at 70–71; West, *supra* note 44, at 77–79; F. COHEN, HANDBOOK OF FEDERAL INDIAN LAW 123 (1942) (powers of internal sovereignty are limited only by treaties and express legislation by Congress).

47. *E.g.*, California v. Cabazon Band of Mission Indians, 480 U.S. 202, 216 (1987) (state interests might be sufficient to sustain state assertion of authority even if federal preemption applies). *See also infra* note 96 and accompanying text.

48. A discussion of the foundations of tribal sovereignty is beyond the scope of this article. We simply note the fact that tribal governments are distinct, independent political communities, Worcester v. Georgia, 31 U.S. (6 Pet.) 515, 559 (1832), with inherent attributes of sovereignty, United States v. Mazurie, 419 U.S. 544, 557 (1975). The tribes' inherent sovereign powers are presumed to be retained unless "withdrawn by treaty or statute, or by implication as a necessary result of their dependent status." United States v. Wheeler, 435 U.S. 313, 323 (1978).

49. __ U.S. __, 113 S.Ct. 2309 (1993).

50. *See, e.g.*, Merrion v. Jicarilla Apache Tribe, 455 U.S. 130 (1982); Montana v. United States, 450 U.S. 544 (1981); Rice v. Rehner, 463 U.S. 713 (1983); *Brendale* 492 U.S. 408, County of Yakima v. Confederated Tribes and Bands of the Yakima Indian Nation, __ U.S. __, 112 S.Ct. 683 (1992); and *Bourland*, 113 S.Ct. 2309. *See also* Joseph William Singer, *Sovereignty and Property*, 86 Nw. U. L. REV. 1 (1991) (criticizing transformation of sovereignty into property issues and vice versa to the disadvantage of Indian interests).

Historically, the Court has recognized two sources of tribal regulatory authority: inherent tribal sovereignty[51] and the power to exclude nonmembers from tribal lands.[52] More recent Supreme Court opinions, however, indicate a retreat from the Court's earlier holdings. In an attempt to restrict the tribes' power over nonmembers, the Court has now stated that the tribes' power to regulate nonmembers stems soley from the tribes' power to exclude,[53] and that the tribes' inherent sovereign power as a basis for regulatory jurisdiction has been implicitly divested. Thus, in instances where a tribe can no longer exclude nonmembers from lands within its territory, the Court argues that the tribe has also lost the power to regulate those nonmembers' conduct. Yet, the Court has conceded that a tribe still may regulate or tax nonmembers living or conducting acitivities on fee lands in two special instances under the *Montana* test: where the nonmembers have entered into consensual relations with a tribe or its members, or where the nonmembers' activities infringe upon or have a direct effect on the tribe's political integrity, economic security, or health or welfare.[54]

The flaw in the Court's analysis is that the tribes' remaining regulatory authority over nonmembers' activities on fee lands cannot stem from the tribes' power to exclude. They have none. Rather, the tribes' remaining regulatory authority must stem from retained inherent

---

51. The Supreme Court has said, "The power to tax is an essential attribute of Indian sovereignty because it is a necessary instrument of self-government and territorial management." *Merrion*, 455 U.S. at 137. *See also* Powers of Indian Tribes, Op. Sol., Dept. Int., 55 I.D. 14, 46 (1934) (opinion stating that a tribe possesses the power of taxation which may be exercised over members and nonmembers); *Kerr-McGee Corp. v. Navajo Tribe*, 471 U.S. 195, 198–99 (1985) (discussing tribal power to tax as unconditioned on Secretarial approval).

In *Kerr-McGee*, the Court emphasized the federal government's commitment to the goal of promoting tribal self-government in relationship to the tribal power to tax. *Kerr-McGee*, 471 U.S. at 200–201. "The power to tax members and non-Indians alike is surely and essential attribute of such self-government; the Navajos can gain independence from the Federal Government only by financing their own police force, schools, and social programs." *Kerr-McGee*, 471 U.S. at 201.

In *Washington v. Confederated Tribes of the Colville Indian Reservation*, 447 U.S. 134 (1980), the Supreme Court held that "[t]he power to tax transactions occurring on trust lands and significantly involving a tribe or its members is a fundamental attribute of sovereignty which the tribes retain unless divested of it by federal law or necessary implication of their dependent status." *Colville*, 447 U.S. at 152.

52. *See, e.g., Brendale*, 492 U.S. at 425; *Merrion*, 455 U.S. at 137, 141–42.

53. *See* discussion of *Bourland, infra* notes 58–65 and accompanying text.

54. *Brendale*, 492 U.S. at 428; *Yakima*, 112 S.Ct. at 692; *Bourland*, 113 S.Ct. at 2320. *See also* West, *supra* note 44, at 81–82 (criticizing Justice White's narrow application of the *Montana* exceptions in his plurality opinion in *Brendale*).

sovereignty.[55] Thus, despite the Court's pronouncements to the contrary, tribal regulatory authority continues to derive from two sources—the power to exclude and inherent tribal sovereignty.

2. The Bourland Analysis

The Supreme Court's decision in *Bourland* illustrates its confusion over the scope of tribal regulatory power. In *Bourland*, the Supreme Court held that the Cheyenne River Sioux Tribe does not have the power to regulate non-Indian hunting and fishing in the reservoir behind the Oahe Dam which inundates a portion of the Cheyenne River Reservation.

In the 1950s, under congressional pressure, the tribe relinquished 104,000 acres of its land to the government for the Oahe Dam and reservoir.[56] The Cheyenne River Act permitted the tribe to continue to hunt and fish in the reservoir, "subject, however, to regulations governing the corresponding use by other citizens of the United States."[57] It was undisputed on appeal that the portion of the reservation taken for the reservoir retained its reservation status. For a time both the tribe and the state regulated public hunting and fishing within the reservation. In 1988 the tribe announced that henceforth it would not recognize state game licenses and that non-Indian hunters would be subject to prosecution in tribal court (and civil penalties) unless licensed by the tribe. The state sued.

---

55. The Court has so held:

> Even though the ownership of land and the creation of local governments by non-Indians established their legitimate presence on Indian land, the [*Buster*] court held that the Tribe retained its power to tax. The court concluded that "[n]either the United States, nor a state, nor any other sovereignty loses the power to govern the people within its borders by the existence of towns and cities therein endowed with the usual powers of municipalities, *nor by the ownership nor occupancy of the land within its territorial jurisdiction by citizens or foreigners.*" This result confirms that the Tribe's authority to tax derives not from its power to exclude, but from its power to govern and to raise revenues to pay for the costs of government.

Merrion, 455 U.S. at 143, *citing* Buster v. Wright, 135 F. 947, 952 (8th Cir. 1905), *appeal dismissed*, 203 U.S. 599 (1906) (emphasis in original).

56. Cheyenne River Act of Sept. 3, 1954, 68 Stat. 1191. *See generally* Michael L. Lawson, Dammed Indians: The Pick–Sloan Plan and the Missouri River Sioux, 1944–1980 (1982) (documenting the destruction wreaked upon the Sioux by the Missouri River dams). Although the *Bourland* Court suggests that the Cheyenne River Sioux consented to the taking of their lands for the Oahe dam and reservoir, 113 S.Ct. at 2313–14 (1993), anyone who doubts that the tribes on whose reservations Pick–Sloan reservoirs were located were under duress should examine the photograph of George Gillette, the Tribal Chairman of the Three Affiliated Tribes of the Fort Berthold Reservation, who broke down in tears while signing the contract with the Army Corps of Engineers for the Garrison dam and reservoir. *Reproduced in* Native American Testimony: A Chronicle of Indian–White Relations from Prophecy to the Present, 1492–1992, 343 (Peter Nabokov, ed., 1991).

57. Cheyenne River Act, *supra* note 56, at 1193.

Writing for the Court, Justice Clarence Thomas agreed that prior to the taking, the tribe had the power to exclude non-Indians, and therefore "arguably" had the power to regulate them.[58] But, citing the *Montana* and *Brendale* cases, he said that when a tribe conveys land to non-Indians, it loses its right to exclusive use of the land as well as its regulatory jurisdiction over the land.[59] Justice Thomas said that in taking the tribal land and opening it up for public use, Congress eliminated the tribe's regulatory jurisdiction by transferring it to the US Army Corps of Engineers.[60]

Justice Thomas further wrote that *Montana* means that when Congress has "broadly opened up such land to non-Indians, the effect of the transfer is the destruction of preexisting Indian rights to regulatory control."[61] With respect to the tribe's argument that it had "inherent sovereignty" over all parts of its reservation, Justice Thomas repeated language from the *Montana* case that "exercise of tribal power beyond what is necessary to protect tribal self-government or to control internal relations is inconsistent with the dependent status of the tribes, and so cannot survive without express congressional delegation." Thomas also found that there was no evidence of such a congressional delegation in this instance.[62] He then turned to whether the *Montana* exceptions applied. The trial court had found they did not, but the appellate court did not rule on this issue. The Supreme Court referred this question back to the appeals court to decide.[63]

Thus, according to the Court in *Bourland*: (1) tribal regulatory authority over non-Indians stems solely from the power to exclude; (2) tribal regulatory authority over non-Indians disappears whenever a tribe

---

58. *Bourland*, 113 S.Ct. at 2316.

59. *Id.*

60. *Id.* at 2316–17. This holding, like the holdings of the *Montana* and *Brendale* cases, is contrary to longstanding policy of the Department of Interior, that "the powers of an Indian tribe [over property] are not limited to such powers as it may exercise in its capacity as a landowner. In its capacity as a sovereign, and in the exercise of self-government, it may exercise powers similar to those exercised by any State or nation in regulating the use and disposition of private property, save insofar as it is restricted by specific statutes of Congress." Powers of Indian Tribes, *supra* note 50, at 55. This statement is reproduced verbatim in the original edition of FELIX S. COHEN, HANDBOOK OF FEDERAL INDIAN LAW 145 (1942).

61. *Id.* at 2318. Justice Blackmun anticipated this result in *Brendale*, stating that Justice Stevens's opinion, which grounded tribal regulatory jurisdiction in the power to exclude, "appears implicitly to conclude that tribes have no inherent authority over non-Indians on reservation lands. . . . [T]his conclusion stands in flat contradiction to every relevant Indian sovereignty case that this Court has decided." *Brendale*, 492 U.S. at 462–63 (Blackmun, J., concurring in part and dissenting in part).

62. *Bourland*, 113 S.Ct. at 2319.

63. *Id.* at 2320.

loses the power to exclude those non-Indians; (3) but, tribal regulatory authority over non-Indians may exist if Congress expressly delegates that power; and, (4) tribal regulatory authority over non-Indians also may exist if either of the two *Montana* exceptions come into play.

The inconsistency in Justice Thomas's analysis lies in his dismissal of the idea that the tribe's own inherent sovereignty provides a source of regulatory power over non-Indians on non-Indian lands. For instance, Justice Thomas wrote that "regulatory authority goes hand in hand with the power to exclude."[64] He also added that "after *Montana*, tribal sovereignty over nonmembers cannot survive without express congressional delegation, 450 U.S. at 564, and is therefore *not* inherent."[65] But, as Justice Thomas admits, a tribe may exercise regulatory authority, without congressional delegation, over non-Indians on fee lands in two instances. The only basis for such regulatory jurisidiction is that "Indian tribes retain *inherent sovereign power* to exercise some forms of civil jurisdiction over non-Indians on their reservations, even on non-Indian fee lands."[66] Thus, inherent sovereignty remains a source of tribal regulatory power, despite the *Bourland* Court's attempts to bury it.

Although the Supreme Court's recent rulings do not eliminate inherent tribal authority as a basis for regulatory power over non-Indians, the fact remains that such power is viewed with suspicion by the non-Indian community and is often the subject of judicial challenge. In the next section, we discuss a key aspect of the courts' concerns with tribal regulatory authority over non-Indians.

C. Consent as a Limit on Tribal Powers over Nonmembers

As descibed earlier, the Supreme Court has retreated from the view that tribal regulatory authority stems from inherent tribal sovereignty. Although *Duro v. Reina*[67] is set in a criminal context, the Supreme Court's opinion in that case indicates that in the context of tribal civil regulatory authority as well, the principle of consent of the governed is a key factor in the Court's application of the implicit divestiture rule.[68] In Duro, the Court stated that:

> [A] basic attribute of sovereignty is the power to enforce laws against all who come within the sovereign's territory, whether citizens or aliens.

---

64. *Id.* at 2317, n.11, *citing Brendale*, 492 U.S. at 423–424.

65. *Id.* at 2320, n.15, *citing Montana*, 450 U.S. 544.

66. *Montana*, 450 U.S. at 565.

67. 495 U.S. 676 (1990).

68. That the Court should emphasize consent of the governed as a basis for tribal sovereignty is somewhat ironic given the fact that Indian tribes have rarely been given the opportunity to consent to federal actions. *See supra* notes 33–38 and accompanying text.

Oliphant recognized that the tribes can no longer be described as sovereigns in this sense. Rather, as our discussion in *Wheeler* reveals, the retained sovereignty of the tribes is that needed to control their own internal relations, and to preserve their own unique customs and social order.[69]

Although the *Duro* court recognized that a tribe's civil jurisdiction over nonmembers is broader than its criminal jurisdiction,[70] the Court stated: "[W]e hesitate to adopt a view of tribal sovereignty that would single out a group of citizens, nonmember Indians, for trial by political bodies that do not include them."[71] Thus, the Court said that in the criminal context:

> The retained sovereignty of the tribe is but a recognition of certain additional authority the tribes maintain over Indians who consent to be tribal members. . . . A tribe's additional authority comes from the *consent of its members*, and so in the criminal sphere membership marks the bounds of tribal authority.[72]

The Court declared that tribal courts are "influenced by the unique customs, languages, and usages" of the tribes, that they are "often 'subordinate to the political branches of tribal governments,' and legal methods may depend on 'unspoken practices and norms.'"[73] Therefore, "[t]he special nature of the tribunals at issue makes a focus on *consent* and the protections of citizenship most appropriate."[74] The Court then reinvented the basis for tribal criminal jurisdiction over nonmembers by saying:

> Retained criminal jurisidiction over members is accepted by our precedents and justified by the voluntary character of tribal membership and the concomitant right of participation in a tribal government, *the authority of which rests on consent*.[75]

The Supreme Court's decision in *Duro* was subsequently overturned by Congress in 1990 and 1991 through legislation affirming the power of tribes to execise inherent criminal jurisdiction over all Indians.[76] Congress

---

69. *Duro*, 495 U.S. at 685–86.

70. "Our decisions recognize broader retained tribal powers outside the criminal context. . . . Civil authority may also be present in areas such as zoning where the exercise of tribal authority is vital to the maintenance of tribal integrity and self-determination." *Id.* at 687–88.

71. *Id.* at 693.

72. *Id.* (emphasis added).

73. *Id., citing* FELIX S. COHEN, HANDBOOK OF FEDERAL INDIAN LAW 334–35 (Rennard Strickland, et al., eds. 1982)

74. *Id.* (emphasis added).

75. *Id.* at 694 (emphasis added).

76. *See* Act of Nov. 5, 1990, Pub. L. No. 101–511, § 8077(b)–(d), 104 Stat. 1892 (codified as amended at 25 U.S.C. § 1301(2)–(4) (1988)), and Act of Oct. 28, 1991, Pub. L. No. 102–137, 105 Stat. 646 (repealing sunset provision in Act of Nov. 5, 1990). *See generally*, Nell Jessup Newton, *Permanent Legislation to Correct Duro v. Reina*, 17 AM. IND. L. REV. 109 (1992).

did so in response to public outcry, led by both tribal and state coalitions, who were angered at the effect of the *Duro* ruling, which had created severe law enforcement problems on Indian reservations. In overturning the Supreme Court's holding, Congress chose to affirm the inherent criminal jurisdiction of tribes over nonmember Indians, rather than delegate tribal jurisdiction. Congressional affirmation thus rejected the Supreme Court's conclusion that tribes had been implicitly divested of inherent authority over nonmember Indians.[77]

Non-Indians persistently claim that tribal authority over them is government without representation, thereby advancing personal rights arguments against tribal sovereignty.[78] We expect that non-Indians will continue to challenge tribal regulatory actions on these and other grounds. Professor Richard Collins has suggested that the plenary power of Congress over the tribes provides tribes with a response to this argument, because non-Indians are represented in Congress. Plenary power therefore "gives democratic legitimacy to tribal jurisdiction over non-Indians."[79] While we are inclined to agree with this line of reasoning, tribal governments should try to find ways to address the concerns of non-Indian reservation residents other than telling them to take their case to Congress.

To the extent that the lower federal courts adopt the Supreme Court's assumption that the principle of consent of the governed provides a basis for limiting or implicitly divesting tribal powers over non-Indians, such challenges may prevail in court.[80] Conversely, to the extent that tribes involve non-Indians in the process of developing and carrying out the exercise of tribal regulatory authority over nonmembers, the courts may be

---

77. The Supreme Court's decision in *Duro* was based on federal common law, not the Constitution. In creating federal common law, the federal courts attempt to divine Congressional intent. Thus, where a court mistakenly interprets Congressional intent, Congress retains the power to "correct" the court's interpretation through subsequent legislation. *Duro* is such a case.

78. Collins, *supra* note 33, at 385. While we agree with Professor Collins that this claim "has obvious force," in *Merrion*, the Supreme Court said, "Indian sovereignty is not conditioned on the assent of a nonmember; to the contrary, the nonmember's presence and conduct on Indian lands are conditioned by the limitations the tribe may choose to impose." 455 U.S. at 147.

79. *Id.* at 386. *See* Article 25(b) of the International Civil and Political Rights Covenant, *supra* note 18.

80. *See, e.g.*, Duncan Energy Co. v. Three Affiliated Tribes of the Fort Berthold Reservation, No. A1–91–222 (D.N.D. filed Sept. 28, 1993) (order granting summary judgment), in which the District Court struck down the Tribe's employment ordinance and oil and gas production tax as to various oil and energy companies operating on fee lands within the Fort Berthold Reservation. The Court stated, "[n]o doubt George III had some worthy projects in mind in the 1770s, but taxation without representation was not popular with the colonists then and still doesn't seem terribly just." *Id.*, slip op. at 6.

more inclined to sustain such exercises of tribal authority. To the extent that nonmembers feel that tribal regulatory programs actually provide them with ways to deal with their concerns, to become a part of the program if they so desire, many such cases may be resolved without recourse to the federal courts. Part IV of this article explores a framework for providing nonmembers and non-Indians with a way to be involved in tribal decision making in the substantive area of environmental protection, but first we present an overview of relevant federal law.

D. Federal Environmental Law in Indian Country

Governmental programs for environmental protection are a relatively recent manifestation of the social compact. In the 1960s and early 1970s, a significant portion of the US public became aware of a wide range of environmental problems and demanded that Congress take action. In response, Congress enacted a number of statutes to protect and restore the environment.

Most federal environmental laws enacted over the past two decades forge a partnership between the federal government and the states. Under these federal statutes, states have substantial responsibilities and may take on additional "delegable" responsibilities if they so choose. States assume the additional responsibilities to avoid direct control by the EPA. Federal laws generally do not preempt state laws, but do establish an overall framework, along with some minimum requirements for state environmental protection programs. States may establish requirements that are more stringent, and they may enact laws to cover subjects not covered by the federal laws. Thus, citizens can take their environmental concerns to the federal or the state sovereign or both.

For the most part, federal environmental laws enacted in the 1970s included few specific references to Indian tribes or Indian lands. Congress did not demonstrate much awareness of, or concern for, reservation environments, and tribes generally had more pressing concerns. This was, after all, the early years of the self-determination era in federal Indian policy,[81] and many tribal governments were engaged in taking control of basic governmental programs like health care, education, and social services.[82]

---

81. *See* COHEN, *supra* note 30, at 180–206 (discussing the self-determination era). The Indian Self-Determination and Education Assistance Act of 1975, Pub. L. No. 93–638, 88 Stat. 2206 (1975) (codified as amended at 25 U.S.C. §§ 13a, 450–450n, 455–458e (1988))— the statute establishing a framework for tribal governments taking over programs that would otherwise be administered by the Bureau of Indian Affairs or Indian Health Service—had not even been enacted when several of the major federal environmental statutes became law.

82. Some tribes were engaged in environmental issues. *E.g.*, the Northern Cheyenne Tribe redesignated its reservation from class II to class I under the Clean Air Act. *See* Nance v. EPA, 645 F.2d 701 (9th Cir. 1981), *cert. denied*, 454 U.S. 1081 (1981).

In 1984, the EPA adopted a "Policy for the Administration of En-vironmental Programs on Indian Reservations,"[83] in which it recognized tribal governments as sovereign entities, which are "the primary parties for setting standards, making environmental policy decisions and managing programs for reservations, consistent with Agency standards and regula-tions."[84] Pursuant to this policy, the EPA encourages and assists tribes to assume regulatory responsibilities, but "[u]ntil Tribal Governments are willing and able to assume full responsibility for delegable programs, [the policy of] the Agency [is to] retain responsibility for managing programs for reservations (unless the State has an express grant of jurisdiction from Congress sufficient to support delegation to the State Government)."[85]

Given the prominent role of the states in carrying out federal environ-mental laws and the history of conflicts between tribes and states, it was to be expected that some states would not embrace the EPA policy. In a leading case,[86] the state of Washington asserted jurisdiction over all per-sons, Indians and non-Indians, within reservation boundaries for the pur-pose of regulating hazardous wastes under the Resource Conservation and Recovery Act (RCRA).[87] The court upheld the EPA's decision not to approve the state's program with respect to Indian reservations, based in

---

83. Environmental Protection Agency, *EPA Policy Statement for the Administration of Environmental Programs on Indian Reservations* (Nov. 8, 1984) (on file with the COLO. J. INT'L ENVTL. L. & POL'Y).

84. *Id.*

85. *Id.* In addition to the EPA's 1984 policy, *supra* note 83, in 1991 EPA issued a document entitled "Federal, Tribal and State Roles in the Protection and Regulation of Reservation Environments," which was distributed as an attachment to Memorandum from William K. Reilly, EPA Administrator, to Assistant Administrators, General Counsel, Inspector General, Regional Administrators, Associate Administrators, and Staff Office Directors (Jul. 10, 1991) [hereinafter *Reilly Memorandum*], reaffirming the 1984 policy. (On file with the COLO. J. INT'L ENVTL. L. & POL'Y).

86. Washington Dept. of Ecology v. EPA, 752 F.2d 1465 (9th Cir. 1985). In this case, when the state of Washington applied to the EPA for approval of its hazardous waste regulatory program under the Resource Conservation and Recovery Act (RCRA), it sought authorization from the EPA to apply its program to both Indian and non-Indian residents of Indian reservations within the state's borders. *Id.* at 1467. This case has been the subject of numerous articles in the legal literature, *e.g.*, Leslie Allen, *Who Should Control Hazardous Waste on Native American Lands? Looking Beyond Washington Department of Ecology v. EPA*, 14 ECOLOGY L.Q. 69 (1987); Richard A. Du Bey, et al., *Protection of the Reservation Environment: Hazardous Waste Management on Indian Lands*, 18 ENVTL. L. 449 (1988); Note, *Regulatory Jurisdiction over Non-Indian Hazardous Waste in Indian Country*, 72 IOWA L. REV. 1091 (1987); Note, *Environmental Law—Federal Indian Law—Recent Developments*—State of Washington, Department of Ecology v. United States Equal Protec-tion Agency, 27 NAT. RESOURCES J. 739 (1987). *See also* Judith V. Royster & Rory SnowArrow Fausett, *supra* note 44, at 629–38.

87. 42 U.S.C. §§ 6901–6992k (1988). Hazardous waste regulation is governed by RCRA §§ 3001–3023, 42 U.S.C. §§ 6921–6939e (1988).

part on the EPA's policy for Indian lands.[88] The court acknowledged the state's "vital interest" in the effective regulation of hazardous wastes throughout the state, including Indian reservations, but reasoned that federal enforcement by the EPA would be sufficient to protect the state and its citizens.[89]

In recent years, Congress has amended many of the federal laws in ways that are generally consistent with the EPA's 1984 policy—in essence ratifying the EPA's policy. These laws now provide that tribes may, if they choose, assume roles similar to the roles performed by states.[90] In response to the mandates of these amended statutes, the EPA has issued numerous amendments to its regulations to establish procedures for tribes to be treated as states for a wide variety of purposes.[91] In addition, Congress has

---

88. Washington Dept. of Ecology v. EPA, 752 F.2d at 1469. Because the state's application to EPA sought approval to regulate all persons within reservations, the court expressly did not decide whether the state could have created a program that, within reservations, would have regulated only non-Indians. *Id.* at 1468.

89. *Id.* at 1472. Regulatory programs such as the hazardous waste program under the RCRA charge the EPA with primary responsibility, a role that states can take over with EPA approval. *See* 40 C.F.R. §§ 271, 272 (1992). For such programs, the EPA can simply retain authority over reservations when states apply for primacy. Some programs established by the federal laws, however, begin by placing the primary responsibility on states, e.g., the solid waste management program under the RCRA which the EPA does not administer directly, although the EPA has established nationally applicable standards. 40 C.F.R. § 258 (1992). The prohibitions of the RCRA relating to solid waste have been held to apply in Indian country, Blue Legs v. U.S. Bureau of Indian Affairs, 867 F.2d 1094 (8th Cir. 1989), but the great majority of waste disposal sites in Indian country nevertheless are not in compliance with EPA standards. This is due in part to a lack of federal financial and technical assistance to tribes and in part to a lack of clarity regarding the responsibilities of federal agencies. *See* S. Rep. No. 370, 102d Cong., 2d Sess, 2–3 (1992).

90. Safe Drinking Water Act (SDWA), 42 U.S.C. § 300j–11(a)(1) (1988) (treating tribes as states for certain purposes); Comprehensive Environmental Response, Compensation, and Liability Act of 1980 (CERCLA, also known as "Superfund"), 42 U.S.C. § 9626 (1988) (treating tribes substantially the same as states for certain purposes); Clean Water Act (CWA), 33 U.S.C. § 1377 (1988) (treating tribes as states for certain purposes); Clean Air Act (CAA), 42 U.S.C. § 7601(d) (1988) (treating tribes as states for certain purposes). *See generally* David F. Coursen, *Tribes as States: Indian Tribal Authority to Regulate and Enforce Federal Environmental Law and Regulations*, 23 ELR 10579 (Oct. 1993); *see also* Steven Berlant, *Responding to the Dangers Posed by Hazardous Substances: An Overview of CERCLA's Liability and Cost Recovery Provisions as they Relate to Indian Tribes*, 15 AM. INDIAN L. REV. 279 (1990); Royster & Fausett, *supra* note 44; Jana L. Walker & Kevin Gover, *Commercial Solid and Hazardous Waste Disposal Projects on Indian Lands*, 10 YALE J.ON REG. 229, 232–35 (1993); Suagee, *supra* note 7 at 704–08.

91. *E.g.*, Safe Drinking Water Act regulations: 40 C.F.R. §§ 35, 124, 141–46 (1992); Clean Water Act regulations for Water Quality standards: 40 C.F.R. § 131 (1992); Clean Water Act regulations for the § 404 program (dredging and filling waters, particularly wetlands): 40 C.F.R. §§ 232, 233 (1992); Clean Water Act regulations for grants: 40 C.F.R. §§ 35, 130 (1992); Comprehensive Environmental Response, Compensation, and Liability Act regulations for cooperative agreement: 40 C.F.R. § 35 (1992); Emergency Planning and Community Right-to-Know Act reporting requirements: 40 C.F.R. §§ 350, 355, 370, 372 (1992). *See generally* Coursen, *supra* note 90, at 10,582–84.

enacted a law providing the EPA with a mandate to provide general assistance to tribes in building the capacity to plan, develop, and implement environmental regulatory programs.[92]

These changes in the federal laws present tribal governments with an historic opportunity and an enormous challenge. Obviously, tribes that succeed in fashioning effective environmental regulatory programs will be better able to preserve the quality of their reservation environments for the benefit of present and future generations of tribal members and to protect and restore the natural environments that sustain tribal cultures.

Perhaps as important in the context of American democracy, effective tribal programs will serve a broad range of public interests that extend well beyond reservation boundaries. In doing so, tribes may find that important non-Indian interest groups will come to regard tribes as indispensable units of government in our federal system. Because important public interests are involved, it is not surprising that EPA regulations require tribes that are treated as states to provide meaningful opportunities for public involvement.[93]

After all, the tribes are being asked to help carry out federal laws. Like the states, tribes are charged with making many of the basic policy decisions,[94] and they may adopt standards that are more stringent than

---

92. Indian Environmental General Assistance Act of 1992, Pub. L. No. 102–497, 106 Stat. 3258 (1992)(codified at 42 U.S.C. § 4368b; amended by Pub. L. No. 103–155, 107 Stat. 1523 (1993)) (extending authorization of appropriations through FY 1998 and requiring an annual report to Congress by the EPA). The EPA General Assistance Program is the successor to its "multi-media" program for Indian tribes, which was authorized in annual appropriations acts for the departments of Veterans Affairs and Housing and Urban Development and Independent Agencies for FY 1991 and FY 1992. Pub. L. No. 101–507, 104 Stat. 1351, 1372 (1990); Pub. L. No. 102–139, 105 Stat. 736, 762 (1991). In addition to the EPA General Assistance Program, Congress also has given a mandate to the Administration for Native Americans in the Department of Health and Human Services to provide financial assistance to tribes to build their capacities to administer environmental protection programs. See Indian Regulatory Enhancement Act of 1990, Pub. L. No. 101–408, § 2, 104 Stat. 883 (1990)(amending § 803 of the Native American Programs Act of 1974, 42 U.S.C. § 2991b).

93. See 40 CFR § 25 (1992). In particular, 40 CFR § 25.10 (1992) establishes minimal requirements for rule making by states, including tribes treated as states, although these requirements do not preempt the requirements of a state administrative procedure act, if one exists. The EPA encourages tribal governments to enact administrative procedure acts, and many have done so. See Reilly Memorandum, supra note 85, at 4–5. In some cases, public involvement requirements for tribes treated as states are based on federal statute, e.g., § 303(c) of the Clean Water Act, 33 U.S.C. § 1313(c), requires a state to hold a public hearing at least once every three years to review, modify and adopt water quality standards. Accordingly, while the general EPA regulations governing state rulemaking provide that a public hearing is optional, EPA regulations for setting water quality standards make clear that, in this context, a public hearing is mandatory. 40 CFR § 131.20.

94. E.g., designating use classifications for bodies of water under the Clean Water Act, Clean Water Act § 303(c)(2)(A), 33 U.S.C. § 1313(c)(2)(A) (1988), 40 C.F.R. § 131.10 (1992); redesignating air quality classification, Clean Air Act § 164, 42 U.S.C. § 7474 (1988), 40 C.F.R. § 52.21(g) (1992).

federal minimum requirements[95] and enact their own laws to address environmental concerns that are not covered by the federal laws. But when tribes are treated as states for the purpose of carrying out federal environmental law, in addition to acting in their own sovereign capacity, they are acting for the federal sovereign as well, carrying out the social compact between the American people and our national government.

Tribes should regard the current federal policy for environmental protection in Indian country as a window of opportunity, one that may not remain open indefinitely if tribes do not accept the challenges that this opportunity presents. Moreover, given the recent judicial erosion of the tribal right of self-government and the increasing use by federal courts of the implicit divestiture rule and the balancing of governmental interests analysis in Indian law cases,[96] if tribes do not establish effective environmental regulatory programs, some states will assert that there is a void and that state interests justify state regulatory jurisdiction. Some of the states can be expected to assert jurisdiction regardless of what tribes do. In such cases, judicial resolution may turn on whether the EPA has acted in accordance with its stated policy and actually has retained primary enforcement authority over the reservation as a "single administrative unit."[97]

If a tribe has not established a program under a particular federal statute, the tribe should be sure that the EPA is committed to federal enforcement so that there is no enforcement void. If there is in fact a void, a federal court may be receptive to a state's argument that, on balance, its interests justify state regulatory jurisdiction. Given the language in the federal statutes authorizing tribes to be treated as states, and given the

---

95. *E.g.*, states may adopt water quality standards and effluent limitations that are more stringent than those in effect under the Act. Clean Water Act § 510, 33 U.S.C. § 1370 (1988). The EPA has construed this section of the Act to be applicable to tribes treated as states. 56 Fed. Reg. 64,876 (1991) (codified at 40 C.F.R. § 131 (1992)).

96. *See* notes 44–47, *supra* and accompanying text.

97. In addition to EPA's 1984 policy, *supra* note 83, in *Reilly Memorandum, supra* note 85, EPA has stated:

> Consistent with EPA Indian Policy and the interests of administrative clarity, the Agency will view Indian reservations as single administrative units for regulatory purposes. Hence, as a general rule, the agency will authorize a tribal or state government to manage reservation programs only where that government can demonstrate adequate jurisdiction over pollution sources throughout the reservation. Where, however, a tribe cannot demonstrate jurisdiction over one or more reservation sources, the Agency will retain enforcement primacy for those sources. Until EPA formally authorizes a state or tribal program, the Agency retains full responsibility for program management. Where EPA retains such responsibility, it will carry out its duties in accordance with the principles set out in the EPA Indian Policy.

Id. at 3–4.

EPA's policy for implementing the federal statutes,[98] a reviewing court should find that the field of environmental regulation within Indian country has been preempted by federal law, that tribal civil regulatory authority over non-trust lands within the reservation boundaries has not been implicitly divested, and that there is no need to engage in a balancing of governmental interests.[99] Even if the courts take this approach and find that the field has been preempted, under the Supreme Court's rulings the federal courts will still give some consideration to the interests advanced by a state.[100] If there is no tribal program and if federal enforcement is lax, a court might find the interests of the state sufficient to justify jurisdiction.[101]

Tribal governments have taken on a variety of roles in environmental protection and restoration. Changes made in the federal environmental laws, in conjunction with the actions of the EPA in carrrying out its policy for Indian reservations, have supported the efforts of tribal governments to build environmental protection regulatory programs. As a result, many tribes have made substantial progress in doing so. Although Indian tribes and nations generally did not consent to the taking of their lands so that nonmembers could become landowners within reservations, nonmembers have become a substantial part of the popululation of many reservations and a majority on some. As discussed earlier, the concept of sovereignty embodies not only power but also responsibility. For tribal governments, this means not only responsibility toward past, present, and future generations of tribal members and toward culturally important plant and animal

---

98. *See* EPA Policy, *supra* note 83, as elaborated in the *Reilly Memorandum*, *supra* note 85. In addition, the preamble to the final rules for treatment of tribes as states for the purpose of adopting water quality standards, *supra* note 90, explains the EPA's position that the Clean Water Act does not constitute a delegation of authority to tribes but that, rather, like states, tribes that adopt water quality standards do so as an exercise of their own sovereignty. 56 Fed. Reg. 64,876–80, *supra* note 95. While the EPA requires each tribe to demonstrate that it has the requisite authority, the EPA also indicates that the showing a tribe must make is relatively simple, including the assertion that impairment of reservation waters by the activities of non-Indians "would have a serious and substantial effect on the health and welfare of the Tribe." *Id.* at 64,879.

99. For a more detailed discussion of the balancing of governmental interests analysis in the context of environmental protection, *see* Royster & Fausett, *supra* note 44, at 649–59.

100. The Supreme Court has said that even the assertion of state authority is preempted if it would interfere with "federal and tribal interests reflected in federal law, unless the state interests at stake are sufficient to justify the assertion of state authority." New Mexico v. Mescalero Apache Tribe, 462 U.S. 324, 334 (1983), *quoted in* California v. Cabazon Band of Mission Indians, 480 U.S. 202, 216 (1987).

101. A state might argue that this constitutes "exceptional circumstances" justifying state regulatory jurisdiction even over reservation Indians. *See* note 47 *supra* and accompanying text. *See also* Royster & Fausett, *supra* note 44, at 605, nn.88, 89 (summarizing court opinions that suggest or apply the "exceptional circumstances" factor). In the absence of an effective tribal program, an actual EPA presence may be necessary to disarm such an argument.

species and sacred places, but also toward nonmembers, both Indian and non-Indian, who reside within reservation boundaries. Unless tribal governments act responsibly with respect to the rights and interests of nonmembers, nonmembers can be expected to take their cases to other sovereigns such as the federal government and the states. No doubt many nonmembers will take their cases to other sovereigns regardless of what tribal governments do, but tribal governments' actions can influence how those other sovereigns respond.

We believe that the field of environmental protection provides a context in which tribes can show the rest of American society that they are fully capable of handling the responsibilities of sovereignty. By attending to the legitimate rights and interests of the governed—tribal members, nonmember Indians, and non-Indians—tribes will find that their environmental protection programs will become not only effective but also resilient. Resiliency will prove to be a critical characteristic if tribal programs are to withstand the challenges that they are sure to face. Although the American public shows strong general support for environmental protection, the objectives of environmental protection programs often conflict with powerful economic interests. The more effective the public perceives an environmental protection program to be in protecting public interests, the greater the likelihood that the program will have critical public support when it comes under attack.

IV. A TRIBAL ENVIRONMENTAL REVIEW PROCESS

As tribal governments assume a growing range of responsibilities in the field of environmental protection, they are inclined to use the same types of tools used by both federal and state governments, including the enactment of laws, adoption of regulations, and establishment of administrative agencies. Regulatory programs should be considered only part of the mix and, in order to control environmental problems effectively, governmental economic policies should operate to make market prices reflect the true costs of products. One way that this may be done is by eliminating government subsidies to environmentally destructive industries.[102] Although there is merit to such an argument, environmental

---

102. One also might argue that the governmental tools used by the federal and state governments should not be assumed to be essential ingredients of environmental protection programs in indigenous territories, because traditional cultural values such as reverence for the natural world and consensus decision making may operate to control environmentally destructive "development" and other activities that nonindigenous governments typically control through regulatory programs. We are concerned in this article, however, with reservations that have substantial populations of persons who are not tribal members.

regulatory programs have become a fact of life in most of the United States, and it should be taken as a given that the next several years will see substantial growth in tribal regulatory programs. The focus for tribal governments should be on how to build *effective* environmental regulatory programs given the constraints that many tribes face, such as limited financial and human resources.

But how should tribal governments go about building effective programs? Tribal governments typically do not have sources of revenue comparable to those of the federal and state governments.[103] Nor do tribes typically have large numbers of tribal members with advanced degrees in environmental sciences from which candidates can be selected for positions in tribal regulatory agencies. For the most part, tribes cannot be expected to build replicas of the federal EPA, the Fish and Wildlife Service, or the Advisory Council on Historic Preservation in the immediate future. Even if many tribes could do so, it may not be the best use of their human and financial resources. Despite limited resources, tribal governments can nevertheless establish effective environmental regulatory programs. In this part of the article, we outline an approach that tribes should consider in building their programs.

A. A "Blanket" Environmental Review Process

We suggest that tribes strategically plan their approach to building environmental regulatory programs. At an early point in the development of its environmental program, a tribe's political leaders and staff should proactively and comprehensively think about the environment and about how all the various regulatory programs that they might eventually decide to establish should fit together. One of the first steps should be the enactment of a tribal code that establishes an overall, or "blanket," environmental review requirement for proposed development activities on lands under tribal jurisdiction.

A blanket environmental review process can serve two basic purposes. First, by establishing such a process, a tribal government could assert control over a broad range of activities that may cause adverse environmental and cultural impacts, and second, such a review process could serve to enfranchise the reservation populace, Indian and non-Indian, by providing a structure through which interested individuals and groups could become involved in the tribal decision-making process. In other

---

103. Many tribal governments do have revenue streams from gaming facilities, and such revenues typically are used to support a wide range of governmental programs and services, including environmental regulatory programs. Many tribes also collect some tax revenues. As a general rule, however, the revenues available to tribal governments are not comparable to those of the states.

words, the environmental review process should not simply be an assertion of tribal governmental authority but rather a genuine manifestation of the social compact.

1. Making the NEPA Serve Tribal Purposes

One approach to establish a blanket tribal environmental review process is to make the existing federal environmental review process work to serve tribal interests. Many kinds of activities that cause environmental impacts in Indian country involve some kind of federal agency action. If a federal action is a prerequisite for or an indispensable aspect of an activity that causes environmental impacts (such as federal permitting of a non-federal entity), the responsible federal agency must comply with the review process established under the National Environmental Policy Act (NEPA).[104] The NEPA has been described as a statute of constitutional dimensions because it constitutes a kind of social compact that empowers citizens to participate in the decisions of government agencies affecting the environment.[105]

The NEPA requires the responsible federal agency to prepare an environmental impact statement (EIS) prior to taking any "major Federal action significantly affecting the quality of the human environment."[106] This requirement has been implemented through regulations issued by the President's Council on Environmental Quality (CEQ).[107] Among other things, the CEQ regulations establish a screening process to help federal agencies determine which proposed actions require an EIS and which require a less detailed environmental assessment (EA). Although the NEPA is the blanket federal environmental review process, there are numerous other federal environmental review and consultation require-ments that are concerned with particular kinds of resources or aspects of the natural world.[108] If an EIS is prepared for a proposed federal action, the CEQ regulations mandate that the EIS should also address compliance with any other federal environmental laws that apply to the proposed action.[109]

---

104. 42 U.S.C. §§ 4321–4347 (1988). *See generally* Dean B. Suagee, *The Application of the National Environmental Policy Act to "Development" in Indian Country*, 16 AM. INDIAN L. REV. 377 (1991).

105. Environmental Law Institute, NEPA Deskbook at v. (1989). One of us has observed that tribal leaders do not appear to have shared this view of the NEPA, suggesting that this is in part because the NEPA "was fashioned by the dominant American society and unilaterally imposed on federal actions affecting Indian lands." Suagee, *supra* note 104, at 463.

106. 42 U.S.C. § 4332(2)(C) (1988).

107. 40 CFR §§ 1500–1508 (1992).

108. One of these other requirements, the consultation process established under section 106 of the National Historic Preservation Act, 16 U.S.C. § 470f(1988), is discussed briefly later in this article. *See* notes 140–150 *infra* and accompanying text.

109. 40 CFR § 1502.25(a).

Similarly, if an EA is required, the EA should at least identify any other federal requirements that would apply.

Because the NEPA applies to a variety of actions in Indian country that cause environmental impacts, tribes can serve their interests in having an effective environmental review process by becoming actively involved in, and asserting control over, the federal NEPA process within their reservations.[110] Two key methods of ensuring involvement are to have tribal staff prepare and review NEPA documents and for tribal officials to wait for NEPA documents to be prepared and reviewed before making tribal decisions on proposed actions. Another key step that tribes can take is to enact tribal laws that expressly require the preparation of an EA when any federal agency is considering a proposed action that may affect important tribal interests. For agencies within the Department of the Interior, including the Bureau of Indian Affairs (BIA), the department's procedures for implementing the CEQ's NEPA regulations expressly require preparation of an EA prior to any proposed federal action that would violate a tribal law.[111] Thus, it would be quite simple to make Interior agencies, including the BIA, prepare EAs before they take or approve actions that may adversely affect important tribal interests by enacting a tribal law requiring an EA for certain kinds of actions. Practically speaking, in some cases, litigation may be necessary to force federal agencies to comply.

2. Federal Help in Fashioning a Review Process

One reason tribes should pay particular attention to the NEPA stems from the fact that while all federal agencies are subject to it, no single federal agency has a lead role in overseeing federal agency compliance. The EPA serves as a clearinghouse for NEPA documents and customarily comments on NEPA documents prepared by other agencies,[112] but it has no enforcement role. Because the EPA does not have a delegable program that states or tribes can take over, it does not have a grant program for the specific purpose of helping tribes develop and sustain their NEPA capabilities.

---

110. *See* Suagee, *supra* note 104, at 426–27.

111. 516 DM [Departmental Manual] 2, app. 2, § 2.10. *See* Suagee, *supra* note 104, at 398 n.79.

112. The EPA's role in reviewing and commenting on the EISs prepared by other agencies is based on section 309 of the Clean Air Act, 42 U.S.C. § 7609 (1988), which also directs the EPA to determine whether the proposed federal action that is the subject of an EIS would be "unsatisfactory from the standpoint of public health or welfare or environmental quality" and, in any such case, to refer the matter to the Council on Environmental Quality. The CEQ regulations establish a process for dealing with such "pre-decision referrals," a process that also allows federal agencies other than the EPA to refer matters to the CEQ. 40 CFR § 1504 (1992). The CEQ cannot order an agency to act in a certain way, but it may refer the matter to the president.

If tribes do not choose to make this one of their own environmental priorities, neither the EPA nor any other federal agency is likely to make this an area of emphasis. Tribes that do choose to make this a priority, however, might use the EPA's general environmental assistance program for tribes[113] to help them develop the capacity to administer a blanket tribal environmental review process.[114] Another source of federal assistance is the Administration for Native Americans.[115]

B. Toward a Tribal "Mini-NEPA"

Beyond making federal agencies comply with NEPA in a way that serves tribal interests, tribal governments can establish their own overall or "blanket" environmental review processes. Because the NEPA process applies to so many actions, tribes should use the NEPA process in building their own review frameworks. Many states have enacted this kind of legislation, and such state statutes are often called "mini-NEPAs."[116] Although state mini-NEPAs may be used as models in developing tribal mini-NEPAs, state mini-NEPAs exist in a context of state environmental laws and land use regulatory laws—much of which may not be very relevant to Indian country. We have fashioned a model mini-NEPA for tribes[117] that is based on the federal NEPA and on the Model Land Development Code,[118] published by the American Law Institute (ALI) in 1976. The

---

113. *See* note 95, *supra*. The EPA issued an interim final rule for the Indian Environmental General Assistance Program of 1992, and 58 Fed. Reg. 63,876 (1993).

114. The statute provides that funding provided to tribes is to be used for "planning, developing, and establishing the capability to implement programs administered by" the EPA. 42 U.S.C. § 4368b(f) (1988). The EPA's interim final rule suggests that this EPA will apply this requirement with flexibility. The preamble to the final interim rule states:

The primary purpose of these assistance agreements is to support the development of elements of a core environmental protection program, such as: . . . ;

Providing for tribal capacity-building to assure an environmental presence for identifying programs and projects . . . .;

Fostering compliance with federal environmental statutes by developing appropriate tribal environmental programs, ordinances and services; and

Establishing a communications capability to work with federal, state, local and other tribal environmental officials.

58 Fed. Reg. 63876 (1993). Establishing a tribal core environmental program that includes a blanket environmental review process would fit well with EPA's characterization of the primary purpose of this program. In addition, since EPA encourages tribes to adopt tribal administrative procedure acts, *see* note 96 *supra*, presumably the General Assistance Program could be used for purposes related to a tribal APA, including training for tribal agency staff.

115. *See* note 95, *supra*.

116. *See* Suagee, *supra* note 104, at 427 n.218.

117. Dean B. Suagee, Hobbs, Straus, Dean & Wilder, "A Model Tribal Environmental Review Code: Analysis and Draft Text" (unpublished paper presented at the National Tribal Environmental Council First Annual Conference, Albuquerque, N.M., November 14–18, 1993) (hereinafter *"Model Tribal Code"*) (on file with the COLO. J. INT'L L. & POL'Y).

118. MODEL LAND DEV. CODE (1976) (complete text adopted by the ALI at Washington, D.C., May 21, 1975, and reporter's commentary).

ALI's Model Code was the culmination of a fifteen-year effort to remake state zoning and subdivision laws, which were regarded as flawed and outdated mechanisms for exercising governmental police power to control land use in the interests of public health, safety and welfare.[119] Although the ALI's Model Code has not been widely adopted by the states to date, we think that it is a major improvement over traditional zoning and subdivision laws and have drawn upon it in fashioning a model tribal mini-NEPA.

1. A Blanket "Development" Permit

One of the key concepts in the ALI's Model Land Development Code is the requirement of a permit for any kind of activity that falls within the statutory definition of "development."[120] The NEPA itself does not establish a permit requirement; but instead, it applies to any federal action that may significantly affect the human environment. If a tribal government is to carry out an environmental review process for development activities within its reservation, there should be a mechanism through which each activity can be carefully considered by the tribe. One such mechanism is to require any proponent of a development project to come before a tribal agency and obtain a development permit.

A permit process is, of course, not necessary for a tribe to exercise control over development on tribally owned land, but a permit process could facilitate tribal environmental review. For development on individual Indian lands or on fee lands, a permit requirement could act as a critical mechanism, allowing a tribe to assert the full measure of its sovereign authority to protect important tribal interests, including public health and safety and respect for tribal environmental and cultural values. If the tribal permit requirement is crafted to protect tribal interests that meet the second prong of the *Montana* test—if the regulated conduct "threatens or has some direct effect on the political integrity, the economic security, or the health or welfare of the tribe"[121]—then the tribal permit requirement should withstand judicial attack even though a tribal zoning ordinance might not.

In our draft tribal mini-NEPA, the term "development" is broadly defined in the statutory language to include any building operation, any material change in a structure, or any material change in the use or appearance of land. A tribe using our draft as a model might expressly

---

119. *Id.* at ix–x.

120. The definition of "development" is in Section 201 of our draft *Model Tribal Code, supra* note 117. In the remainder of this article we generally have omitted specific references to our draft *Model Tribal Code*. For further discussion of the definition of "development," see the ALI MODEL LAND DEV. CODE, *supra* note 118, at 16–26. *See also* Suagee, *supra* note 107, at 429–44.

121. *Montana*, 450 U.S. at 566.

exclude certain kinds of development activities that usually have minimal adverse environmental impacts. In addition, our draft provides that the tribal Environmental Review Commission, which would be established by the tribal code, would have authority to issue rules to define a category of "low-impact" development for which the permit process would be a largely ministerial function.

2. A Tribal Environmental Review Commission

Our draft calls for the establishment of a tribal Environmental Review Commission (ERC)[122] charged with reviewing permit applications for development proposals. The ERC's primary mission would be to issue or deny permits, and it would have the power to include conditions in permits that it does issue. Appeals from ERC decisions should be provided in tribal court.

The tribal governing body would delegate authority to the ERC to develop and promulgate rules, although the tribal governing body might choose to reserve to itself the power of legislative veto over the ERC's rules.[123] If a tribe has enacted its own administrative procedure act (APA), the ERC should be governed by the tribal APA.[124] If a tribe has not adopted its own APA, then the tribal environmental review code might expressly require the ERC to follow EPA requirements for rule making by states, which also apply to tribes treated as states.[125] We suggest that the ERC be directed to hold public meetings, and possibly public hearings, as part of its rule-making process.

The ERC would consist of three commissioners appointed to staggered terms by the tribal governing body.[126] Ideally, the ERC should have

---

122. We have used this name for the Commission because it describes the Commission's primary role, but a different name might be preferable for a particular tribe.

123. In Immigration and Naturalization Service v. Chadha, 462 U.S. 919 (1983), the Supreme Court held a legislative veto of federal agency regulations unconstitutional (actions of one House of Congress under Section 244(c)(2) of the Immigration and Nationality Act, 8 U.S.C. § 1254 (1988), violated "strictures" of the US Constitution, namely, separation of powers, and the presentment and bicameral requirements of Art. I, §§ 1,7). A tribal government would not be constitutionally barred from exercising a legislative veto of tribal agency rulemaking because tribes are not bound by the "strictures" of the US Constitution. *See* Santa Clara Pueblo v. Martinez, 436 U.S. 49, 56 (1978); Talton v. Mayes, 163 U.S. 376, 384 (1896).

124. If a tribe has adopted an APA, it nevertheless may be advisable to review the APA in conjunction with consideration of the enactment of a tribal environmental review code, particularly if the scope of the tribal APA is not sufficiently broad to cover the full range of activities that the ERC will be authorized to carry out.

125. *See* 40 CFR § 25, discussed in note 93, *supra*.

126. Many alternatives could be imagined. For example, the commissioners might be elected. Three was suggested because we are trying to fashion a process that can be used by small tribes. For large tribes, a larger number of commissioners might be desirable. If there are many nonmember landowners within reservation boundaries, a tribe might want to consider including one or more nonmembers on the ERC or providing some other structured way for nonmembers to have input into the ERC.

some professional staff, but initially it could depend on the staff of relevant tribal agencies, such as a tribal Environmental Protection or Natural Resources Department. The ERC itself would not be composed of tribal staff, however; instead, it would be an independent, quasi-judicial tribal administrative agency. The ERC would have authority to review development permit applications from tribal government agencies and instrumentalities and to hold administrative hearings as part of the application process. The ERC also would be charged with a role in enforcing the tribal environmental review code by holding adjudicatory hearings on alleged violations.

In addition, although the draft only hints at this possibility, the tribal governing body might delegate authority to the ERC to administer one or more of the EPA's delegable regulatory programs, such as setting water quality standards under the Clean Water Act or regulating public water systems under the Safe Drinking Water Act.[127] Tribal leaders should be aware that the EPA, in its rule-making documents for these statutes, has expressed concerns regarding possible conflicts of interest when the regulatory agency and the regulated entity are both tribal entities.[128] Tribal delegation of authority to an independent tribal agency such as an ERC would be one way to address the EPA's concerns.

3. Tribal Land Use and Development Plan

One of the main functions of the ERC would be to determine whether or not the development proposed in an application for a permit would be consistent with the tribe's land-use and development plan. This plan would be similar to a land-use plan adopted pursuant to a zoning code but could be more flexible. Rather than providing that certain kinds of development can only take place in certain areas, as zoning codes do, the plan might describe the kinds of development that the tribe wants to encourage and provide a set of standards for the ERC to use in determining whether development proposed in an application is consistent with the plan. The plan also might include areas of special tribal concern in which development proposals would be strictly scrutinized. The plan would not be developed by the ERC but by tribal staff in an appropriate department of tribal government. The ERC, however, would be directed to facilitate public involvement in reviewing the tribe's plan, including for example, a hearing on the plan similar to a rule-making procedure. The ERC also

---

127. *See* notes 90–91, *supra.*

128. 53 Fed. Reg. 37,401 (1988) (discussing regulatory independence in the context of the Safe Drinking Water Act); 56 Fed. Reg. 64,876 (1991) (discussing regulatory independence in the context of water quality standards and National Pollutant Discharge Elimination System (NPDES) permits under the Clean Water Act).

would be directed to make recommendations to the tribal governing body regarding the plan. The adoption of the plan would be by action of the tribal governing body.

4. Application for a Development Permit

The draft code establishes two procedures that would apply to development permits: one for "low-impact" development and one for "general" development. For low-impact development, the procedure would be very simple. The applicant would certify that the proposal meets the criteria established by the ERC for low-impact development, and the applicant would agree to comply with any conditions imposed by the ERC in issuing a permit. Low-impact permits could be issued by the chairperson of the ERC without holding a hearing.

For "general" permits, the applicant normally would be required to prepare a draft environmental assessment (EA) and to include it with the application. If the proposed development fits within a categorical exclusion under the ERC's rules, then an EA would not be required. In addition, if ERC staff determine that the environmental impacts of the proposed development are sufficiently addressed in an earlier EA or EIS, then the staff would advise the applicant that a new EA is not necessary. The ERC staff would be authorized to assist applicants in the preparation of EAs and to charge fees for this service. Making the proponent of an action bear the responsibility for, or at least the cost of, preparation of an EA is consistent with BIA policy,[129] although this policy is often overlooked in practice. The ERC staff would review applications to determine their adequacy, as well as the adequacy of any EA prepared by an applicant, and to determine consistency with the tribal land-use and development plan. The ERC staff would submit a report to the Commission providing staff assessment of these and other issues.

An important reason for incorporating EA preparation in the permit application is that for many kinds of development proposals in Indian country, some kind of federal agency action will be required. Although it may not be apparent at the outset that a federal action will be required, if it turns out that it is, a previously prepared EA will tend to expedite the federal NEPA process. Another reason for requiring an EA is that in many cases the applicant for the permit will be a federal agency, and federal agencies are familiar with EA preparation. Moreover, as was already discussed, if tribal law says that federal agencies are required to prepare EAs for certain kinds of actions, the agencies' own procedures require

---

129. 30 BIAM Supp. 1, § 4.2; see also 516 DM § 3.6.

them to comply with the tribal law. A final, and perhaps most important, reason for using an EA as part of a tribal environmental review process, is simply that EAs work. They have proven to be effective tools for evaluating the environmental impacts of proposed actions and for formulating measures to avoid or mitigate adverse impacts.

5. Action on Permit Applications

Decisions on permit applications would be made by the Commission. Permits for low-impact development would be issued by the chairperson. General permits would be issued by the full Commission, after holding an informal administrative hearing. Requiring a hearing recognizes that in many tribes important decisions affecting Indian communities are reached only after people have had an opportunity to talk things out. This hearing requirement should not become excessively formal. While it could be called something other than a "hearing," non-Indian applicants for tribal permits probably expect that they will be given a hearing,[130] and this is an expectation that we believe tribes would be well-advised to honor. After the hearing, the Commission would render its decision, subject to appeal to tribal court.

6. Enforcement

Enforcement presents practical problems for tribal governments, in part because recent Supreme Court decisions seem to invite non-Indians to challenge tribal jurisdiction. Our draft would charge the ERC with authority to investigate alleged violations of the code, and it would charge the chairperson of the ERC with the duty of issuing notices of violation and cease and desist orders. The ERC would serve an adjudicatory role by holding a hearing on any such notice or order to determine if a violation of the code had occurred. The ERC could assess civil penalties, and it could order a violator to take corrective action.[131] Any tribe that adopts a code based on our model draft should carefully consider issues relating to enforcement through consultation with tribal legal counsel.

---

130. A hearing is widely regarded as an essential element of due process of law when property interests are affected by government action, and tribal governments are prohibited by the Indian Civil Rights Act from depriving any person of property without due process of law. Indian Civil Rights Act of 1968, 25 U.S.C. § 1302(8)(1988). Although the Indian Civil Rights Act was imposed upon tribes by Congress through an exercise of its plenary power, see COHEN supra note 30 at 666–70, tribal officials should be aware that the right to a hearing is also protected by the Article 8 of the International Covenant on Civil and Political Rights, supra note 18, that is, it is a universal human rights standard.

131. A tribe may choose to use the sanction of exclusion of nonmembers from the tribe's reservation, but this is not included in our draft, in part because the reliance of Supreme Court Justices on the power to exclude nonmembers as the basis for tribal jurisdiction over nonmembers is wrong. See notes 57–65, supra.

C. How Big Should the Blanket Be?

A tribe which establishes a blanket tribal environmental review process would build a framework for taking on regulatory roles, or review and consultation roles, with respect to particular aspects of environmental protection that are priorities for the tribe. Some of the possibilities are obvious. For example, the ERC might be delegated authority from the tribal governing body to promulgate rules setting water quality standards under the Clean Water Act.[132] If a tribe does this, EPA's rules provide that it must also take on the certification process under section 401 of the Clean Water Act.[133] The tribal governing body may want to delegate this function, which is technical and to some extent ministerial, to tribal staff, such as the head of the tribe's environmental protection or natural resources department, with a right of appeal to the ERC. A tribe may want to limit the responsibilities that it assumes under the Clean Water Act. For example, a tribe may decide to let the EPA continue to issue section 402 permits (National Pollutant Discharge Elimination System or "NPDES")[134] to enforce the tribal water quality standards.

If air pollution is a problem on a reservation, the tribal governing body may want to delegate to the ERC authority to develop a tribal implementation plan under the Clean Air Act.[135] On the other hand, if air quality is currently pristine but potentially threatened by off-reservation development, the tribal governing body might delegate authority to the ERC to conduct a study leading to redesignation from Class II air quality to Class I.[136]

The role of an ERC need not be limited to programs administered by the EPA. A tribal ERC might also be charged with duties pursuant to environmental laws administered by other federal agencies or with duties under tribal laws that have no direct counterpart in federal law. For example, tribes for which anadromous fish runs have great cultural and economic importance have enacted tribal regulations on activities that affect fish habitat. The ERC could be charged with making sure that applicants for development permits are in compliance with the tribal fish

---

132. 40 C.F.R. § 131 (1992). *See* note 90, *supra.*

133. 56 Fed. Reg. 64,876 (1991).

134. 33 U.S.C. § 1342 (1988). Any person discharging pollutants into waters of the United States within a reservation without a section 402 permit, without compliance with the terms of a section 402 permit, and not otherwise permissible under the Clean Water Act, would be subject to an enforcement action by the EPA under section 309 of the Act. 33 U.S.C. § 1319 (1988).

135. Clean Air Act, § 110(o), 42 U.S.C. § 7410(o) (1988).

136. Clean Air Act, § 164(c), 42 U.S.C. § 7474(c) (1988).

habitat regulations. The list of options under tribal law is limited only by the range of interests that a tribe seeks to protect and the need for efficiency in the legislation that the tribe chooses to enact. Rather than enact a number of separate tribal laws protecting different aspects of the environment, the tribe could include some of those aspects in parts of its comprehensive environmental review code.[137] Thus, a tribe might protect other aspects of the environment through its land-use and development plan rather than through separate tribal legislation.

The ERC may not be charged with lead responsibility for all of a tribe's environmental protection program, but, through its permit process, the ERC should exercise a review function over the whole scope of tribal environmental programs. For example, if another tribal agency or department is charged as lead for setting water quality standards, the ERC should ensure that no development takes place without certification under section 401 of the Clean Water Act and the issuance of a permit under section 402 or 404, if applicable. A tribal government, particularly for one of the larger tribes, might establish advisory committees or review commissions for specific aspects of its environmental program, which would operate under the blanket of the ERC. In such cases, non-Indians with appropriate expertise or representatives of important non-Indian interest groups such as non-Indian fee landowners, might be appointed to serve on such advisory committees or review commissions. This would help to give non-Indians a sense of enfranchisement and also would allow the tribe to make use of their expertise.

The ERC's duties should not necessarily be limited to lands within a tribe's jurisdiction. Tribes are routinely provided copies of NEPA documents prepared by federal agencies for proposed federal actions near reservations that may affect off-reservation resources in which tribes have treaty or statutory rights. Pursuant to the federal cultural resources laws discussed later,[138] tribes also have rights to notice and consultation when proposed federal actions may affect places that have religious or cultural importance or when such actions may cause disturbance of Indian graves.

---

137. The *Model Tribal Code* lists the following subjects that might be covered in additional subtitles of a tribal environmental protection code: cultural preservation and cultural resources conservation, public water systems, water quality and wetlands, waste management and recycling, air quality, hazardous and toxic substances, emergency response plan, and community right-to-know.

138. *See* notes 140–156, *infra* and accompanying text.

A tribal ERC could be designated by the tribal governing body to serve as the initial point of contact for all such notices received from federal and state agencies and from other tribes. The ERC could ensure that the appropriate tribal staff and officials, as well as community organizations or religious societies, are informed about particular proposed off-reservation actions. The ERC also could be charged with responding to such notices on behalf of the tribe.[139] Serving this function would be more important for some tribes than for others, depending on the nature of the off-reservation rights and interests of particular tribes.

Even though most tribes do not have the resources to pursue all of these options, many are already pursuing some of them. Establishing a blanket environmental review process would mean that, for those aspects of environmental regulation for which a tribe has not yet established a program, or for which it may not intend to establish a program, there would nevertheless be a review process through which the tribe would be exercising a measure of control. In addition, in the event that a tribe's regulatory jurisdiction is challenged in the context of a particular proposed action and the court engages in a balancing of interests analysis, the tribe will have a stronger case if it has established some kind of program of its own.

D. Bringing Cultural Resources Under the Blanket

Tribes sorting out their environmental protection priorities should place emphasis on the protection of the cultural as well as the natural environment. From an Indian perspective, of course, one might say that the natural environment *is* the cultural environment. In this article, we focus on the protection and conservation of those things and places that federal agencies describe as "cultural resources," a term that includes historic buildings and places as well as archaeological resources. There are three major federal statutes that are particularly relevant to the protection and conservation of cultural resources: the National Historic Preservation Act of 1966 (NHPA),[140] the Archaeological Resources Protection Act (ARPA),[141] and the Native American Graves Protection and Repatriation Act (NAGPRA).[142] These statutes and the implementing regulations establish a framework for avoiding inadvertent damage or destruction to historically or culturally significant places as a result of development activities.[143]

---

139. If the Native American Free Exercise of Religion Act (NAFERA), S. 6456 (May 25, 1993), is enacted into law with notice and consultation provisions substantially similar to those contained in the bill, a tribal ERC could be designated the point of contact to receive notice from federal agencies.

140. 16 U.S.C. § 470 (1988).

141. 16 U.S.C. §§ 470aa–470ll (1988).

142. 25 U.S.C. §§ 3001–3013 (1988).

143. *See generally* Dean B. Suagee and Karen J. Funk, *Cultural Resources Conservation in Indian Country,* 7 NAT. RESOURCES & ENV'T, no. 4, 30 (Spring 1993). *See also* Suagee, *supra* note 7, at 706–12.

Tribal laws can make these federal statutes more effective in protecting tribal interests.[144]

The NHPA is a multifaceted statute that seeks to protect properties that have historic significance. The National Park Service (NPS), an agency within the Department of the Interior, is the lead federal agency for most aspects of the NHPA. The NHPA authorized the creation of the National Register of Historic Places, and the NPS has established criteria and procedures for determining eligibility for the National Register.[145] Places that hold religious or cultural importance for Indian tribes are eligible for listing on the National Register.[146] The NHPA also created an independent agency, the Advisory Council on Historic Preservation, and charged it with reviewing proposed federal or federally assisted "undertakings" that may affect properties listed, or eligible for listing, on the National Register. The Advisory Council's mandate for this review function is found in Section 106 of the NHPA,[147] and the review process has come to be called the Section 106 consultation process.

Like the federal environmental laws administered by the EPA, the NHPA is carried out through a partnership with the states. The NPS provides financial assistance on a recurrent basis to State Historic Preservation Officers (SHPOs), and the Advisory Council, in its regulations for carrying out the Section 106 process,[148] has assigned a major role to the SHPOs. Amendments to the NHPA enacted in 1992 authorize tribes, at their option, to take over any or all of the functions of the SHPOs within reservation boundaries.[149] A tribal program designed to carry out the NHPA

---

144. Our *Model Tribal Code* does not include express provisions to cover cultural resources in the tribal environmental review process. *See Model Tribal Code, supra* note 117. Code language to do this could delegate authority to the ERC or to a separate cultural commission to fill in the details through rule making. If the tribal governing body delegates the authority to deal with cultural resources to an agency or commission other than the ERC, cultural resources concerns nevertheless should be one of the aspects of environmental protection that the ERC considers before issuing a development permit.

145. 36 C.F.R. § 60 (1992).

146. Reclamation Projects Authorization and Adjustment Act of 1992, Pub. L. No. 102–575, § 4006(a)(2), 106 Stat. 4600 (1992) (amending 16 U.S.C. § 470a (1988)). The statutory language expressly provides for properties of religious or cultural importance to an Indian tribe or Native Hawaiian organization and confirms the prior administrative practice; *see* National Park Service, *Guidelines for Evaluating and Documenting Traditional Cultural Properties*, National Register Bulletin 38.

147. 16 U.S.C. § 470f (1988).

148. 36 C.F.R. § 800 (1993).

149. Pub. L. No. 102–575, § 4006(a)(2) (1992) (amending 16 U.S.C. § 470a (1988)). The term "tribal lands" is defined as "(A) all lands within the exterior boundaries of any Indian reservation; and (B) all dependent Indian communities." *Id.* at § 4019(a)(12) (amending 16 U.S.C. § 470w (1988)). If a tribe has taken over the SHPO's role in the section 106 process and a federal undertaking would affect private lands within reservation boundaries, the private landowner(s) may request the SHPO to participate in the section 106 consultation process in addition to the tribal historic preservation official (amending 16 U.S.C. 470a(d)(2)(D)(iii) (1988).

within reservation boundaries might include the establishment of a tribal register of historic places, including traditional cultural properties. This would help to ensure that tribal cultural values, as well as national interests in historic preservation, are considered in the environmental review of proposed federal actions.

From an Indian perspective, a key provision of the NHPA, as amended in 1992, is that if a proposed federal undertaking might affect a place that has religious or cultural importance to a tribe, and if the place is eligible for the National Register, the tribe has a right to receive notice and to be involved in the section 106 consultation process.[150] This applies to properties outside of reservation boundaries—even on private lands—if there is a federal action involved. A tribe need not have a program established under the NHPA nor have taken over the role of the SHPO to be entitled to notice and consultation under this amended provision of the NHPA.

The ARPA was enacted in 1979 and includes express provisions governing the excavation of archaeological resources on Indian lands. Archaeological resources cannot be excavated on Indian lands without a permit issued under the authority of the Secretary of the Interior. The ARPA does provide exceptions for the tribe itself and for a tribal member if the tribe has enacted a law regulating the subject matter.[151] Any ARPA permit issued for Indian lands requires consent of the tribe with jurisdiction over the lands and, in the case of individually owned Indian lands, consent of the Indian landowner(s) as well.[152] Thus, a tribe can control archaeological excavations on Indian lands simply by denying consent or by granting consent subject to specified conditions, which must be included in the permit. The ARPA also provides that tribes have a right to notice from a federal agency prior to the issuance of an ARPA permit for work on federal lands that might affect a site that holds religious or cultural importance for the tribe.[153]

Enacted in 1990, the NAGPRA includes provisions that enhance the authority of tribes to control the excavation of graves within reservation boundaries and on federal lands. The mechanism that the NAGPRA uses to

---

150. Pub. L. No. 102–575, § 4006(a)(2) (1992) (amending 16 U.S.C. § 470a (1988)). In addition, section 110 of the NHPA as amended now provides that, each federal agency must carry out its process for identifying and evaluating historic properties in consultation with, inter alia, Indian tribes and Native Hawaiian organizations. Pub. L. No. 102–575 (amending 16 U.S.C. § 470h–2 (1988)).
    151. 16 U.S.C. § 470cc(g) (1988). *See also* 43 C.F.R. § 7.
    152. 16 U.S.C. § 470cc(g) (1988), 43 C.F.R. § 7.9(c).
    153. 16 U.S.C. § 470cc(c) (1988), 43 C.F.R. § 7.7.

accomplish this is the issuance of a permit under the ARPA.[154] The NAGPRA expressly covers all lands within reservation boundaries[155] and represents congressional recognition that tribes have important interests in the graves of their ancestors, even though the land on which graves are located may have passed out of Indian ownership.[156] Thus, a tribal environmental review code that includes the graves of ancestors located on fee lands within reservations in its coverage should satisfy the second prong of the *Montana* test.[157] If a tribe is concerned with protecting the graves of its ancestors that are located on lands within reservation boundaries but which have passed out of Indian trust status, then these cultural resource concerns should be covered by the blanket of the tribe's environmental review code.

E. How Can Mainstream Environmental Groups Help?

In recent years several major American environmental groups have been engaged in efforts to make their organizations more responsive to the concerns of minority groups within the American society. Some of these efforts have focused on increasing dialogue and interaction among environmental group leaders and tribal leaders.[158] Many tribal leaders and environmental leaders now realize that when they take a position on an environmental issue, both groups often find themselves standing on common ground. We think that the environmental community should seek out ways to support tribal governments in the development and implementation of their environmental protection programs. By helping tribes to build their programs in ways that respect tribal sovereignty and tribal cultural values,

---

154. 25 U.S.C. § 3002(c) (1988).

155. 25 U.S.C. § 3001(15) (1988) (defining "tribal lands" to include all lands within the boundaries of an Indian reservation and all dependent Indian communities, as well as certain lands held for Native Hawaiian organizations). Although NAGPRA applies to all lands within the reservation boundaries, the coverage of ARPA within reservations is limited to "Indian lands," a term which is defined as lands held in Indian trust or subject to a federally imposed restraint on alienation. 16 U.S.C. § 470bb(4) (1988). NAGPRA provides that "cultural items" located on fee lands within reservation boundaries cannot be lawfully excavated without an ARPA permit, 25 U.S.C. § 3002(c) (1988), but the Bureau of Indian Affairs has taken the position that it lacks authority to issue ARPA permits for fee lands. 58 Fed. Reg. 65,246 (1993). Thus, any excavation of "cultural items" located on fee lands within the reservation boundaries appears to be illegal, which is surely not what Congress intended. Congress should fix this problem by amending ARPA to apply to all lands within reservation boundaries.

156. The rationale for this congressional recognition is based, in part, on the common law principle that interred human remains are not treated as property. *See* Jack F. Trope & Walter T. Echo-Hawk, *The Native American Graves Protection and Repatriation Act: Background and Legislative History*, 24 ARIZ. ST. L.J. 35, 47–48, 59–60 (1992).

157. *See* notes 50-55, *supra* and accompanying text.

158. At the National Tribal Environmental Council First Annual Conference, in Albuquerque, N.M., on April 14–18, 1993, John Echohawk, Executive Director of the Native American Rights Fund and a member of the Board of Trustees of the Natural Resources Defense Council, made a presentation on the efforts of the environmental groups to build better relationships with tribes and tribal leaders.

environmental groups can also help tribal governments to build a sense of enfranchisement among the reservation populace, Indian and non-Indian alike.

Primarily, environmentalists need to understand tribal sovereignty. To do this they need some knowledge of history. Indian law is a complex field in which environmental activists cannot become experts overnight. It is encouraging that some of the national environmental groups have made room for Indian lawyers on their boards, although the larger society needs a lot more education than what a few Indian lawyers can reasonably be expected to provide. The larger society needs to learn quite a bit of history as a prerequisite for learning Indian law. An important way for the major environmental groups to help with this learning would be to turn some of their attention to monitoring federal land managing agencies in their im-plemention of the 1992 amendments to the NHPA.[159] All federal public lands in North America were once Indian lands, and many Indians continue to use areas within public lands for cultural or religious purposes. Federal NHPA programs could help the larger society to understand how tribes used these lands in the past, which would help to build public support for protecting present-day Indian uses of public lands.

Major environmental groups can lend support to tribal environmental programs in a variety of other ways. For example, the groups have a great deal of expertise in legislative advocacy both in Congress and in state legislatures. Many of the major groups have joined with tribes, intertribal organizations, religious groups, and civil rights groups in the campaign to enact the Native American Free Exercise of Religion Act.[160] Groups also should be helping tribes to enact amendments to federal environmental laws to address tribal concerns,[161] and when they take positions on pending amendments to federal laws, the major groups should have a process in

---

159. *See* notes 149 & 150, *supra* and accompanying text.

160. *See* note 139 *supra*. A number of national environmental groups are involved in the NAFERA coalition (copy of list of coalition members on file with the COLO. J. INT'L L. & POL'Y). *See also* Michael J. Simpson, *Accommodating Indian Religions: Proposed 1993 Amendement to the American Indian Religious Freedom Act,* 54 MONT. L. REV. 19 (1993).

161. *E.g.*, proposing amendments to the Resource Conservation and Recovery Act ,42 U.S.C. §§ 6901–6992k (1988). The Act has not yet been amended to authorize treatment of tribes as states. In the 102d Congress, the Senate Indian Affairs Committee reported a bill specifically concerned with waste management in Indian country. Sen. Rep. 370, 102d Cong., 2d Sess. (1992) (to accompany S. 1687, the Indian Tribal Government Waste Management Act of 1992). For a variety of reasons, this bill was not enacted. *See* statements of Senators Inouye, McCain, Moynihan, Chafee and Baucus, 138 Cong. Rec. S 7059–60 (daily edition, October 5, 1992). The national environmental groups could take a step toward building some rapport with tribes by including support for tribal RCRA provisions in their legislative advocacy.

place to formulate a position on tribal provisions in such bills. Tribal governments have a much stronger presence in the nation's capital than they did twenty years ago, but a lot of legislation still works its way through Congress with little consideration given to its potential impact in Indian country. Major environmental groups could help to ensure that federal environmental laws include well-considered provisions relating to Indian country, provisions that recognize and affirm inherent tribal sovereignty over all lands within reservation boundaries, thus making it clear that this aspect of tribal sovereignty has not been implicitly divested with respect to non-Indians.

Another way to help support tribal environmental protection programs would be to create a bank of technical expertise that would be available to tribal governments. Many environmental professionals could afford to donate some time to help a tribal government build a program; others would be glad to work for tribes for reasonable compensation. Environmental groups could work to create a mechanism to link non-Indian environmental professionals with tribes in need of help. The possibilities are practically limitless and could include using outside professionals as consultants or appointing respected academic specialists to positions on advisory committees or on the tribal ERC.[162] We think that non-Indians subject to tribal regulatory jurisdiction are less likely to challenge it if they perceive that the tribe's program is doing a good job, and that the major environmental groups could help tribes to earn this perception by building excellent programs. In addition, environmental groups that work with indigenous peoples in other parts of the world might find that it would help to build rapport and trust if the US groups have some Indian professionals in prominent positions.

We recognize that there are some people living within reservation boundaries who will resist tribal jurisdiction regardless of the lengths to which a tribe goes to enfranchise nonmembers and regardless of the expertise of the people involved in the tribal program. In such cases, one approach would be to buy out such people. The Nature Conservancy is one environmental group devoted to the acquisition of environmentally important areas. In many cases its acquisitions are subsequently transferred to units of government. Their operating principle is that sometimes the best way to protect an environmentally important piece of Mother Earth is to buy it. We would like to see the Nature Conservancy and other organiza-

---

162. For example, environmental groups could help tribes assemble the expertise to act as trustees for natural resource damages under the Comprehensive Environmental Response, Compensation and Liability Act (CERCLA). 42 U.S.C. § 9607(f) (1988).

tions work with tribal leaders to establish a program for the reacquisition of lands within reservation boundaries that have passed out of Indian trust status. A program could also be developed to help tribes reacquire culturally important lands outside reservation boundaries.

V. CONCLUSION

In the era when the human rights of indigenous peoples are recognized in international law, indigenous peoples and the states of the world will be engaged in fashioning new arrangements for indigenous self-government. The new arrangements between states and indigenous peoples will be recorded in a variety of legal instruments, including international treaties and domestic legislation. Whether or not states are as concerned about the human rights of indigenous peoples as they are that some indigenous peoples may demand complete independence, states must come to the bargaining table prepared to provide indigenous peoples with resources to help empower them in the exercise of self-government. International organizations and nongovernmental organizations must also be prepared to help.

As they fashion new arrangements, indigenous peoples and states will be looking for working models wherever they may be found. They will surely look to the United States as one of the states of the world with long-standing indigenous self-government, a flawed model to be sure, but a working model just the same. A key aspect of the US model that may be broadly applicable to other countries is the role of the national government in promoting the autonomy of indigenous peoples and in protecting indigenous self-government against infringements by sub-national units of government.

We would like to see Congress and the Executive demonstrate some awareness of the human rights dimensions of their actions relating to the roles of tribal governments in carrying out environmental protection regulatory programs. We believe that the judicially created "implicit divestiture" rule violates the emerging human rights norms supporting self-government for indigenous peoples, and we think that Congress should recognize this conflict and expressly reject the implicit divestiture rule. In addition to taking such actions to support the human rights of indigenous peoples of the United States, the United States should make the human rights of indigenous peoples a central concern in its dealings with the community of nations. As a leader in the international human rights movement, the United States should aspire to be an example for the rest of the world in its relations with indigenous peoples, and the United States should live up to such aspirations.

We believe the existence of functioning tribal government environmental regulatory programs in the United States will help to make indigenous self-government in other parts of the world not just a right but also a fact. The existence of working tribal programs in the United States will help to change the terms of the debate from whether indigenous peoples should be engaged in this aspect of governmental authority to a focus on how indigenous peoples can carry out this governmental responsibility effectively. Tribal governments should acknowledge that nonmembers have legitimate interests and find ways to enfranchise them, while still being faithful to tribal cultural values. These factors will help to make tribal environmental regulatory programs become not just functional but truly strong, because they will derive their just power from the consent of the governed.

Indigenous Peoples Displaced from Their Environment: Is There Adequate Protection?

Maria Stavropoulou[†]

Indigenous peoples have a special right to their environment.[1] As a result, they must be afforded even stronger protection than others against removal from their environment. Should displacement take place, they should be guaranteed full protection and assisted in returning to their original lands as soon as possible. This article examines the current international legal structure regarding the displacement of indigenous peoples from their lands, points out some of its inconsistencies, and attempts to combine certain principles of human rights law, refugee law, and international environmental law in a comprehensive protection framework.

I. INDIGENOUS PEOPLES AND THEIR RIGHT TO THEIR ENVIRONMENT: A SUMMARY OF THE ISSUES

A universally accepted definition of the term "indigenous peoples" remains, after decades of discussion, elusive. The use of the word "people" or "peoples" is not consistent in United Nations (UN) documents[2] and there are, even among indigenous groups themselves, disagreements and concerns about the appropriateness of each term.[3]

Even the utility of the concept "indigenous peoples" is now being questioned. It has been persuasively argued, for instance, that since the Second World War, the concept has been used to represent certain groups as either "pathetic" or "romantic," thus bracketing them outside the

---

† Assistant to the Representative of the UN Secretary General on Internally Displaced Persons.

1. This can be concluded from various trends in current international law. *See infra* part I.

2. *See, e.g.,* HURST HANNUM, AUTONOMY, SOVEREIGNTY AND SELF-DETERMINATION 88 (1990).

3. *See, e.g., Report of the Working Group on Indigenous Populations on its eleventh session*, U.N. Commission on Human Rights, Sub-Comm. on Prevention of Discrimination and Protection of Minorities, 11th Sess., Agenda Item 14, U.N. Doc. E/CN.4/Sub.2/1993/29 paras. 62–67 (1993) [hereinafter *Report of the Working Group*].

"modern" world and, in effect, excluding them from all developments that affect them directly.[4]

For the working purposes of this paper, however, it is not necessary to engage in a discussion of these thorny issues. Assuming that a certain group of people is identified as "indigenous" or tribal, it is important to define the specific components of certain rights, such as the right to life, the right to lands and territories, the right to natural resources, and the right to protection of the environment.

How clearly are these rights established currently in international law? There is no doubt that in the case of indigenous peoples, these rights are much more closely interconnected than in the case of other groups. As has been noted elsewhere:

> [w]ith rich social traditions and vital economic practices integral to the physical area in which they occur, these communities depend upon a healthy environment. To be sure, possessing little or no technological capability, these communities *are* their environment—profoundly integrated and deeply dependent.[5]

Unquestionably, the disruption of the relationship between indigenous peoples and their environment threatens their very existence as a people — not only their cultural existence, but also their physical well-being.[6] International human rights treaties address those threats.[7] But the cumbersome mechanisms available under UN and other intergovernmental regimes,[8] compounded by the lack of a definition of and consensus on the term "collective rights" in the case of indigenous peoples,[9] render the right to their environment nonjusticiable.

---

4. *See generally*, Chris Tennant, *"A Permanent Hope for Humanity": The Representation of Indigenous Peoples in the International Legal Literature from 1945–1992*, Hum. Rts. Q. (forthcoming 1994).

5. William Andrew Shutkin, *International Human Rights Law and the Earth: The Protection of Indigenous Peoples and the Environment*, 31 Va. J. Int'l L. 479, 480 (1991) (emphasis in original).

6. *See id.*, at 488–493 for a general discussion on the existing international law and the protection of indigenous cultures and the environment. The right to life and personal security, the freedom from cruel, inhuman or degrading treatment, from arbitrary exile, from interference with his or her privacy, family and home, the right to seek and enjoy asylum in other countries, the right to own property, the right to an adequate standard of living are just a few of the human rights currently protected under international law. *See* the Intertational Bill of Human Rights, *infra* note 7.

7. *See* the International Bill of Human Rights, which includes the Universal Declaration of Human Rights, adopted Dec. 10, 1948, G.A. Res. 217 A (III), U.N. Doc. A/810 (1948); the International Covenant of Civil and Political Rights, adopted Dec. 16, 1966, G.A. Res. 2200A (XXI), art. 49; and the International Covenant of Economic, Social and Cultural Rights, adopted Dec. 16, 1966, 2200 (XXI), art. 27.

8. Shutkin, *supra* note 5, at 488–493.

It has been stated that "[b]ecause migration is a last resort, the rising number of environmental refugees should be seen as an important indicator of the extent and severity of worldwide environmental deterioration."[10] Displacement of indigenous peoples from their land is perhaps the harshest consequence of damage caused to the environment upon which they depend. To respond to this problem, complementary protection measures from existing international regimes must be examined. Because responding to the symptom sometimes beneficially affects the cause, it is hoped that this exercise in analysis of complementary international law regimes will develop and strengthen the right to the environment, which has not yet been firmly established in international human rights law.[11]

II. ENVIRONMENT-RELATED DISPLACEMENT: AN OVER-VIEW OF THE PHENOMENON AND ITS CAUSES

It has been observed that more and more people are forced to move away from their homes for reasons related to the environment.[12] Examining why this movement is so provides the factual framework of the legal analysis regarding displacement due to environmental damage.

According to one formulation,[13] the reasons for environment–related displacement usually are:

- elemental disruptions (such as cyclones and volcanoes);
- biological disruptions (such as locusts);
- slow-onset disruptions (such as drought);
- accidental disruptions;
- disruptions caused by development and urbanization;

---

9. *See, e.g., Report of the Working Group, supra* note 3, at paras. 68–69. For many indigenous peoples land and environment claims are inherently "collective," and have to be exercised as such, contrary to the "individual nature" that traditional human rights are considered to have in the Western tradition.

10. Jodi L. Jacobson, *Environmental Refugees: Nature's Warning System,* in 16 POPULI 29, 30 (March 1989).

11. *See* Shutkin, *supra* note 5, at 505–506. As long as the right to the environment remains theoretical it is essentially non-justiciable. "No environmental right exists *per se* as positive international law"; but such a right "might well develop in the future so as to protect the whole of nature, including human societies."

12. This observation applies more generally to groups other than indigenous peoples. The number of displaced persons due to environmental causes generally was thought to be approximately 10 million in 1989 overall. *See* Jodi Jacobson, *supra* note 10, at 40.

13. REFUGEE POLICY GROUP ET AL., MIGRATION AND THE ENVIRONMENT, 11 (1992). The report identifies both root and proximate causes; it also offers a categorization of the types of movement (small or large scale; emergency versus slow-onset; temporary, extended and permanent; internal and international) and the relevant needs for protection (report available from author).

- environmental warfare.[14]

Apart, perhaps, from such instances as earthquakes or volcanic eruptions,[15] every other listed cause for displacement could in theory be attributed to a human activity or at least be aggravated by it, even if it is seemingly accidental.[16] It has also been asserted that the populations affected the most by elemental disruptions are vulnerable groups in developing countries, such as indigenous peoples and the poor.[17]

A distinction is often made between root causes and proximate causes of a mass population movement. Recent studies in economics, anthropology, demography, and political science have highlighted the complexity and interlinkage of these root causes. Although war is often cited as a major cause of environmental destruction and mass movements of people,[18] other causes are more difficult to pinpoint. Faulty agricultural and development policies, sometimes dictated by donors, are one example.[19] Additional examples include transmigration schemes, internal colonization programs,[20] political or social conflicts and *their* root causes.[21] Any or all of

---

14. For other descriptions of the causes of environmental displacement, *see generally*, Jacobson, *supra* note 10 (noting case studies in Africa, Latin America, Bangladesh, Seveso and Bhopal that lend support to the fact that this type of displacement is serious in numbers and in scope); Lazarus, *New Strangers at the Door?* in REFUGEES Dec.1990, at 14, 15; Peter Newhouse, *Global Warning* in REFUGEES, Dec. 1992, at 14, 17 (July 1992, discussing early warning mechanisms for ensuing famines).

15. Even this could be disputed. For instance, a nuclear explosion near a volcano might trigger a volcanic eruption.

16. *See, e.g., Impacts Assessment of Climate Change, The Policymakers' Summary of the Report of Working Group II to the Intergovernmental Panel on Climate Change* (DASETT, 1990); Jacobson, *supra* note 10, at 33–38; *see also*, INDEPENDENT COMMISSION ON INTERNATIONAL HUMANITARIAN ISSUES, THE DYNAMICS OF DISPLACEMENT 11 (1986) [hereinafter THE DYNAMICS OF DISPLACEMENT].

For an analysis of the causes of famine, *see generally*, FRANCIS MADING DENG & LARRY MINEAR, THE CHALLENGES OF FAMINE RELIEF: EMERGENCY OPERATIONS IN THE SUDAN (1992).

17. *See* MIGRATION AND THE ENVIRONMENT, *supra* note 13 at 11.

18. *See, e.g.*, Zdanek Cervenka, *The Relationship Between Armed Conflict and Environmental Degradation in Africa*, ECOLOGY AND POLITICS—ENVIRONMENTAL STRESS AND SECURITY IN AFRICA 25 et. seq. (1989, Mohamad Salih et al., eds.) [hereinafter ECOLOGY AND POLITICS].

19. *See, e.g.*, Ved P. Nanda, *Human Rights and Environmental Considerations in the Lending Policies of International Development Agencies—An Introduction* 17 DENV. J. INT'L L. & POL'Y 29 (1989); *see, also*, Zygmunt J.B. Plater, *Damming the Third World: Multilateral Development Banks, Environmental Diseconomies, and International Reform Pressures on the Lending Process, id.*, 121; James C.N. Paul, *International Development Agencies, Human Rights and Humane Development Projects, id.* at 67; Michael Cernea, *Involuntary Resettlement and Development: Preventing Adverse Social Effects*, FINANCE AND DEVELOPMENT, Sept. 1988, at 44 (for a short overview of the relevant considerations).

these causes can affect indigenous communities established in a particular territory.

While population movement itself may cause direct environmental degradation, other related conflicts and tensions have also been well-documented.[22] Famine is one of the most serious causes of displacement. Some scholars have observed that "it is the person to whom food is not redistributed who is obliged to wear on the land, thus causing degradation;" this same person ultimately becomes a refugee.[23] Furthermore, circumstances specific to a geographical region may compound or complicate problems. For example, the "fluid boundaries of the Western African states, while facilitating the movement of refugees, cause economic imbalances through the smuggling of goods and food and create competition over the scant social and public services."[24]

A closely related issue is the extent to which environmental degradation *causes* political conflict and war. Although this claim is less-easily established, mass population migrations to urban centers, to richer ecological territories inhabited by other groups, or across national borders are obvious recipes for such results.[25] Indigenous peoples forced to assimilate into new areas may suffer from discrimination, if not outright hostility, from the local population.[26]

---

20. I.L.O., PARTIAL REVISION OF THE INDIGENOUS AND TRIBAL POPULATIONS CONVENTION, 1957 (No. 107), Report VI (1) at 65. International Labour Conference, 75th Sess. (1988) [*hereinafter* PARTIAL REVISION].

21. *See generally* ECOLOGY AND POLITICS, *supra* note 18. Through its case studies, this book lends much support to the interrelation between political conflict and environmental degradation, the *first* symptom of which is the appearance of "ecological refugees" in urban centers, areas inhabited by other groups, or across national borders.

22. *See, e.g.,* Byaruga Emanueto Foster, *The Rwandese Refugees in Uganda,* in ECOLOGY AND POLITICS, *supra* note 18, at 145.

For other tensions apart from environmental ones caused by people displaced because of famine, *see,* Okwudiba Nnoli, *Refugees and Regional Conflict in West Africa,* in ECOLOGY AND POLITICS, *supra* note 18, at 169.

"Vulnerability, land degradation and overpopulation all have to do with the political nature of resource allocation . . . . High population mobility caused by desertification [causes] conflicts [which] arrest development efforts and divert resources from economic and social planning priorities." *Id.* at 16.

23. *See* ECOLOGY AND POLITICS, *supra* note 18, at 10.

24. *Id.* at 16.

25. *Id.* at 10–12. For a critical appraisal of the relevant discussions, *see* Astri Suhrke, *Pressure Points: Environmental Degradation, Migration and Social Conflict,* Occasional Series of the Project on Environmental Change and Acute Conflict No.3, 3 (Joint Project of the University of Toronto and the American Academy of Arts and Sciences, March 1993) at 15.

Several cases of disrupted relationships between indigenous peoples and their environment have been documented in the international literature.[27] The general paradigm of indigeneous peoples' displacement tends to be that of environmental damage caused by colonialism, by attempts to assimilate the indigenous group, or by efforts to use their lands for development purposes. However, the causes of displacement are much broader and varied, as previously demonstrated, and can often be hidden in the history of a particular community and its relationship with the surrounding world. In any event, every type of forced displacement places the people affected in an extremely vulnerable position, one in which their very lives are often threatened.[28] Displacement, therefore, must be regulated and, if not prohibited, at least strictly limited to those few instances of absolute necessity.

III. INTERNATIONAL LEGAL INSTRUMENTS CONCERNING DISPLACEMENT OF INDIGENOUS PEOPLES FROM THEIR ENVIRONMENT

The purpose of this section is to clarify the extent to which international environmental law restricts the displacement of indigenous peoples because of damage to their environment.[29] Two types of environmental law provisions are examined: first, general international environmental law,

---

26. At the same time it must be pointed out that these disruptions will not always cause people to move, especially in large numbers. Depending on the underlying or intervening factors such as the political structures, the security situation, international assistance etc., people may be prepared to stay and try to cope with the situation, especially if the disruption is of the slow-onset type. *See* MIGRATION AND THE ENVIRONMENT, *supra* note 13, at 15 seq.; *see also* Suhrke, *supra* note 25, at 7. According to Suhrke, the most problematic areas are those where fragile environments are inhabited by large and poor populations which engage in civil strife, leaving a very small margin for disaster. *Id.* at 33.

27. One of the less known cases, that of the Wanniya-Laeto of Sri Lanka is a case that illustrates quite explicitly the complexity of the root causes and the different ways the issues can manifest themselves. *See generally* WIVECA ANN-CHATRIN STEGEBORN, NATURE CONSERVATION, HUMAN RIGHTS AND INDIGENOUS PEOPLE: THE WANNIYA-LAETO (VEDDHAS) OF SRI LANKA (1993); *see also generally* Ashley Barr, *Sri Lanka: "Truth" Seeking Among the Veddhas,* 6 HARV. HUM. RTS. J. 247 (1993).

For a discussion of the threats posed to the Huaorani people in Equador by the construction of a network of roads through the forest they inhabit for purposes of oil exploration, *see* Shutkin, *supra* note 5, at 493–499. For a broader discussion in the case of the cultures of the low-lying islands in the Caribbean, South Pacific, and Indian Oceans because of the global climate change, *see id.* at 499–502. For a legal analysis of the case of the Nauru people, now pending in its substantive phase before the International Court of Justice, *see* Anthony Anghie, *The Heart of My Home: Environmental Damage, Colonialism and the Nauru Case* HARV. INT'L L. J. *(forthcoming* 1994) (draft unpublished paper, March 1993). For a reference to the Orissa tribals of India, *see* Suhrke, *supra* note 25.

28. *See, e.g.,* Anghie, *supra* note 27.

and second, provisions with environmental law content found in international instruments specific to indigenous peoples.[30]

A. General International Environmental Law

International environmental law is characterized by an abundance of soft-law instruments such as nonbinding declarations, especially regarding the displacement of indigenous peoples. The clauses most pertinent to displacement can be found in the Stockholm[31] and Rio[32] declarations, as well as in the World Charter for Nature[33] and Agenda 21.[34] Although none of these four instruments is binding law, the process has led to the evolution of several principles, some of which may already be considered customary law.[35] The following is a compilation of some of these principles:

- War and armed conflict should be prohibited insofar as they result both in displacement and environmental damage, which may cause further displacement.[36]

---

29. For a discussion of the legal rules and principles in the context of displacement, risk of displacement, environmental law and the rights of indigenous people applying in the case of the Nauru people, *see* Anghie, *id.*

30. Various provisions contained in the Universal Declaration of Human Rights, *supra* note 7, in the International Covenant of Civil and Political Rights, *supra* note 7, and on Economic, Social and Cultural Rights, *supra* note 7, as well as other regional and international instruments may be violated in cases of arbitrary displacement whether resulting from to environmental or other causes. *See, e.g.,* Julia Hausermann, *Root Causes of Displacement: The Legal Framework for International Concern and Action* (paper published by Rights and Humanity, 1986).

31. Stockholm Declaration on the Human Environment: U.N. Doc. A/Conf.48/14/Rev.1 (1972), *reprinted in,* 11 I.L.M. 1416 [hereinafter Stockholm Declaration].

32. Rio Declaration on Environment and Development, U.N. Doc. A/CONF.151/5/Rev.1 (1991), Adopted 14 June 1992, 31 I.L.M. 874 (1992). In its Preamble the Rio Declaration "reaffirms" the Stockholm Declaration; therefore, presumably, the principles therein are not withdrawn [hereinafter the Rio Declaration].

33. The World Charter for Nature, Adopted by the U.N. General Assembly on Oct. 28, 1982, G.A. Res. 37/7, U.N. Doc. A/37/51 (1983), *reprinted in* 22 I.L.M. 455 (1983). This non-binding instrument contains some of the principles mentioned in the Stockholm and Rio declarations; its importance lies in the fact that it has been adopted by the United Nations General Assembly [hereinafter the World Charter for Nature].

34. Agenda 21, United Nations Conference on Environment and Development, U.N. Doc. A/CONF.151/26 (1992) [hereinafter Agenda 21]. It is obvious that the issues addressed in the UNCED agenda go a long way towards reducing migration pressure from both environmental degradation and under-development. Refugee Policy Group et al., *supra* note 13, at 41. There is little point, therefore, in trying to extract from the whole of the agenda statements to this effect. Certain thematic chapters, however, are more pertinent to the discussions in this paper.

35. For instance the principle that states are internationally responsible for damage occurring outside their borders as a consequence of activities taking place within their jurisdiction. *See, e.g,* Shutkin, *supra* note 5, n.17 at 483; Anghie, *supra* note 27, at 68.

- Attention and efforts should focus on safeguarding sustainable development,[37] especially in the most vulnerable areas more prone to disaster and
  to generating refugees and displaced persons.[38]

- Appropriate assessment in planning and carrying out development policies
  and projects should be ensured. This assessment should include the

---

36. Principle 24 of the Rio Declaration, *supra* note 32, states that "warfare is inherently destructive of sustainable development"; it is, therefore, broader than Prinicple 26 of the Stockholm, *supra* note 31, which mentions nuclear weapons and "other means of mass destruction" but does not proscribe war and "other means of mass destruction." *See also* the World Charter for Nature *supra* note 33, para. 20: "Military activities damaging to nature shall be avoided."

37. "Life-threatening effects of environmental exploitation include the destruction of natural areas used for subsistence hunting and farming . . . . Concerning the potential impact of global climate change, a similar diminution or even decimation of natural resources necessary to sustain life is possible." Shutkin, *supra*, note 5, n.59 at 491 and accompanying text.

See also Rio Declaration, *supra* note 32, principle 14 (requiring states not to transfer hazardous activities). *See also,* Agenda 21, *supra* note 34, at § I, chap. 5, 43 seq., on demographic dynamics and sustainability. *See especially id.*, para. 5.20, at 38: "Research should be conducted on how environmental factors interact with socio-economic factors as a cause of migration"; *id.* para. 5.34, at 38: "Demographic concerns, including concerns for environmental migrants and displaced people, should be incorporated in the programmes for sustainable development of relevant international and regional institutions"; *id.*, para. 5.39, at 40: "The capacity of the relevant United Nations organs, organizations and bodies, international and regional intergovernmental bodies, non-governmental organizations and local communities should, as appropriate, be enhanced to help countries develop sustainable development policies on request, and as appropriate, provide assistance to environmental migrants and displaced people." *See also id.*, § II, Chapt. 14 at 76 on promoting sustainable agriculture and rural development. *See also id.*, § II, Chaps. 19,20,22, at 217 et seq. on environmentally sound management of toxic chemicals, hazardous wastes, and radioactive wastes.

See also the World Charter for Nature, *supra* note 33, para. 8 ("[i]n formulating long-term plans for economic development, population growth and the improvement of standards of living, due account shall be taken of the long-term capacity of natural systems to ensure the subsistence and settlement of the populations concerned . . . ."), para. 11 ("[a]ctivities which might have an impact on nature shall be controlled, and the best available technologies that minimize significant risks *to nature or other adverse effects* shall be used . . . .") (emphasis added).

38. Principle 9 of the Stockholm Declaration, *supra* note 31, provides:

"Environmental deficiencies generated by the conditions of under-development and natural disasters pose grave problems and can best be remedied by
accelerated development through the transfer of substantial quantities of financial and technological assistance as a supplement to the domestic effort of the
developing countries and such timely assistance as may be required."

To say how broadly or narrowly this provision can be construed is almost as difficult as trying to ascertain the forces that generate the environmental deficiencies mentioned in this provision. There is at least some basis, however, for a requirement for international cooperation and assistance when "grave problems" are caused by these deficiencies.

See also Agenda 21, *supra* note 34, § I, chap. 27, at 65 on promoting sustainable human settlement development. *See especially id.,* para. 7.30 (i), at 73: "Promote understanding among policy makers of the adverse consequences of unplanned settlements in environmentally vulnerable areas and of the appropriate national and local land-use and settlement policies required for this purpose;" Programme area (F) at 81: "Promoting human settlement, planning and management in disaster-prone areas."

participation of those affected, especially if policies and projects result in displacement and forced resettlement.[39]

- International organizations, states, nongovernmental organizations, and the like should cooperate fully and effectively, especially where they are involved in activities that may have adverse effects on the environment.[40]

- Measures to alleviate absolute poverty should be adopted, especially in order to address the type of poverty that results in distress flights of people from famine.[41]

- Legal instruments should be adopted to deal with the environmental damge *caused* by policies that generate forced migration and the resulting collateral problems.[42]

- To provide for the preceding principles, legislation should be adopted[43] that makes the "right to the environment" justiciable.[44]

---

39. Principles 13, 14, and 15 of the Stockholm Declaration, *supra* note 31, are quite explicit in requiring states to integrate and plan appropriately their development policies so as to maximize environmental protection and economic and social benefits for all. Principle 17 of the Rio Declaration, *supra* note 32, specifically requires environmental impact assessments to be conducted before activities likely to have adverse environmental effects are undertaken. On the question of participation, *see* Agenda 21, *supra* note 34, § III, chap. 24 at 4 on the global action for women towards sustainable and equitable development; *also id.* Vol. III, at 39 seq. on strengthening the role of farmers. *See also*, the World Charter for Nature, *supra* note 33, para.23 ("[a]ll persons, in accordance with their national legislation, shall have the opportunity to participate, individually or with others, in the formulation of decisions of direct concern to their environment, and shall have access to means of redress when their environment has suffered damage or degradation").

40. Principle 25 of the Stockholm Declaration, *supra* note 31, requires states to ensure that international organizations play "a co-ordinated, efficient and dynamic role for the protection and improvement of the environment." Despite its vague characterizations, the provision requires at least prudence on the part of international organizations when implicated in projects that could have adverse effects on the environment and cause displacement. Principle 15, *id.*, provides that "projects which are designed for colonialist and racist domination must be abandoned."

See also, the World Charter for Nature, *supra* note 33, para. 21: "States and . . . other public authorities, international organizations, individuals . . . shall: . . . (d) Ensure that activities within their jurisdictions or control do not cause damage to the natural systems located within other States or in the areas beyond the limits of national jurisdiction."

41. For instance, Principle 4 of the Rio Declaration, *supra* note 32, introduces the concept of sustainable development and Principle 5 centers on the "essential task of eradicating poverty as an inspensible requirement for sustainable development." Principle 8 centers on unsustainable patterns of production and consumption and the promotion of appropriate demographic policies. To the extent that poverty and unsustainable development are causes of displacement, these provisions provide a basis, albeit weak, to the concept that displacement is an indication that they have not been observed. *See also,* Agenda 21 *supra* note 24, § I, chap. 3 at 21–26, on combating poverty; *See also id.*, § II, chap. 12 at 46–66, on managing fragile ecosystems: combating desertification and drought.

42. It has been argued that refugee generating policies could be considered under the principles enunciated under the Trail Smelter Arbitration, *infra* note 96, to the extent that they cause damage to other countries. *See* Jack Garvey, *The New Asylum Seekers: Addressing their Origin in* DAVID MARTIN, REFUGEE LAW IN THE 1980s: THE NEW ASYLUM SEEKERS 183, 187 (1986). When a refugee influx actually results in environmental damage this will be presumably even more true.

In some cases regarding indigenous peoples, these principles have
been brought before international courts and similar fora to the extent that
they coincided or overlapped with other international instruments of binding force.[45]

B. Law Relating to Indigenous Peoples

Indigenous peoples have been traditionally considered distinct communities with specially recognized rights.[46] Some of these rights include
the right to their environment, lands, and resources and the right not to be
arbitrarily removed from their territories.

The first legal instrument that specifically provided for such rights
was the 1957 International Labour Organization (ILO) Convention 107,[47]
eventually replaced in 1989 by Convention 169.[48] The original convention
was replaced because it had been criticized[49] for attempting to assimilate
indigenous peoples in accordance with the prevalent attitudes of the imme-

---

43. Principle 11 of the Rio Declaration, *supra* note 32, requires the states to enact
"effective environmental legislation." This formulation may require states to provide specifically for the elimination or mitigation of the environmental causes of displacement, although
it is so broad that such an argument cannot be too forceful. *See also* Agenda 21, *supra* note
34, at 99 seq. § I, chap. 8, at 91–107, on "Integrating environment and development in
decision-making" and especially on "providing an effective legal and regulatory framework"
Id. Programme (B) at 96.

44. Principle 1 of the Stockholm Declaration, *supra* note 31, contains such a tentative
formulation:

> Man has the fundamental right to freedom, equality and adequate conditions of
> life, in an environment of a quality that permits a life of dignity and well-being
> . . . . [P]olicies promoting or perpetuating *apartheid*, racial segregation, dis-
> crimination, colonial and other forms of oppression and foreign domination
> stand condemned and must be eliminated.

Principle 1 of the Rio Declaration, *supra* note 32, is the equivalent to Stockholm
Principle 1 and the second part of principle 2 is analogous to Stockholm Principle 21.

For a discussion of the developments in this area and a relevant analysis *see, e.g.,*
Shutkin, *supra* note 5, at 502.

45. *See, e.g.,* Shutkin, *supra* note 5 (discussing the case of the Huaorani); ORGANIZA-
TION OF THE AMERICAN STATES, INTER-AMERICAN COMMISSION ON HUMAN RIGHTS, REPORT
ON THE SITUATION OF HUMAN RIGHTS OF A SEGMENT OF THE NICARAGUAN POPULATION OF
MISKITO ORIGIN (1984). For a discussion on state obligations with respect to environment
and other states and the common environment, the conditions of state responsibility, possible
state defenses, international law remedies, local and private remedies, *see*, Restatement
(Third) of the Foreign Relations Law of the U.S. Vol. 2, Part VI: The Law of the Environment
(1987).

46. *See* Part 1, *supra.*

47. Convention Concerning the Protection and Integration of Indigenous and Other
Tribal and Semi-Tribal Populations in Independent Countries, Jun. 26, 1957, 328 U.N.T.S.
247 [hereinafter ILO Convention 107], *reprinted in* SARDAR SAROVAR 18 (Report of the
Independent Review, 1992).

48. Convention Concerning Indigenous and Tribal Peoples in Independent Countries,
Jun. 27, 1989, 28 I.L.M. 1382 [hereinafter ILO Convention 169], *reprinted in* BASIC
DOCUMENTS ON HUMAN RIGHTS (Ian Brownlie, ed., 1992).

diate post-war period.[50] As the ILO objective evolved into a more complex appreciation of the relationship between international institutions, states, and indigenous peoples—including the recognition of a degree of autonomy for indigenous peoples[51] — replacing Convention 107 became a necessity.[52]

Both ILO conventions address the question of displacement. The provisions attempt to restrict arbitrary forced removal from the land and provide for basic guarantees, such as the participation of the affected group in the processes that affect them.[53] Convention 107 assumes both that assimilation should not be too harsh and that it will be more effective if indigenous peoples are willing participants.[54] Convention 169 ostensibly aims at ensuring "respect for the cultures, ways of life and traditional institutions of these peoples," as well as "effective involvement of these peoples in decisions that affect them."[55] Both conventions, despite their different wording, have been criticized for tolerating, if not legitimizing, dispossession whenever a government wishes to put indigenous peoples' lands to alternative use.[56]

If taken at face value, however, both conventions recognize the rights of indigenous peoples over their traditional lands and resources. These rights have been reiterated in the guidelines of international financing institutions, which address the issue of development-induced displacement.[57] These institutional guidelines may have established the groundwork for additional binding international law.

---

49. *See generally*, PARTIAL REVISION, *supra* note 20.

50. In the late 1950's, when the 107 Convention was being discussed by the Conference, it was "felt that integration [of the indigenous peoples] into the dominant national society offered the best chance for these groups to become a part of the development process of the countries in which they live." *Id.* at 18.

51. *See* Tennant, *supra* note 4, for a full analysis of these developments.

52. *See generally*, PARTIAL REVISION, *supra* note 20.

53. *See* Convention 107, *supra* note 47, arts. 11 and 12; *see also* ILO Convention 169, *supra* note 48, arts. 14(1), 16.

54. *See* Tennant, *supra* note 4.

55. *See* PARTIAL REVISION, *supra* note 20, at 18–19.

56. *See* PARTIAL REVISION, *supra* note 20, at 62 (discussing ILO Convention 107). *See* Sub-Commission on Prevention of Discrimination and Protection of Minorities, *The Human Rights Dimensions of Population Transfer, including the Implantation of Settlers*, item 8 of the provisional agenda, U.N. doc. E/CN.4/Sub.2/1993/17, paras. 253–261 (1993) (discussing ILO Convention 169).

57. *See, e.g.*, The World Bank Operational Directive 4.30 (June 29, 1990). The World Bank is said to define "tribal people" as ethnic groups exhibiting certain characteristics and to follow a policy that "would provide assistance to development projects in areas being used or occupied by tribal people only if such projects include adequate measures to safeguard the integrity and well-being of those concerned and [only] if the World Bank is satisfied that the borrowing government or agency supports and can implement such measures effectively." PARTIAL REVISION, *supra* note 20, at 12.

For instance, the much-debated Draft Declaration on the Rights of Indigenous Peoples[58] includes a number of extraordinarily progressive clauses.[59] It provides for prevention of, and redress for, dispossession of lands and territories. It also contains detailed descriptions of the traditional rights to land and resources, ownership of lands traditionally occupied, the right to the protection of the environment, the prohibition of military activities in indigenous peoples' lands and territories, and decision-making power concerning those lands and resources.[60]

Despite this fairly strong and detailed legal framework, questions remain regarding specific definitions of vague terms, such as "free and

---

58. *See Report of the Working Group on Indigenous Populations on Its Eleventh Session,* U.N. Comm. on Human Rights, Sub-Comm. on Prevention of Discrimination and Protection of Minorities, 11th Sess., Annex I, Agenda Item 14, U.N. Doc. E/CN.4/Sub.2/1993/29 (1993) (hereinafter Draft Declaration).

59. *Id.*

Article 8: Indigenous peoples have the *collective* and individual right not to be subjected to ethnocide and cultural genocide, *including prevention of and redress for:* . . .

(b) Any action which has the aim or effect of dispossessing them of their lands, territories or resources. . . .

Article 25: Indigenous peoples have the right to maintain and strengthen their distinctive spiritual and material relationship with the lands, territories, waters and coastal seas and other resources which they have traditionally owned or otherwise occupied or used, and to uphold their responsibilities to future generations in this regard.

Article 26: Indigenous peoples have the right to own, develop, control and use the lands and territories, including the total environment of the lands, air, waters, coastal seas, sea-ice, flora and fauna and other resources which they have traditionally owned or otherwise occupied or used. This includes the right to the full recognition of their laws, traditions and customs, land-tenure systems and institutions for the development and management of resources, and the right to effective measures by States to prevent any interference with, alienation of or encroachment upon these rights.

Article 28: Indigenous peoples have the right to the conservation...and protection of the total environment and the productive capacity of their lands, territories and resources, as well as to assistance for this purpose from States and through international cooperation. *Military activities shall not take place in the lands and territories of indigenous peoples,* unless otherwise freely agreed upon by the peoples concerned.

States shall take effective measures to ensure that *no storage or disposal of hazardous materials* shall take place in the lands and territories of indigenous peoples. . . .

Article 30: Indigenous peoples have the right to determine and develop priorities and strategies for the development or use of their lands, territories and other resources, including the right to require that States obtain their free and informed consent prior to the approval of any project affecting their lands, territories and other resources, particularly in connection with the development, utilization or exploitation of mineral, water or other resources. Pursuant to agreement with the indigenous peoples concerned, just and fair compensation shall be provided for any such activities and measures taken to mitigate adverse environmental, economic, social, cultural or spiritual impact (emphasis added).

60. *See id. generally.*

informed consent" and "effective measures." The Draft Declaration was not adopted at the last session of the Working Group, despite raised expectations due in part to 1993 having been declared the International Year of the World's Indigenous Peoples. Nevertheless, the Draft Declaration is already significantly impacting the rights of indigenous peoples and other related discussions.[61]

Finally, the Rio Declaration refers to indigenous peoples and their communities,[62] and Agenda 21 provides, inter alia, for the recognition and strengthening of the role of indigenous peoples and their communities, for the protection of their lands from environmentally unsound policies, and for the development of "national dispute-resolution arrangements in relation to settlement of land and resource-management concerns."[63]

IV. THE SHORTCOMINGS OF INTERNATIONAL HUMANITARIAN AND REFUGEE LAW IN THE PROTECTION OF INDIGENOUS PEOPLES

Although a complete prohibition against the arbitrary displacement of indigenous peoples would be ideal, in reality displacement will continue to occur. Indigenous peoples displaced because of damage to the environment will continue to suffer as much as, if not more than, all other refugees and displaced persons,[64] simply because they are being forced out of their homes and homelands for reasons beyond their control. Current international protection regimes have often proven inadequate in protecting displaced indigenous peoples. This section discusses those shortcomings and attempts to pull together principles from existing protection regimes that could be used to enhance the rights of displaced indigenous persons.

---

61. The drafting of the Draft Declaration has brought together every year increasing numbers of organizations of indigenous peoples, who participate as observers in the biweekly sessions of the Working Group on Indigenous Populations of the Sub-Commission on Prevention of Discrimination and Protection of Minorities. *See generally*, Draft Declaration, *supra* note 58. Indigenous peoples have been actively encouraged in the past twenty years to participate in the processes that affect them. *See* PARTIAL REVISION, *supra* note 20, at 13. Whether their participation legitimizes those processes that affect them, however, has been questioned. *See, e.g.,* Tennant, *supra* note 4.

62. Principle 21, Rio Declaration, *supra* note 32.

63. Agenda 21, *supra* note 34, § III, chap. 26, at 15–18. *See especially* paras. 26.1, 26.3, 26.6 (a).

64. *See* Shutkin, *supra* note 5.

A. A Summary of Protection Regimes Available for Displaced Persons

"Protection" has been defined as a concept that refers to a tripartite relationship between the protecting entity, the protected party, and a third party or force of nature against which protection is required.[65] A state is expected to protect the rights of *all* its citizens; when it fails to do so, other states or the international community are expected to fill the gap.[66]

Two main international regimes are available for the protection of displaced persons: refugee law and humanitarian law. Persons in fear of persecution because of their religion, race, nationality, political opinion, or membership in a particular social group, and who have crossed an international border, are protected mainly under the 1951 Geneva Convention Relating to the Status of Refugees.[67] A particular and individualized fear must be shown, as opposed to a fear of generalized violence,[68] in order to fall under, and thus benefit from, the characterization as a "refugee" under the Convention's definition. However, in the last two decades, regional instruments and UN practice have expanded this restricted definition of "refugee" in certain cases to include victims of war or generalized violence.[69] The UN High Commissioner for Refugees is mandated to provide protection and assistance to refugees.[70]

In times of war, whether international or internal, some persons will benefit from the 1949 Geneva Conventions,[71] and the two Additional Protocols of 1977.[72] Those benefitting include civilian populations and prisoners of war, whether displaced or not. These instruments are said to codify the largest part of international humanitarian law.[73] The Internation-

---

65. Atle Grahl-Madsen, *Protection of Refugees by their Country of Origin*, 11 YALE J. INT'L L., 362, 366 (1986). *See also*, for description of the spectrum of activities that protection includes, *id.*, at 364.

66. In the case of refugees these are, for example, the country of asylum and the United Nations High Commission for Refugees (UNHCR).

67. Convention Relating to the Status of Refugees, July 28, 1951, 189 U.N.T.S 137.

68. *See generally* JAMES HATHAWAY, THE LAW RELATING TO REFUGEE STATUS (1991).

69. *E.g.,* Convention Governing the Specific Aspects of Refugee Problems in Africa, Sept. 10, 1969, 189 U.N.T.S. 150; Convention on Asylum, Feb. 20, 1928, 132 L.N.T.S. 323; Convention on Territorial Asylum, Mar. 28, 1954, 161 B.F.S.P. 566.

70. G.A. Res. 429(v), U.N. GAOR, 5th Sess., Supp. 20 at 48, U.N. Doc. A/1775 (1950).

71. Convention Relative to the Protection of Civilian Persons in Time of War, Aug. 12, 1949, 75 U.N.T.S. 287.

72. Protocol Additional to the Geneva Conventions of 12 August 1949, and Relating to the Protection of Victims of International Armed Conflicts [hereinafter Protocol I], June 8, 1977, 16 I.L.M. 1391; Protocol Additional to the Geneva Conventions of 12 August 1949, and Relating to the Protection of Victims of non-International Armed Conflicts [hereinafter Protocol II], June 8, 1977, 16 I.L.M. 1442.

73. *See generally*, THEODORE MERON, HUMAN RIGHTS IN INTERNAL STRIFE: THEIR INTERNATIONAL PROTECTION (1987).

al Committee of the Red Cross monitors the enforcement of these instruments.

Internally displaced persons fall outside the scope of the 1951 Geneva Convention because they have not crossed an international border. Unless the conditions required for the application of the 1949 Convention and the 1977 Protocols are met, internally displaced refugees are not protected under international humanitarian law either.[74]

B. The Term "Environmental Refugee" and Its Implications for Refugee Law

Thus, as international law stands today, indigenous people who seek asylum in a third country will be protected as refugees if they can show that they fear being persecuted by the government in their country of origin because of their religion, race, nationality (including ethnic origin), membership in a particular social group or political opinion. Furthermore, indigenous people who are being victimized in the course of an armed conflict may occasionally fall under the protection regime established by international humanitarian law.[75]

Otherwise, as is generally acknowledged, people displaced because of environment-related reasons fall into a category where there is little legal and institutional protection provided by international legal instruments. Unless the environmental degradation is a consequence of an armed conflict or there is a mixture of environmental and political causes so the resulting displacement is covered under the regimes previously mentioned this type of displacement is not regulated in any coherent manner. As a result, those affected are not covered by an international protection regime.[76]

---

74. *See, e.g., Comprehensive Study by Mr. Francis M. Deng, Representative of the Secretary-General on the Human Rights Issues Related to Internally Displaced Persons,* U.N. Economic and Social Council, Commission on Human Rights, 49th sess., Provisional Agenda item 11(a), paras. 62–70 U.N. Doc. E/CN.4/1993/35 (1993). Occasionally UNHCR will provide assistance and protection to internally displaced persons, especially if they are mixed with people who sought asylum abroad and have recently returned to their country of origin (the so-called "returnees"). United Nations, Economic and Social Council, Commission on Human Rights, Note on International Protection U.N. doc. no. A/AC.96/815 (1993). For an overview of the existing institutions in the international field dealing with persons displaced because of environmental disasters, *see generally* MIGRATION AND THE ENVIRONMENT, *supra* note 13.

75. This will depend on the type of armed conflict, on the population in question, and on whether the state affected has acceded to the humanitarian law instruments.

76. Suzan Forbes Martin attributes this to the following factors: unclear mandates, lack of coordination, lack of resources, and seemingly competing or contradictory interests of the organizations concerned with environmental migration. *See*, Suzan Forbes Martin, *The Inhospitable Earth,* 89 REFUGEES 13, 14 (1992).

In the case of indigenous peoples, the lack of protection is compounded because, more often than not, they are displaced or forcibly transferred within their own country and continue to fall under the jurisdiction of that same state. As a result, those displaced cannot enjoy asylum in a third country or take advantage of any other form of international protection.

Because of this gap in the law relating to displacement caused by damage to the environment, some have advocated an expansion of the Geneva 1951 Convention refugee definition to include so-called "environmental refugees."[77]

"Environmental refugees" were first defined, without any reference to the 1951 Convention, as "those people who have been forced to leave their traditional habitat, temporarily or permanently, because of a marked environmental disruption (natural and/or triggered by people) that jeopardized their existence and/or seriously affected the quality of their life."[78]

This definition has been criticized as erasing the distinction between (1) refugees and migrants and (2) refugees and internally displaced persons.[79] But such distinctions are important; it has been observed that "the category to which a person is assigned can determine whether that person receives aid and/or protection from the international community or gains legal entry into another country."[80]

Strictly speaking, it is accurate to say that an "environmental refugee" (that is, a person in need of international protection) is a person who is both a refugee in the 1951 Convention sense (that is, he or she has a well-founded *fear of persecution*) and, *in addition*, has been displaced because of environmental reasons. Even so, it has been conceded that environmental migrants (persons not covered by the 1951 Convention) also are in need of assistance.[81]

By focusing on persecution, the definition of "environmental refugee" does not disturb the existing refugee regime and points out that certain persons affected by environmental degradation will be protected under

---

77. *See, e.g.,* Lazarus, *supra* note 14, at 15. "[O]ne might legitimately ask whether the international community's growing efforts to prevent environmental crises should not be accompanied by a formal extension of the refugee concept."

78. MIGRATION AND THE ENVIRONMENT, *supra* note 13, at 8, *citing* ESSAM EL-HINNAWI, ENVIRONMENTAL REFUGEES (1985). Other similar definitions have been also proposed. *See, e.g., generally,* JODI JACOBSON, ENVIRONMENTAL REFUGEES (1988).

79. *See* Suhrke, *supra* note 25; MIGRATION AND THE ENVIRONMENT, *supra* note 13, at 22–23.

80. *See* MIGRATION AND THE ENVIRONMENT, *supra* note 13, at 22–24, 51.

81. *Id.*

current refugee law. It adds little, however, to the search for better protection standards for those persons fleeing environmental degradation. They remain unprotected because they are not "persecuted" in the traditional sense.

For instance, in many cases of environmental migration, coercion may be present even if "persecution" itself is not easily discernible.[82] This may be true in the case of famine. Defining the term "environmental refugee" with exclusive reference to the terms of the 1951 Convention may easily lead to an inequitable conclusion. For example, those who flee from hunger are not environmental refugees, but simply environmental migrants who have fled their homes voluntarily to seek better lives elsewhere.[83]

It has been noted that absolute poverty[84] rarely produces truly massive migrations of people. At the same time, however, such a population movement can occur in cases where the distinction between flight from violence and flight from hunger is erased.[85] Indigenous peoples are often perceived as very poor, although their existence is usually not threatened until some disruption to their environment causes them to lose their means of subsistence. This disruption may well be caused by outside force or violence. Although the element of individual persecution will not always be evident, it has been observed that there is a greater tendency now within the refugee regime to treat such persons as refugees.[86]

It has been suggested "that the concept of environmental refugee must refer to especially vulnerable people who are displaced due to extreme environmental degradation. While all economic change involves an element of degradation, the critical question is whether a renewed equilibrium

---

82. For a discussion of the meaning of persecution and its interpretation in the context of the 1951 Convention, see HATHAWAY, supra note 68, at 99 seq. Generally, it means "constant threat to basic human rights." Although this constant threat may will be the basis of coercion, the term "persecution" implies the existence of a "target" and does not cover situations in which the person is a "victim" rather than a target. For an analysis of this distinction, see generally, ARISTIDE ZOLBERG ET AL., ESCAPE FROM VIOLENCE: CONFLICT AND THE REFUGEE CRISIS IN THE DEVELOPING WORLD (1989).

83. See MIGRATION AND THE ENVIRONMENT, supra note 13, at 51. The Waniya-Laeto seem to have been victims of this restricted refugee definition: although their displacement is still the cause of many human rights violations, no protection is available for them in the form of an international presence. They do not fall under the 1951 Refugee Convention, since they are still in their own country; and even if they had crossed the border, they might still not be protected. The cause for their displacement—damage to their environment due to development policies—would also not be considered to be covered under the refugee definition. See, supra note 13.

84. See generally, AMARTYA SEN, POVERTY AND FAMINES—AN ESSAY ON DEPRIVATION (1991).

85. See ARISTIDE ZOLBERG ET AL., supra note 82, at 260–261.

86. Id.

will develop."[87] Thus, the concept of sustainable development is linked to the definition of the term "environmental refugee." This definition also takes into account the role of the government and the time given to the displaced to cope with the situation (that is, with the circumstances under which the displacement took place).[88]

In the case of indigenous peoples, the extent and degree of their protection depends largely on the circumstances in each specific instance. For example, if their physical and cultural existence following their displacement is seriously endangered, if damage to their environment is deliberately carried out to induce displacement and thus eliminate them as an indigenous people, and if this destruction of their environment renders their return impossible, indigenous peoples should be afforded protection and rights similar to those provided for refugees and embodied in the 1951 Refugee Convention. If the definition previously referred to was applied, many indigenous peoples would be defined as persons in need of international protection, because the damage to their environment threatens their existence.

V. CONCLUSION: LINKING INTERNATIONAL ENVIRONMENTAL AND REFUGEE LAW— THE CASE OF THE INDIGENOUS PEOPLES

There are many areas of international law that address the issue of indigenous peoples' displacement from their environment. Environmental law seeks to limit the environmental damage that forces people from their traditional lands and subsistence practices. The law specific to indigenous peoples provides for their special rights with regard to their environment. Refugee law and humanitarian law, although they are not applied specifically to displaced indigenous peoples, can occasionally provide a legal basis for their protection.

These legal doctrines must be linked, however, to provide a comprehensive response to such displacement. Otherwise, each of these regimes will continue to evolve independently, leaving a vulnerable portion of the world's population unprotected. For instance, because refugee law doctrine has not been applied to the displacement of indigenous

---

87. Suhrke, *supra* note 25, at 9. The paper describes the various positions taken by sociologists and anthropologists to define the phenomenon. In relation to the definitional aspect discussed here it concludes that "[w]hether a given population ends up as destitute refugees or can transform themselves into successful migrants will in the first instance depend on conditions of social peace and the resources available for policy intervention." *Id.* at 15.

88. *See id.* at 9.

peoples per se,[89] in part because it has developed with reference to the 1951 Refugee Convention,[90] other regimes are attempting to address the needs of displaced indigenous peoples under different legal frameworks.

An example of such a linkage regarding indigenous peoples' right to return to their lands, or to compensation following displacement, may be found in the Draft Declaration on the Rights of Indigenous Peoples.[91] This Draft contains some striking provisions:

> Article 27: Indigenous peoples have the right to the *restitution* of the lands, territories and resources which they have traditionally owned or otherwise occupied or used, and which have been confiscated, occupied, used *or damaged* without their free and informed consent. Where this is not possible, they have the right to just and fair *compensation*. Unless otherwise freely agreed upon by the peoples concerned, compensation shall take the form of lands, territories and resources equal in quality, size and legal status.
>
> Article 28: Indigenous peoples have the right to the . . . *restoration* . . . of the total environment and the *productive capacity* of their lands, territories and resources, as well as to *assistance for this purpose from States and through international cooperation.*[92]

Such rights are unprecedented in traditional refugee law doctrine.[93] It seems that any projected repatriation of indigenous refugees would have to take into account the rights included in these two provisions and guarantee them as fully as possible. It would further appear that in other cases of

---

89. UNHCR has, however, expressed some interest in designing assistance according to the specific needs of indigenous refugees, including cultural specificity and promotion of international instruments specifically dealing with their rights, and analyzing the causes and dynamics of forced migration of indigenous peoples. *See 2nd Inter-agency Technical Consultation on Indigenous and Tribal Peoples, Final Report* (unpublished document, on file with author, Dec. 1991).

90. Convention relating to the Status of Refugees, *supra* note 67.

91. *See* Draft Declaration, *supra* note 58. In this regard, the ILO Conventions also include certain pertinent provisions. *See, e.g.,* ILO Convention 107, *supra* note 47, arts. 12, 16(1).

92. Draft Declaration, *supra* note 58, at arts. 27, 28 (emphasis added).

93. The principles guiding voluntary repatriation of refugees usually refer to the best interests of the refugee, the voluntary nature of the return, and the carrying out of the return under conditions of safety and dignity. *See, e.g., Report on Action Taken By UNHCR On the Recommendations of the Temporary Excom Working Group,* Office of the United Nations High Commissioner For Refugees (UNHCR) — Executive Committee, 41st Sess., concl. 18, 40, U.N. Doc. A/AC.96/761 (1990). Lately UNHCR has been addressing the question of voluntary repatriation as "a long-term, multi-dimensional and complex process" that should result in truly durable solutions and is now elaborating new guidelines for the involvement of the office in voluntary repatriation exercises. *Information Note on the Development of UNHCR's Guidelines on the Protection Aspects of Voluntary Repatriation,* Sub-Committee of the Whole on International Protection, 23rd mtg., U.N. Doc. EC/SCP/80 (1993).

refugee movements, refugees might, depending on the circumstances of each case, be in a similar situation and be able to raise claims of a similar nature.[94]

There is room for protection in existing environmental instruments. For example, Principle 22 of the Stockholm Declaration provides that States "shall *co-operate to develop* the international law relating to liability and compensation for the victims of pollution *and other environmental damage* caused by activities within the jurisdiction of such states *to areas beyond their jurisdiction.*"[95] This "undertaking to co-operate," as well as all similar "undertakings," can be characterized as rather weak and as giving no claims to those affected by such damage. On the other hand, it does lend support to the concept of liability for damage resulting *outside* the home country.[96]

Principle 13 of the Rio Declaration requires States to develop *national* laws regarding "liability and compensation for the victims of pollution and *other environmental damage,*" in addition to the requirements stated in Stockholm Principle 22.[97] This is probably the most important development since the Stockholm Declaration in the area of environment-related displacement. It was mentioned earlier that many of the environmental causes of displacement can ultimately be traced to human activity, although doing so may be extremely complicated and difficult.[98] This difficulty, however, does not neutralize the need for clear legal provisions that can be used by the "victims" in order to claim compensation more effectively. Rather, that difficulty demonstrates even more vividly the need for clear provisions.

In addition to the rights of compensation and restitution, however, the issue of protecting displaced indigenous peoples should be elaborated

---

The questions of the right to return and the right to compensation have been also raised in the context of the rights of refugees, although to a limited extent. On the right to return, *see generally* Gervaise Coles, *The Human Rights Approach to the Solution of the Refugee Problem: A Theoretical and Practical Enquiry, in* A. NASH, HUMAN RIGHTS AND THE PROTECTION OF REFUGEES UNDER INTERNATIONAL LAW, at 195 (1988). On the right to compensation, *see* Luke T. Lee, *The Cairo Declaration of Principles of International Law on Compensation to Refugees,* 87 AM. J. INT'L L. 157 (1993).

94. In reality it may well be the case that these standards are rarely applied or fully respected even in the cases they are provided for.

95. Stockholm Declaration, *supra* note 31 (emphasis added).

96. This principle is now considered to have binding force as it has been articulated in a number of cases by the International Court of Justice. *See* Trail Smelter Case (U.S. v. Canada), 3 R.I.A.A. 1907 (Apr. 16, 1938); Lac Lanoux Case (Fr. v. Spain), 53 AM. J. INT'L L. 156 (Nov. 16, 1957).

97. Rio Declaration, *supra* note 32, at principle 13.

98. *See* notes 15–17, *supra* and accompanying text.

further. Compensation, return, and restitution to undamaged traditional lands are ideal solutions that may well remain unimplemented in many instances. On the other hand, protection as conceived of in refugee law can be vital while indigenous peoples remain displaced, insofar as it provides certain principles guaranteeing their life and security. These fundamental provisions would include the following elements:

- The serious consequences of displacement of indigenous peoples, due to the disruption of their relationship to their environment, should influence their determination as refugee or vulnerable groups.

- Displaced indigenous peoples should be provided with adequate relief, rehabilitation assistance, and physical protection. There should be guarantees for their basic human rights.

- The return of indigenous peoples to their homelands, if at all possible, should be accelerated and facilitated, and its voluntary nature should be monitored. In the case that return is not a viable solution, they should be assisted in remaining within the host community or, if that is not possible, they should be assisted with their resettlement and provided with rehabilitation and development assistance.

- In all the aforementioned cases the specific nature of indigenous peoples' needs should be taken into account, especially those relating to the violation of their land and environment rights.

These elements form the content of refugee protection in general terms. The importance of applying them in the case of forced removal of an indigenous people from its homeland should not be forgotten or underestimated. Although it is arguable that in one form or another all of these rights are provided for in international human rights and environmental law, it may at the same time prove beneficial to cross-examine the international regimes of refugee law and environmental law and establish links that will serve to strengthen them both.

Traditional Ecological Knowledge and Environmental Futures

Winona LaDuke[†]

Traditional ecological knowledge is the culturally and spiritually based way in which indigenous peoples relate to their ecosystems. This knowledge is founded on spiritual-cultural instructions from "time immemorial" and on generations of careful observation within an ecosystem of continuous residence. I believe that this knowledge represents the clearest empirically based system for resource management and ecosystem protection in North America, and I will argue that native societies' knowledge surpasses the scientific and social knowledge of the dominant society in its ability to provide information and a management style for environmental planning. Frankly, these native societies have existed as the only example of sustainable living in North America for more than 300 years.

This essay discusses the foundation of traditional ecological knowledge and traditional legal systems, the implications of colonialism on these systems, and the challenges faced by the environmental movement and native peoples in building a common appreciation for what is common ground—Anishinabeg Akiing—the people's land.

> *I had a fish net out in a lake and at first I was getting quite a few fish in it. But there was an otter in the lake and he was eating the fish in the net. After a while, fish stopped coming into the net. They knew there was a predator there. So similarly game know about the presence of hunters as well. The Cree say, "all creatures are watching you. They know everything you are doing. Animals are aware of your activities." In the past, animals talked to people. In a sense, there is still communication between animals and hunters. You can predict where the black bear is likely to den. Even though the black bear zigzigs before retreating into his den to hibernate, tries to shake you off his trail, you can still predict where he is likely to go to. When he approaches his den entrance, he makes tracks backwards, loses his tracks in the bush, and makes a long detour before coming into the den. The hunter tries to*

† Member of the Mississippi Band Anishinabe and Campaign Director of the White Earth Land Recovery Program, a reservation-based land and environmental advocacy and acquisition organization on the White Earth Reservation of Anishinabeg in northern Minnesota.

*think what the bear is thinking. Their minds touch. The hunter and the
bear have parallel knowledge, and they share that knowledge. So in a
sense they communicate.*[1]

To be secure that one will be able to harvest enough involves more
than skill; it also involves careful observation of the ecosystem and careful
behavior determined by social values and cultural practices.

"Minobimaatisiiwin,"[2] or the "good life," is the basic objective of the
Anishinabeg and Cree[3] people who have historically, and to this day,
occupied a great portion of the north-central region of the North American
continent. An alternative interpretation of the word is "continuous rebirth."
This is how we traditionally understand the world and how indigenous
societies have come to live within natural law. Two tenets are essential to
this paradigm: cyclical thinking and reciprocal relations and responsibilities to the Earth and creation. Cyclical thinking, common to most
indigenous or land-based cultures and value systems, is an understanding
that the world (time, and all parts of the natural order—including the moon,
the tides, women, lives, seasons, or age) flows in cycles. Within this
understanding is a clear sense of birth and rebirth and a knowledge that
what one does today will affect one in the future, on the return. A second
concept, reciprocal relations, defines responsibilities and ways of relating
between humans and the ecosystem. Simply stated, the resources of the
economic system, whether they be wild rice or deer, are recognized as
animate and, as such, gifts from the Creator. Within that context, one could
not take life without a reciprocal offering, usually tobacco or some other
recognition of the Anishinabeg's reliance on the Creator. There must
always be this reciprocity. Additionally, assumed in the "code of ethics" is
an understanding that "you take only what you need, and you leave the
rest."

Implicit in the concept of Minobimaatisiiwin is a continuous inhabita-
tion of place, an intimate understanding of the relationship between
humans and the ecosystem, and the need to maintain that balance. These
values and basic tenets of culture made it possible for the Cree, Ojibway,
and many other indigenous peoples to maintain economic, political,

---

1. Fikret Berkes, *Environmental Philosophy of the Chisasibi Cree People of James
Bay Brock University, in* TRADITIONAL KNOWLEDGE AND RENEWABLE RESOURCE MANAGE-
MENT IN NORTHERN REGIONS (Occasional Paper No. 23), at 7, 10 (Milton M.R. Freeman &
Ludwig N. Carbyn, eds. 1988).
    2. "Minobimaatisiiwin" can be literally translated as the "good life"—"mino" means
"good" and "bimatissiiwin" mean "life" in the language of the Anishinaabeg people.
    3. Anishinabeg, which means "the people," are also called the Ojibway or Chippewa,
and are an Algonkinspeaking people who reside in the Great Lakes region. The Cree or
Eeyou, which can be translated as "the people" in their language, are close relatives of the
Anishinaabeg.

religious, and other institutions for generations in a manner that would today be characterized as sustainable.[4]

I. A MODEL

By its very nature, "development"—or, concomitantly, an "economic system" based on these ascribed Indigenous values—must be decentralized, self-reliant, and very closely based on the carrying capacity of that ecosystem. By example, the nature of northern indigenous economies has been a diversified mix of hunting, harvesting, and gardening, all utilizing a balance of human intervention or care, in accordance with these religious and cultural systems' reliance upon the wealth and generosity of nature. Because by their very nature indigenous cultures are not in an adversarial relationship with nature, this reliance is recognized as correct and positive.

> *A hunter always speaks as if the animals are in control of the hunt. The success of the hunt depends on the animals: the hunter is successful if the animal decides to make himself available. The hunters have no power over the game, animals have the last say as to whether they will be caught.* [5]

The Anishinabeg or Ojibway nation, for example, encompasses people and land within four Canadian provinces and five US states. This nation has a shared common culture, history, governance, language, and land base—the five indicators, according to international law,[6] of the existence of a nation of people. This nation historically and correctly functions within a decentralized economic and political system, with much of the governance left to local bands (like villages or counties) through clan and extended family systems. The vast natural wealth of this region and the resource management systems of the Anishinabeg have enabled people to prosper for many generations. In one study of Anishinabeg harvesting technologies and systems, a scientist noted:

> Economically, these family territories in the Timiskaming band were regulated in a very wise and interesting manner. The game was kept account of very closely, proprietors knowing about how abundant each kind of animal was. Hence they could regulate the killing so as not to deplete the stock. Beaver was made the object of the most careful "farming" an account being kept of the numbers of occupants old and young to each "cabin . . . ."[7]

---

4. For discussion, *see generally*, Colin Scott, *Knowledge Discussion Among Cree Hunters: Metaphors and Literal Understanding*, LXXV JOURNAL DE SOCIETE ANTHROPOLOGIC, 1989, at 193, 193-208.

5. Berkes, *supra* note 1, at 10.

6. Jason W. Clay, *What's a Nation?*, MOTHER JONES, Nov.–Dec. 1990, at 28.

7. Frank G. Speck, *The Family Hunting Band as the Basis of Algonkian Social Organization*, 17 AMERICAN ANTHROPOLOGIST, 289, 296 (1915).

The killing of game was regulated by each family. . . .[8]

The Anishinabeg employed a resource management system that used techniques for sustained yield. Such systems show a high degree of unification of conception and execution (possible because the "scientist" is the "resource manager"). There has only been limited imitation of this system by the scientific community.[9]

This system has allowed traditional land-based economies to prosper. Conceptually, the system provides for both domestic production and production for exchange or export. Hence, whether the resource is wild rice or white fish, the extended family as a production unit harvests within a social and resource management code that insures sustained yield. Traditional management practices have often been dismissed by North American settlers as useless in the current circumstances of more significant populations. However, it is important to note that previous North American indigenous populations were substantially higher than they are now. This indicates that these management practices were applied in greater population densities, an argument which is useful in countering the perceptions that all Native American practices have occurred with very low populations. I believe there is a more substantial question meriting discussion: Can North American society craft the social fabric to secure a traditional management practice, based on consensual understanding and a collective process?

II. COLONIALISM AND UNDERDEVELOPMENT

The governance of this land by traditional ecological knowledge has been adversely affected by genocide, colonialism, and subsequent circumstances that need to be considered in the current dialogue on North American resource management, the role of the environmental movement, and indigenous peoples. The holocaust of America is unmatched on a world scale, and its aftermath caused the disruption necessary to unseat many of our indigenous economic and governmental systems. There can be no accurate estimate of the number of people killed since the invasion, but one estimate provides for 112,554,000 indigenous people in the western hemisphere in 1492 and an estimated 28,554,000 in 1980. Needless to say, this is a significant depopulation.[10] This intentional and unintentional genocide facilitated a subsequent process of colonialism, which served to

---

8. *See generally, id.* at 289–305.

9. Peter J. Usher, *Property Rights: The Basis of Wildlife Management, in* NATIONAL AND REGIONAL INTERESTS IN THE NORTH 389, 408–09 (1984).

10. Robert Venables, *The Cost of Columbus: Was There a Holocaust?*, NORTHEAST INDIAN Q., Fall 1990, at 29, 30 n.7.

establish a new set of relations between indigenous nations and colonial or "settler" nations in the Americas.

Three basic concepts govern relations between colonial "settlers" and indigenous nations. Colonialism has been extended through a set of "center periphery relations" in which the center has expanded through: (1) the cultural practice spreading Christianity and, later, Western science and other forms of Western thought; (2) the socioeconomic practice of capitalism; and (3) the military–political practice of colonialism.[11]

These practices have resulted in the establishment of a set of relations between indigenous economies and peoples and the North American colonial economy that are characterized by dependency and underdevelopment. Underdevelopment—or, more accurately, "underdeveloping," because it is an ongoing practice—is the process by which the economy both loses wealth and undergoes the structural transformation which accentuates and institutionalizes this process.[12] This process, underway for at least the past 200 years, is characterized by the appropriation of land and resources from indigenous nations for the purpose of "developing" the US and Canadian economies and, subsequently, the "underdeveloping" of indigenous economies. The resulting loss of wealth (closely related to loss of control over traditional territories) has created a situation in which most indigenous nations are forced to live in circumstances of material poverty. It is no coincidence that Native Americans and Native Hawaiians (as well as First Nations in Canada) are the poorest people both in the United States and on the continent as a whole. As a consequence, indigenous peoples are subjected to an array of socioeconomic and health problems that are a direct consequence of poverty.[13]

In this process of colonialism, and later marginalization, indigenous nations become peripheral to the colonial economy and eventually are involved in a set of relations characterized by dependency. As Latin American scholar Theotonio Dos Santos notes: "By dependence we mean a situation in which the economy of certain countries is conditioned by the development and expansion of another economy to which the former is subjected."[14] These circumstances—and indeed, the forced underdevelopment of sustainable indigenous economic systems for the purpose of

---

11. John Galtung, *Self Reliance: Concepts, Practice and Rationale, in* SELF RELIANCE: A STATEGY FOR DEVELOPMENT 19, 20 (Johan Galtung et al. eds., Bogle-L'Ouverture Publications, Ltd. 1980).

12. SAMIR AMIN, UNEQUAL DEVELOPMENT: AN ESSAY ON THE SOCIAL FORMATIONS OF PERIPHERAL CAPITALISM 201–03 (Brian Pearce, trans., Monthly Review Press 1976).

13. AMERICAN INDIAN POLICY REVIEW COMM., FINAL REPORT SUBMITTED TO CONGRESS MAY 17, 1977 (Comm. Print 1977).

14. Theotonio Dos Santos, *The Structure of Dependence, in* READINGS IN U.S. IMPERIALISM 225, 226 n.1 (K.T. Fann & Donald C. Hodges eds., Porter Sargent 1971).

colonial exploitation of land and resources—are an essential backdrop for any discussion of existing environmental circumstances in the North American community and of any discussion of sustainable development in a North American context. Perhaps most alarming is the understanding that even today this process continues, because a vast portion of the remaining natural resources on the North American continent are still under native lands or, as in the case of the disposal of toxic wastes on Indian reservations, the residual structures of colonialism make native communities focal points for dumping the excrement of industrial society.

III. INDIGENOUS NATIONS TODAY

On a worldwide scale, there are more than 5000 nations and just over 170 states. "Nations" are defined under international law as those in possession of a common language, land base, history, culture and territory, while "states" are usually recognized and seated at the United Nations.[15] North America similarly contains a series of nations, known as "First Nations" in Canada and, with few exceptions, denigrated in the United States by the term "tribes." Demographically, indigenous nations represent the majority population north of the 55th Parallel in Canada (the 50th Parallel in the eastern provinces) and occupy approximately two-thirds of the Canadian landmass.

Although the United States has ten times the population it had during colonial times, Indian people do not represent the majority, except in a few areas, particularly the "Four Corners" region of the United States (so named because four states—Arizona, Utah, New Mexico, and Colorado—all meet at one point) where Ute, Apache, Navajo, and Pueblo people reside. However, inside our reservations, which occupy approximately four percent of our original land base in the United States, Indian people remain the majority population.

In our territories and our communities a mix of old and new coexist sometimes in relative harmony and at other times, in a violent disruption of the traditional way of life. In terms of economic and land tenure systems, the material basis for relating to the ecosystem, most indigenous communities are a melange of colonial and traditional structures and systems. Although US or Canadian laws may restrict and allocate resources and land on reservations (or aboriginal territory), the indigenous practice of "usufruct rights" is often still maintained and, with it, traditional economic and regulatory institutions like the trapline, "rice boss," and family hunting, grazing (for peoples who have livestock), or harvesting territories.

---

15. Clay, *supra* note 6.

These subsistence lifestyles continue to provide a significant source of wealth for domestic economies on the reservation, whether for nutritional consumption or for household use, as in the case of firewood. They also, in many cases, provide the essential ingredients of foreign exchange; wild rice, furs, woven rugs, and silverwork. These native economic and land tenure systems, which are specific to each region, are largely invisible to US and Canadian government agencies' economic analysts who consistently point to native "unemployment" with no recognition of the traditional economy. The Bureau of Indian Affairs labor statistics are categorized by sector, as is most employment data available from the U.S. Census Bureau.

In many northern communities, over half of local food and a significant amount of income is garnered from this traditional economic system. In other cases, for instance on the Northern Cheyenne Reservation in Montana, over ninety percent of the land is held by Cheyenne and is used primarily for ranching. Although they do not represent formal "wage work" in the industrial system, these land-based economies are essential to native communities. The lack of recognition for indigenous economic systems, although it has a long history in the North American colonial view of native peoples, is particularly frustrating in terms of the current debate over development options.

Resource extraction plans or energy mega projects proposed for indigenous lands do not consider the current significance of these economic systems nor their value for the future, as demonstrating what remains of sustainable ways of living in North America. A direct consequence is that environmentally destructive development programs ensue, many times foreclosing the opportunity to continue the lower-scale, intergenerational economic practices that had been underway in the native community.

IV. INDIGENOUS ENVIRONMENTAL ISSUES

The conflict between two paradigms—industrial thinking and indigenous thinking—becomes central to the North American and, indeed to the worldwide, environmental and economic crisis. As native communities struggle to survive, issues of sovereignty and control over natural resources become central to North American resource politics and the challenge for North Americans of conscience. Consider these facts:

  • More than 50 million indigenous peoples inhabit the world's remaining rain forests.

  • More than 1 million indigenous people will be relocated to allow for the development of hydroelectric dam projects in the next decade.

• The United States has detonated all its nuclear weapons in the lands of indigenous people, more than 600 of those tests within land legally belonging to the Shoshone nation.

• One-half of all uranium resources within the borders of the United States lay under native reservations. In 1974, Indians produced 100 percent of all federally controlled uranium.[16]

• One-third of all low-sulfur coal in the western United States is on Indian land, with four of the ten largest coal strip mines in these same areas.[17]

• Over 40 billion board feet of timber stands on Indian reservations— trees now coveted by US timber interests.[18]

• Fifteen of the eighteen recipients of phase one nuclear waste research grants, so-called Monitored Retrievable Nuclear Storage sites, are Indian communities.

• The largest hydroelectric project on the continent, the James Bay Project, is on Cree and Inuit lands in northern Canada.[19]

For many indigenous peoples, the reality is as sociologist Ivan Illich has suggested: development practices are in fact a war on subsistence.

V. MANITOBA HYDRO: A WAR ON SUBSISTENCE

Hydroelectric dams in the north illustrate the battle between the indigenous and industrial the world. The James Bay dams of northern Quebec continue to be a front line environmental struggle, as the pending destruction of the "Amazon of the North" rallies environmentalists and Crees in an ongoing battle with Quebec Hydro.[20] For the past five years, American environmentalists have joined with Cree to stop American export contracts (New York Power Authority, Commonwealth Edison, etc.) and build a coalition which successfully stopped at least one contract. This case is far from isolated; there are dams in Canada west of Quebec that are equally devastating. In the early 1970s, a series of seven dams was built on the Nelson and Churchill River systems. The dams spin out 2,600

---

16. Winona LaDuke, *Native America: The Economics of Radioactive Colonialism*, REVIEW OF RADICAL POLITICAL ECONOMICS, Fall 1983, at 9, 10.

17. *Id.*

18. Interview with Marshall Cutsforth, Bureau of Indian Affairs Office of Trust Responsibility (August 10, 1993).

19. *See* Boyce Richardson, STRANGERS DEVOUR THE LAND (1976).

20. Richardson, *supra* note 18.

megawatts of power. In total, another eleven generating stations are proposed, to spin out an additional 6,000 megawatts.[21]

The Churchill and Nelson River systems drain one of the largest watersheds in North America. They extend from the Rockies in the west to the Mississippi and Lake Superior drainage basin in the south. These rivers ultimately flow into Hudson Bay, the larger bay into which James Bay drains.

One control dam at Missi Falls on the Churchill River illustrates the project's intent. The dam cut the flow from an average of 1,050 cubic meters per second to an average of 150 meters per second and turned all the water back into South Indian Lake.[22]

The Manitoba Hydor dams' location, in the midst of permafrost, causes additional problems. Dr. Robert Newbury of the Freshwater Institute notes: "What made the venture most critical . . . was that it was the first large river diversion and take impoundment in widespread permafrost. When the project was planned, the implications of that were suspected but unproven."[23] The development has inadvertently been an ecological experiment. Because the temperature of the water always exceeds the temperature of the soil, the water causes a constant "melting away" of the shoreline. The annual rate of "shoreline retreat," as it is aptly called, is currently 130 to 140 feet per year. According to the Winnipeg–based Freshwater Institute, it may be 80 years or more before shoreline retreat subsides.[24] This silting—which is another term for shoreline retreat—chokes the reservoirs, causes widespread mercury contamination and the destruction of wildlife.

There is a story told by northern moose hunters about of two hunters on South Indian Lake. They scan the shore for a moose. After much searching, they finally happen upon one. It was a moose, alright, but sinking up to its neck in silt.[25]

It is such ecosystem devastation that caused more than ninety-eight percent of the waterfowl to disappear from the South Indian Lake region in northern Manitoba, according to the Freshwater Institute. Humans have been affected, too. Health surveys demonstrate that one out of every six

---

21. Larry Krotz, *Dammed and Diverted*, CANDIAN GEOGRAPHIC, Feb/Mar. 1991, at 36, 38.

22. *Id.* at 39.

23. *Id.* at 41.

24. *Id.*

25. Information derived from conversation between Alan Ross of Norway House and Randy Kapashesit of Moose Factory, Ontario.

people on the Nelson River suffer from mercury contamination.[26] The dams have also created widespread economic and social disruption.

Two decades ago, seventy-five percent of the food came from the land, as did the majority of local income. Today, that is impossible. Very little comes from the land, and people are forced to buy food at the store, often at prices ten times that in the south.

At the Cree village of Moose Lake, for instance, two-thirds of their land base was flooded and 634 people were moved into a housing project.

Jim Tobacco, Moose Lake Band, said 90 percent of the adults were estimated to have substance abuse problems after the flooding. "There is a very hostile attitude in the community," he laments. "Our young people are always beating each other up. My people don't know who the hell they are. They live month to month on welfare. Our way of life and resources have been destroyed. We were promised benefits from the Hydro Project. Today, we are poor and Manitoba Hydro is rich."

Elsewhere, suicide epidemics plague flooded communities. "There's just a feeling they're being exploited, they're being used," said Alan Ross, Chief of Norway House, another flooded community. His small village had fifteen suicide attempts a month during the 1980s.[27] At Cross Lake, twenty suicides occurred during an eight-month period—ten times the provincial average.[28]

Manitoba government officials are quick to point to the recent "compensation package" worth tens of millions of dollars to these northern villages. But in the face of a near doubling of hydroelectric capacity in the north—from seven dams to eleven, increasing the rate of devastation to the ecosystem and the community—many natives have come to wonder if there is any "just compensation" for the destruction of their way of life.

Manitoba Hydro's impact on northern Cree and Ojibway communities is indicative of the devastation being wrought in Indian Country by development projects. This example also illustrates the complexity of indigenous environmental issues in the larger context of a North American environmental movement and the depth of the problems we collectively face in our strategies. Specifically, I have found four consistent facts. First, Cree and Ojibway economic, cultural, and ecological knowledge and systems are largely dismissed as inevitably outdated and lacking in value in

---

26. Krotz, *supra* note 21, at 42.
27. GEOFFRY YORK, THE DISPOSSESSED: LIFE AND DEATH IN NATIVE CANADA 96–97 (1989).
28. *Id.* at 96.

comparison to the "greater good" associated with hydroelectric dams. The
lack of valuation of traditional economies augments the underrepresenta-
tion of native ways of life in cost/benefit equations. Second, the inevitable
cultural and social devestation wrought by such projects is soft-peddled by
government and, often, by environmentalists, who have become accus-
tomed to viewing "the Natives as steeped with social and health problems
and subsequently have become numb to concern." Third, the Manitoba
Hydro dams, like the Hydro Quebec dams, are a result of shortsighted
development programs (based on continued increases in electrical consumption) and an often compromising environmental movement that trades
nuclear power plants in for hydroelectric dams. Finally, the single largest
contract for Manitoba Hydro dams is with the United States (Northern
States Power), illustrating US environmentalists' ability to subscribe to an
"out of sight/out of mind" allowance that creates "sacrifice areas" in
communities like Moose Lake and in ecosystems like James and Hudson
Bay.

VI. STRATEGIC ERRORS IN THE ENVIRONMENTAL MOVEMENT

The mainstream environmental movement, one that journalist Mark
Dowie suggests is "courting irrelevantism," has historically played into the
colonial mind-set by denying the existence of indigenous ecological
knowledge (except perchance quoting a few words of Chief Seattle) and
the significance of this knowledge in sustainable thinking.

There are numerous examples of the alleged superior knowledge of
(usually) urban-based environmentalists over the knowledge of ecosystems
inherited by indigenous peoples. Just a few:

> • On a reservation in northern Minnesota, White Earth, The Nature
> Conservancy purchased approximately 400 acres of land (to preserve
> "indigenous prairie") from a private, nonabsentee landholder and
> turned it over to the state.

> • A pending lawsuit in New Mexico state court, Ray Graham III v. Sierra
> Club Foundation, is based on Graham's donation of $100,000 to the
> Sierra Club Foundation to purchase land in northern New Mexico for a
> Chicano community sheep ranching project. (Land-based Chicanos
> subscribe to similar value systems as indigenous people and a share
> good portion of common bloodlines.) The Sierra Club Foundation is
> alleged to have purchased other properties instead.[29]

---

29. Interview with Mark Dowie, Editor-at-Large of InterNation.

• As a result of successful organizing work by Greenpeace and animal rights groups, the European Economic Community (EEC) placed a ban on the sale of white coat seal pup pelts. In 1983 the market for pelts of mature seals collapsed as well. In eighteen of twenty Inuit communities in the Northwest Territories, the annual revenue from the sale of sealskin pelts dropped by approximately sixty percent.[30]

• The community of Broughton Island saw its collective income drop from a total of $92,099 in 1981–1982 to $13,504 in 1983–1984. The Inuit of Pangnirtung on Baffin Island made only $42,146 in 1983–1984 in comparison with the $200,714 they had made two years earlier. The income for Resolute, in the High Arctic, fell from $54,841 to $2,383 during the same period. Since the EEC ban there has been a significant increase in social problems in the communities, which until that time had been largely self-sufficient.[31] When asked by a Canadian government committee to report on the impact of the loss of the market for sealskins in Inuit communities, Ms. Rhoda Inusuk, president of the Inuit Tapirisat of Canada replied:

"One of the disasters that has happened as a result is that of youth suicide. We have a very high rate of suicide. The loss is due to the animal rights group. . . . We have the youth problems, drug and alcohol abuse, violence. There is very little employment and when you are hit with something like that, you are bound to see these problems come up as result of that."

• The Great Whale proposed site of the James Bay II Dam is another excellent example: *"What are we conserving the beluga for?"* a Great Whale hunter wonders, noting the community imposed limit of ten, *"So that the power project can kill them all later?"*[32]

Although these instances are not the whole story of the environmental movement in Indian Country, they represent problems that reoccur consistently because, I believe, underlying racism exists in the basically white-dominated environmental organizations. This "environmental racism" in the environmental movement is also indicated by the inability of mainstream organizations to recognize, for instance, the relationship between ecologically destructive development projects (or culturally altering environmental initiatives, like the seal campaign) and cultural and physical devastation and genocide, such as is seen in the Inuit and Cree examples. These so-called "social justice issues" must be recognized as a part of an environmental agenda—for if there is no one left who understands how to care for an ecosystem in a sustainable, practiced manner, it will not be cared for.

---

30. Winona LaDuke, Briefing Paper for the Greenpeace USA Board of Directors on Sovereignty and Native People.
31. *Id.*
32. *Id.*

Finally, the culturally limited worldview of many urban environmentalists serves to drive a wedge between native and settler. So long as the issue of consumption is not addressed, someone's land and lives will be traded for someone else's cappuccino machine. Therefore, arguments made by individuals who support Hydro Quebec's James Bays dams as an alternative to nuclear power means that my children are not to have land or a cultural inheritance so that their grandchildren may retain a level of consumption they feel they deserve.[33]

The challenge that I believe faces the North American environmental movement is to form a meaningful partnership with indigenous communities and peoples. Only then can we address the common issues of environmental degradation and the clear need for a new operating paradigm from which to build a natural resources management system or, more appropriately, a way of managing our relations with the land.

VII. NATIVE SUSTAINABILITY INTO THE TWENTY-FIRST CENTURY

Native people are on the front lines of resistance to many ecologically devastating projects. Whether it is the Cree of James Bay, the Havasupai of the Grand Canyon opposing uranium mining, the Columbia River fishing peoples opposing nuclear contamination at Hanford, the Point Hope Inupiat trying to force the federal government to clean up a nuclear testing site on the North Slope, or the Anishinabeg of northern Wisconsin trying to stop a copper strip mine, we continue vigilant struggles for land, culture, and future generations.

Native peoples are also engaged in proactive struggles to regain control over ecosystems and ways of living. The following are examples of the adaptability of indigenous thinking to community development projects.

A. Zuni

For the past 1,500 years, the Zuni people have farmed in an area that they currently occupy—the Zuni Reservation in central New Mexico. They are famous for their skill and knowledge of farming under difficult conditions. Floodwater irrigation of folk crop varieties in this dry area has been the core of their farming.

---

33. Information derived from the 1992 New England Environmental Conference, Tufts University Filene Center, March 19-21, 1992.

During the past several generations, however, there has been a reduction both in farming and in area farmed from 1,012,000 acres in the mid-1800s to about 1,000 acres today. However, there is now renewed interest and commitment by the Zuni people in agriculture. The Zuni Sustainable Agriculture Project is their response, which they place in the context of the crisis of American "modern" industrial agriculture.[34]

The Zuni note, with some remorse, that in the United States, salt buildup is lowering yields on some thirty percent of irrigated land, and about twenty percent of irrigated land is watered by pumping out groundwater at a rate exceeding its replacement. About seven tons of US cropland topsoil per acre are being lost to wind and water erosion, and approximately 500,000 tons of 600 different types of pesticides are applied annually in the United States. The cumulative impact of this type of agriculture is—from the Zuni, and other indigenous people's, viewpoint— unsustainable.[35]

The intent of the Zuni project is to restore community participation in and control over food production and agriculture through a diversified program of education, research/data collection and analysis, as well as actual farming and technical assistance. The projects are integrated. One example is peach tree orchard restoration and revitalization, which is based on a Zuni system called *dabathishna*, or "field rooting".[36]

Another aspect of the Zuni project is the managing of rainfall runoff into the fields. This project is called *kwa'k'ya,di deyatchinanne*, often translated as "dry farming" in English. At Zuni, however, this English term is misleading. In fact, farmers really do irrigate these fields, but usually with rainfall runoff from surrounding areas or by capturing water from arroyos.

The project is part of the International Union for Conservation of Nature, which recently held an international meeting at Zuni.

B. Anishinabeg Resource Management Initiatives

In the Great Lakes region, a number of Anishinabeg communities have undertaken restorative programs for traditional ecological knowledge and the recovery of control over land on which people live.

---

34. David Cleveland and Daniela Soleri, *The Zuni Sustainable Agriculture Project*, ZUNI FARMING FOR TODAY & TOMORROW (Occasional Newletter), Spring 1993, at 1.

35. Zuni Sustainable Agriculture Project and the Nutria Irrigation Unit, *The Nutria Project*, ZUNI FARMING FOR TODAY & TOMORROW (Occasional Newletter), Spring 1993, at 1, 4.

36. Daniela Soleri with Lygatie Laate, *Peach Tree Care and Propogation: Building on Traditional Knowledge*, ZUNI FARMING FOR TODAY & TOMORROW (Occasional Newletter), Summer 1993, at 1, 2.

On the White Earth reservation in northern Minnesota, the White Earth Land Recovery Project seeks to recover control over more than one-third of all reservation lands in the next two decades. At least that much is held by government agencies, including 21,000 acres designated as a National Wildlife Refuge, which the people seek to have returned. The White Earth people will seek to restore traditional resource management schemes to those parcels they recover.

To the south of White Earth, the Mille Lacs Band of Anishinabeg is litigating against the State of Minnesota, seeking to secure harvesting access to lands within the 1847 treaty boundary that were unceded by the band. These traditional people have been restricted to only 4,000 acres of land, of which only 1,500 are secure for harvesting. The remainder is greatly diminished in wealth by environmental degradation and the encroachment of non-Indian settlers and tourist industries.

The Mille Lacs Commissioner of Natural Resources, Don Wedll, documented the subsistence requirements for the band members' future to establish the amount of territory required by band members to ensure their sustenance. This approach underscores their political strategy, which, in turn, is based on cultural values and long-term self-sufficiency brought about by careful stewardship.

> The economic revenue from natural resources is based on the ability to harvest surplus resources for sale or trade. The using of Natural Resources for economic gains will be secondary to the gathering for feed or herbs. Through [sic] traditionally the Chippewa from Mille Lacs [Anishinabeg] have traded and sold harvestable natural resource[s], Mille Lacs Reservation will insure [sic] the protection of species to any economic gain from our natural resources. The economic gains will be limited to a moderate harvesting and managed so as to insure [sic] the rights of all Band members to harvest and gather food and/or herbs. The economic benefits from natural resources harvesting will be limited to family units and not individual members. It will also be limited to an income guideline.[37]

In northern Wisconsin, similar approaches to securing adequate food, clothing, shelter, and sustenance are forwarded by Anishinabeg bands within the 1847 treaty area. For example, a comanagement plan drafted by native activists Walt Bresette (Anishinaabe) and James Yellowbank (Winnebago) speaks to proposals for indigenous values and the common sense of rural communities trying to survive.

Similarly, the Wabigon Lake Wild Rice Management Program has been advanced by the Anishinabeg of southern Ontario. While Canadian

---

37. *See* Don Wedll, *Mille Lacs Band of Chippewa Indians: Basic Existence Requirements for Harvesting of Natural Resources*, TRIBAL DOCUMENT (1986).

government legislation has demarked wild rice harvesting zones in the area according to resource management districts, the Wabigon Lake people have noted that their traditional territory extends into two districts and that the Canadian government management proposals are not based on traditional resource management practices of the Anishinabeg. The Wabigon Lake Anishinabeg have responded with their own demarcation and regulation program, including provisions for traditional (canoe) harvesting followed by mechanical (airboat) harvesting. Their organically certified wild rice (by the Organic Crop Improvement Association) is marketed internationally, returning substantial revenues to their community and illustrating the potential of using traditional economies and value systems as the foundation for community control of economy and destiny. They have also developed Wabuskang Wildfruits, which hopes to continue marketing 10,000 jars of organically certified blueberry spread annually.[38]

Other examples in the region abound, but perhaps none is so striking as the Menominee Forest Enterprises in northern Wisconsin. This reservation contains the most age and species diversified stands in the region and retains the same amount of timber today as a century ago, all due to indigenous forestry management practices paired with careful harvesting techniques. The Menominee forest is the only "green cross certified" forest in North America.

These examples illustrate the application of traditional ecological knowledge within the cultural areas of those peoples from whom the knowledge originates. Sustainable practice with continuous harvest is critical for the environmental movement to recognize; it is a practice in which humans are a part of the land and of ecosystems. Equally important is applying this knowledge within the cultural fabric of cohesive societies—something that North Americans (including environmentalists) have yet to attain—and linking sustainable practice and governance over territory. There will not be the former without the latter. Native peoples must be accorded the proprietary interest in those lands that sustain their communities; that is the only way that sustainability will be insured. However, this point remains a divisive one in terms of the North American environmental movement.

---

38. *See* Winona LaDuke, *Wabuskang Women's Marketing Collective*, INDIGENOUS WOMAN, Vol. 1, No. 3, at 48.

VIII. COMMON GROUND/COMMON ADVERSARIES AND COMMON SOLUTIONS

A more effective goal for all of us is to get serious about becoming "native to our place." As a culture, we still operate more in the conquering spirit of Columbus and Coronado, than in that of the Natives we conquered. To be native to this place would not mean the end of science or the end or management of our landscape. . . .

Embrace the arrangements that have shaken down in the long evolutionary process and try to mimic them . . . ever mindful that human cleverness must remain subordinate to nature's wisdom.[39]

Wes Jackson, Salina, Kansas

It is time that indigenous peoples' knowledge, experience, ways of living, and struggles to survive are taken seriously by the environmental movement.

Environmentalists who seek principally to defend ecosystems from devastation by hydro dams, clear-cutting, development, or mining have much to gain from an alliance with native people. We have common adversaries, whether they be corporations or governments. For instance, the WISE USE Movement includes organizations like Protect American Rights and Resources (PARR), Equal Rights for Everyone (ERRA), SPAWN, and other groups whose central purpose is to strip native peoples of their rights to govern lands and to secure culture, language, and religion.[40]

Knowing your allies is critically important, as is sharing the power to determine larger political agendas. It is possible that we may have common solutions. An interesting discussion is now underway over the central lands of North America, which illustrates the tensions between indigenous peoples and North Americans or environmentalists.

In the center of the United States, stretching across the Great Plains, is a vast expanse of reservation land—approximately 50 million acres of the most significant native landholdings in the United States. That same region contains a much larger area of indigenous lands—lands reserved under treaties like the 1868 Fort Laramie Treaty with the Lakota nation and the 1853 Ruby Valley Treaty with the Western Shoshone nation. These treaty lands are, in effect, illegally occupied by the United States. These

---

39. Wes Jackson, *Listen to the Land*, THE AMICUS J., Spring 1993, at 32, 33–34.

40. *See* Rudolph Rÿser, *Anti Indian Movement on the Tribal Frontier*, Center for World Indigenous Studies (Occasional Paper No. 16), June 1992, at 3, 3–5.

lands are the subject of discussion in two separate agendas. The *Great Plains Initiative* discusses water allocations in that overdrawn region and the *Buffalo Commons* discusses the future of land tenure within the region. In the case of the Great Plains Initiative (a process underway largely between state and federal governments and environmental groups), native people have rarely been at the table. Proposals for water allocations in the region have yet to address the 50 million acres of reservation lands that have not been allowed "a drink." Instead, these communities have been left "high and dry" by decades of ill-conceived water diversion projects (including Oahe, Garrison, Kerr, and Lake Powell). Native peoples retain legal rights to water their lands and need to be included in the dialogue, something that should be demanded by the environmental movement if it is interested in preserving sustainable cultures. The Mini-Sosi Alliance, for instance, a coalition of Northern Plains indigenous governments created to discuss water issues, is demanding this recognition.

Frank and Debra Popper of Rutgers University put forward the Buffalo Commons initiative in the early 1980s, offering other possibilities. The Poppers undertook a comprehensive study of economics and land-use patterns in the region. They discovered that 110 counties—a quarter of all counties in the western portions of the states of North and South Dakota, Nebraska, Kansas, Oklahoma, and Texas, as well as eastern Montana, Wyoming, Colorado, and New Mexico—had been on shaky financial ground since, essentially, the moment they were expropriated from indigenous peoples. (These counties and those who inhabit them, are also, not surprisingly, engaged in an agriculture policy that, in many cases, is ecologically unsound and which, for instance, results in the seven tons of topsoil loss annually per acre, a rate that is occurring in most of this region.)

This region of approximately 140,000 square miles of prairie is inhabited by approximately 400,000 Euro-Americans in financially stricken counties that attempt to support school districts, road maintenance, fire departments, and social services in the face of dropping populations and subsequent decreases in revenues. The local governments have not been successful in financing all these programs, and most counties are nearly bankrupt. These counties are frequently located not only near Indian reservations but also adjoining a great deal of western federal lands.

The Poppers proposed an interesting idea, which indigenous scholar Ward Churchill takes a step further. The Poppers suggest that the government should cut its proverbial losses and buy out the individual landholdings. The final result, in the Poppers' proposal, would be a commonly held land—the "Buffalo Commons," on which ecological restoration should occur.

Churchill proposes that ecological and cultural restoration should occur, largely by expanding this area to the Indian reservations, the national forests and parklands, and the now-redundant military reservations like the Ellsworth Air Force Base and other similar areas under the Strategic Air Command. These lands are within the unceded territory of the Lakota, Pawnee, Arikara, Hidatsa, Mandan, Crow, Shoshone, Assiniboine, Cheyenne, and Arapaho. Such a proposal would cause relatively little dislocation of non-Indians (thousands annually drain out of these counties in any case) and would provide a fertile area for the recovery of indigenous species and peoples.[41]

The Indigenous Commons region and areas like the Northern Rockies Ecosystem (occupied by peoples such as the Blackfeet, Salish, Kootenai, and Nez Perce), the Nunavat (the newly created Inuit territory in what was formerly the Northwest Territories—an area the size of the Indian subcontinent), James and Hudson Bay, and regions like Anishinabeg Akiing, represent the beginnings of a political decolonization—the dismantling of settler-imposed political and economic institutions—of the continent. Such regions also represent the beginning of a new paradigm or, perhaps, a recovered indigenous paradigm, which has immense value in the context of the North American environmental movement.

IX. THE NEW PARADIGM: STRUCTURAL CHANGE

Long-term solutions are implicitly necessary to sustain the land and resolve the arguments about the land. Cultural diversity is as critical as biological diversity and must be manifested in our methods of relating to the land. Resource and so-called "common property" management policies can neither be conceived nor implemented without reference to the system of property rights, which is, in turn, determined by the fundamental political arrangement of any society. Resource management systems that exist in North American law today rely on a system of property rights that emulate the social values of Euro-American society and have no reference to indigenous values and property rights. As a result, I argue that these systems have no relation to this land.

Property rights, in traditional native society, can be said to rest with the group, the collective. Each band or co-residential group traditionally has maintained the rights to use territory by virtue of occupancy. The connection between the land and the group lies in the ceremony, spiritual

---

41. WARD CHURCHILL, STRUGGLE FOR THE LAND: INDIGENOUS RESISTANCE TO GENOCIDE, ECOCIDE AND EXPROPRIATION IN CONTEMPORARY NORTH AMERICA 421-433 (1993).

instruction, naming, travel knowledge, and intergenerational residence. Traditionally, usufruct rights are allocated to the whole, usually based on extended family/clan allocations, and the property right remains with the collective. To the extent that indigenous peoples have articulated their relationship to the land, they see themselves as belonging to it rather than it to them. Anishinabeg Akiing and Dineh Bii Kaya, both signifying "the people's land," articulate the same principle value or set of values.

Those values deserve a place at the environmental table and in its dialogue. In the consistent dismissal of both native values and property rights in a North American political context, even in the context of the "left" and the environmental movement, there remains a subliminal fear of the indigenous—a residue of colonialism and the colonial mind.

"Management" is a prerogative that flows from the system of property every system of resource management is based on certain assumptions, frequently unstated, that social organization, political authority and property rights, all of which are closely interrelated. As no two societies or cultures are identical in these respects, there can be no such thing as a scientifically or technically neutral management regime that is equally applicable and acceptable to both. Consequently, where two social systems share an interest in the same resource, there must be some accomodation in the sphere of property, as in the system of management, unless one is to be completely obliterated by the other.[42]

We have inherited a dominant system of property and natural resource management that flows from the European industrial mind. Common property, or the perception of common property, governs a substantial portion of land within the United States. The federal government is, after all, the single largest landholder. "Common property" is therefore "state property." This is not a result, however, as many legal scholars will argue, of a legal process, for within each of a series of bounded territories, there is an organized society that has the effective right and ability to use and to manage fish and wildlife while those resources are available. Fish and wildlife are, in effect, communal property. They became state property through various forms of expropriation in the transfer of title that took place across North America, with or without the compliance or agreement of native peoples, and often against their will. Our prevailing conception of common property as state property was imposed not on a lawless, free-for-all situation in which no one owned or had responsibility for anything, but rather on a functions system or communal property that is, in fact managed by the occupying group.[43]

---

42. *See* Usher, *supra* note 9.
43. *Id.*

It is the legacy of colonialism that native peoples' access to resources is seen by many as a social policy issue rather than a fundamental property right issue; this situation continues to be replicated by the North American environmental movement. The environmental movement, therefore, exceeds the charge of contributing to environmental racism and is charged more appropriately with environmental colonialism.

The work underway in communities like Zuni, White Earth, and Menominee is clear evidence of our continuing ability to apply our intellectual and scientific traditions to our ecosystems and harvesting areas. The broader proposals, such as the Indigenous Buffalo Commons and comanagement discussed here and elsewhere, are a challenge to the North American environmental movement.

It is now time for North Americans to work on decolonization. This process must be undertaken with tangible support for indigenous struggles to protect land, territories, and ecosystems. Organizations such as Greenpeace have adopted a policy to recognize indigenous peoples' rights to self-determination and sovereignty and to include that policy in the campaigning framework, whether by supporting native campaigns, by hiring native people, or simply by working cooperatively with native communities on common ground issues. Other alliances, like Sierra Club's and National Resources Defense Council's opposition of James Bay hydroelectric, also show evidence of past cooperation and the promise of more. Proposals like the Northern Rockies Ecosystem Protection Act, which have included native people in their formulation, are of extreme political significance, particularly because those are native lands, sacred areas, and *awessiag* (animals) that environmentalists are discussing. We need to encourage the practice of cooperation, and never relinquish the goal of changing the paradigm.

Decolonization also means support for turning back military, political, economic, cultural, and religious imperialism in North America as a way of securing traditional ways of living on the land and the cultural framework on which they lie. Whether decolonization efforts take place through support of native free exercise of religion legislation or native language restoration, the broader context has imminent value in the specifics of living within the ecosystems.

Finally, we need to focus on enhancing, recovering, and strengthening our traditional ecological knowledge. This needs to occur at the local level of communities, bands, and families as well at the larger level of indigenous nations. In addition, native organizations—such as the Council of Energy Resource Tribes, American Indian Science and Engineering Society, Native American Rights Fund, Indian Law Resource Center,

National Congress of American Indians, Native American Fish and Wildlife Association, and others—should look toward support and training within our own paradigm as opposed to the European industrial worldview. We have much to offer.

Throughout the world, examples abound of traditional knowledge and indigenous law as the foundation for sound policy—in the rain forest, in the South Pacific, and in the Arctic. A new model—an autocthonous one, *springing from this land*—needs to emerge, and I, for one, hope that this movement embraces the challenge with principles and courage. We can only do better by combining these traditions in Anishinabeg Akiing, the peoples' land.

Indigenous Peoples And The Environment: The Case Of The Pastoral Maasai Of Kenya

Joy K. Asiema[†]
Francis D. P. Situma[††]

I. INTRODUCTION

A definition of "indigenous peoples" is notoriously elusive, despite the fact indigenous peoples consider themselves to be distinct peoples. A great variety and number of communities in the world are referred to or refer to themselves as indigenous peoples.[1] National minorities, nomadic peoples, and displaced peoples have been referred to as indigenous, particularly where they have been subjected to discrimination, exploitation, dispossession of their lands, and relocation. Isolated or marginalized groups that have not been subjected to, or subjugated by, colonialism have also been referred to as indigenous because of their historic presence on a particular territory, their preservation of ancestral customs, or their incorporation into a state with different national, social, and cultural characteristics from their own.[2]

Despite these varied definitions, indigenous peoples can be collectively described as people descending from the original inhabitants of an area that has been taken over by more powerful outsiders, with a distinct language, culture, or religion. Most think of themselves as custodians—not owners—of their land and other resources and partly define themselves by reference to the habitat from which they derive their livelihood. They commonly live in, or maintain strong ties to, a subsistence economy; many either are, or are descendants of, hunter-gatherers, fishers, nomadic or

---

† Lecturer at the Kenya School of Law in Nairobi, Kenya, and attorney for the firm of Hamilton Harrison & Mathews, Advocates.

†† Candidate for a Ph.D. at the Fletcher School of Law & Diplomacy at Tufts University in Medford, Mass.

1. Russell L. Barsh, *"Indigenous Peoples, an Emerging Object of International Law,"* 80 AM. J. INT'L L. 369, 373–375 (1986).

2. *Id.*

seasonal herders, shifting forest farmers, or peasant cultivators. Their social relations are often tribal, involving collective or communal management of natural resources, thick networks of bonds among individuals, and group decision making, often by consensus among elders.[3]

More than 300 million indigenous peoples live in more than seventy countries. They inhabit almost every climate zone from the remote arctic regions and the deserts of northern and southern Africa to the Pacific Islands and the rain forests of Asia and South America. Great diversity in language, culture, dress, religion and habit exists among indigenous peoples. At least 5,000 indigenous groups can be distinguished by linguistic and cultural differences or by geographic separation.[4] Although some are pastoralists or hunter-gatherers, others live in cities and participate fully in the culture of their national society.

Of the common traits that indigenous peoples share, probably the most notable are the retention of a strong sense of their distinct culture and a strong identity with their ancestral homelands. They conceive of their land as a substance endowed with sacred meanings, which defines their existence and identity and to which they are inextricably attached. Similarly, the trees, plants, animals, and fish that inhabit the land are not just natural resources in the popular sense but are highly personal beings, which form part of indigenous peoples' social and spiritual universe.

Despite their diversity, indigenous peoples face common problems and concerns. These range from the confiscation of their traditional lands and natural resources which they have depended upon for countless generations, to the adulteration of their indigenous knowledge and practices and erosion of their culture. They seek intellectual property rights to their knowledge about natural resources on their lands, which they have sustainably managed and view themselves as the world's most experienced environmentalists with a role to play in environmental protection and conservation, especially of the ecosystems they have traditionally inhabited.[5]

---

3. *See* INDIGENOUS PEOPLES, A GLOBAL QUEST FOR JUSTICE, A REPORT FOR THE INDEPENDENT COMMISSION ON INTERNATIONAL HUMANITARIAN ISSUES (Julian Burger, ed., 1987).

4. The International Year for the World's Indigenous People, U.N. Doc. DPI/1296–92358 (Nov. 1992).

5. ALAN T. DURNING, GUARDIANS OF THE LAND: INDIGENOUS PEOPLES AND THE HEALTH OF THE EARTH, WORLD WATCH PAPER 112 (1992). *See also* Richard E. Schultes, *Ethnobotanical Conservation and Plant Diversity in the Northwest Amazon*, 7 DIVERSITY (1991).

Although indigenous peoples have existed for a long time, it was not until 1953 that the United Nations (UN) became interested in their welfare. In that year, the International Labour Organization (ILO) launched a study of the persistent violations of their human rights. As a result, in 1957 the ILO General Conference adopted the Convention Concerning the Protection and Integration of Indigenous and Other Tribal and Semi-Tribal Populations in Independent Countries (hereinafter Convention 107).[6] Convention 107, whose main objective was protection and integration of indigenous peoples into the dominant culture of the state, applied to:

> members of tribal or semi-tribal populations in independent countries which are regarded as indigenous on account of their descent from the populations which inhabited the country, or a geographical region of which the country belongs, at the time of conquest or colonisation and which, irrespective of their legal status, live more in conformity with the social, economic and cultural institutions of that time than with the institutions of the nation to which they belong.[7]

Specific provisions were made for land ownership and control,[8] recruitment for and conditions of employment,[9] vocational training,[10] social security and health,[11] education, and the means of communication.[12] Convention 107 entered into force on June 2, 1959, and was ratified by twenty–seven states.

Convention 107 was revised and replaced in 1989 by the Convention Concerning Indigenous and Tribal Peoples in Independent Countries (hereinafter Convention 169).[13] Convention 169 entered into force on September 5, 1991, after ratifications by Bolivia, Colombia, Mexico, and Norway.[14] Convention 107 still remains in force for those States that ratified it but which have not yet ratified Convention 169.[15] The Preamble to Convention 169 recognizes the legitimacy of indigenous peoples' aspirations to exercise control over their own institutions and to maintain and develop their identities, languages, and religions. The Convention defines "indigenous" peoples as:

---

6. Convention Concerning the Protection and Integration of Indigenous and Other Tribal and Semi-Tribal Populations in Independent Countries, June 26, 1957, 328 U.N.T.S. 247 [hereinafter Convention 107].

7. *Id.* at 250, art. 1(1)(b).

8. *Id.* at 256–258, arts. 11–14.

9. *Id.* at 258–260, art. 15.

10. *Id.* at 260, arts. 16–18.

11. *Id.* at 262, arts. 19–20.

12. *Id.* at 262–264, arts. 21–26.

13. Convention Concerning Indigenous and Tribal Peoples in Independent Countries, *adopted* June 27, 1989, reprinted in 28 I.L.M. 1382 [hereinafter Convention 169].

14. *Id.*

15. Convention 107, *supra* note 6, at art. 36(2).

peoples in independent countries who are regarded as indigenous on account of their descent from the populations which inhabited the country, or a geographical region to which the country belongs, at the time of conquest or colonization or the establishment of present State boundaries and who, irrespective of their legal status, retain some or all of their own social, economic, cultural and political institutions.[16]

The Convention qualifies its application by stating that "[s]elf–identification as indigenous or tribal shall be regarded as a fundamental criterion for determining the groups to which this Convention shall apply."[17] This qualification adds a subjective and limiting element to the enumerated criteria and renders the definition awkward. If "indigenous" people do not identify themselves as such, conferring upon them the rights reserved under the Convention is paternalistic and patronizing.

The Convention then sets goals toward which governments should work,[18] lays down guidelines for a participatory approach to decision making,[19] and provides specific provisions for the protection of these peoples' rights.[20] Like Convention 107, Convention 169 expressly recognizes the importance of the territorial basis for indigenous peoples, including their relationship "with the lands or territories, or both as applicable, which they occupy or otherwise use . . . ."[21] Governments are asked to take steps to identify lands that are traditionally occupied by indigenous peoples, to guarantee effective protection of indigenous peoples' rights of ownership and possession,[22] and to safeguard their rights to natural resources in the lands occupied by them, including the use, management, and conservation of these lands.[23] Indigenous peoples shall not be removed from the lands that they occupy except where such removal is "considered necessary as an exceptional measure" and with full compensation for loss or injury suffered by relocation.[24] Whenever possible, they shall have the right to return to their traditional lands as soon as the grounds for relocation cease to exist.[25] If return is not possible, they shall be provided with lands of equal quality and status to those previously occupied.[26]

In 1982 the UN Commission on Human Rights initiated, and the UN Economic and Social Council approved, the formation of the Working

---

16. Convention 169, *supra* note 13, at 1385, art. 1(1)(b).
17. *Id.* at art. 1(2).
18. *Id.* at art. 2.
19. *Id.*
20. *Id.* at 1385–1386, arts. 3–8.
21. *Id.* at 1387, art. 13(1).
22. *Id.* at art. 14(2).
23. *Id.* at art. 15(1).
24. *Id.* at 1387–1389, art. 16(1)–(2).
25. *Id.* at 1388, art. 16(3).
26. *Id.* at art. 16(4).

Group on Indigenous Populations.[27] The group meets each summer to take testimony on the status of indigenous peoples around the world. More significantly, the group is charged with the task of drafting a Declaration of the Rights of Indigenous Peoples, to be adopted by the UN General Assembly.

At the end of its eleventh session in the early fall of 1993, the Working Group agreed upon a Draft Declaration of the Rights of Indigenous Peoples.[28] The forty–five article document covers every conceivable problem related to indigenous peoples' rights, ranging from self–determination and land ownership to the maintenance and development of transfrontier contacts and relations and cooperation in socioeconomic and political activities.[29] The reference to the right of self–determination is purposefully cautious; self-determination is to be exercised within the legal framework of each state. It is limited to internal self-determination and does not permit indigenous peoples to secede.[30]

With respect to environmental conservation, the Draft Declaration recognizes that respect for indigenous knowledge, cultures, and traditional practices contributes to sustainable development and proper management of the environment.[31] It also provides that indigenous peoples have the right to their traditional medicines and health practices, including the right to the protection of vital medicinal plants, animals, and minerals;[32] the right to the conservation, restoration, and protection of the total environment and the productive capacity of their lands, territories and resources with national and international assistance for that purpose;[33] and the right of full ownership, control, and protection of their cultural and intellectual property.[34]

It remains to be seen if governments will be persuaded to accept the Draft Declaration and thereafter work toward negotiating and adopting a legally binding international instrument along the lines of the 1948 Universal Declaration of Human Rights[35] and the subsequent 1966 instruments.[36] This will depend, inter alia, on how politically sensitive the Draft Declara-

---

27. *See* Res. 1982/19 U.N. GAOR, Hum. Rts. Comm. (1982); Res. 1982/34, U.N. GAOR, Econ. and Social Counc. (1982).

28. *Report of the Working Group on Indigenous Populations on its eleventh session,* U.N. Comm. on Human Rights, Sub-Comm. on Prevention of Discrimination and Protection of Minorities, 11th Sess., Annex I, Agenda Item 14, UN Doc. E/CN.4/Sub.2/1993/29 (1993) [hereinafter Draft Declaration].

29. *See id.* arts. 3, 10, 35.

30. *See id.* arts. 1, 31, 37.

31. *See id.* preambular para. 9.

32. *See id.* art. 24.

33. *See id.* art. 28.

34. *See id.* art. 29.

tion provisions are viewed by states, particularly those in Africa and Asia which are anxious about fratricidal civil strife that might arise as a result of emphasizing some of the Draft Declaration's rights.

In order to draw attention to the existence and the needs of indigenous peoples, the 45th Session of the UN General Assembly adopted a resolution on December 18, 1990 proclaiming 1993 the International Year of the World's Indigenous People.[37] The purpose of the proclamation was to strengthen international cooperation in solving problems faced by indigenous communities in areas such as human rights, the environment, development, education, and health.[38] The theme chosen for the year was: "Indigenous People—A New Partnership."[39] This implies that indigenous peoples are equals with all other communities and that the partnership will provide them justice. The climax of the year was the World Conference on Human Rights held in Vienna in June 1993. Indigenous peoples from several countries participated in this conference which provided an international forum for them to discuss their views and concerns.

Kenya sent a delegation of the Maasai to the Vienna Conference. In addition to being the most widely known of the indigenous communities in Kenya, the Maasai are the most suitable Kenyans to attend a conference at which the problems of indigenous peoples are discussed because they have faced the most complex issues as a consequence of Kenyan national development, environmental protection, and wildlife conservation policies. Their traditional lands are home to more varieties of Kenya's flora and fauna than any other single commmunity's lands. They have been custodians of Kenya's wildlife, and their contribution toward environmental and wildlife conservation is invaluable. Although they have had a long–standing proprietary interest in these rich lands, they have suffered great injustices over time.

The remainder of this article discusses the Maasai and their history and explains the environmental and socioeconomic changes to which they have been subjected. It then suggests ways of addressing their struggle with the Kenyan government over environmental conservation in light of the international developments previously discussed.

---

35. Universal Declaration of Human Rights, G.A. Res. 217A (III); U.N. Doc. A/810, at 71 (1948).

36. International Covenant on Economic, Social and Cultural Rights, G.A. Res. 2200 (XXI), 21 U.N. GAOR, Supp. 49, U.N. Doc. A/6316 (1966); International Covenant on Civil and Political Rights, G.A. Res. 2200 (XXI), 21 U.N. GAOR, Supp. 52, U.N. Doc. A/6316 (1966).

37. UN Doc. A/OR/45/Res/164 (1990).

38. *See id.* art 1.

39. UN Doc. A/Res/46/128 (1992) at 2.

II. THE MAASAI AND THEIR HISTORY

Many Western anthropologists and historians who have had contact with the Maasai have come away from the experience with a deep feeling of admiration and affection for them. The Maasai have a unique glory and an unmistakable air of invincibility or superiority. Vincent J. Donovan, a Holy Ghost Father of the Maryknoll Society, who worked as a missionary among the Tanzania Maasai, said:

> One has to see them suddenly silhouetted against the horizon, tall, spare, proud, leaning on their shields and spears and staring silently across the plains, to catch a glimpse of that wisp of history still being lived . . .. There is a trace of ancient Egypt in their finely chiseled features, in their slightly slanted eyes, in their reckoning the beginning of any month by the dying of the moon, in their half forgotten customs and perhaps in their blood.

> Dressed for all the world like Roman soldiers, red from head to feet, red tunics, red helmets made of mud, with spear, shortsword and shield, they stride across the plains and consciousness of Africa, the finest example of what Africa once was.[40]

The Maasai inhabit the Rift Valley area of Kenya which stretches along western Kenya and into northern Tanzania. Those in northwestern Kenya, the Purko Maasai, are sedentary agriculturalists, while those in the southwestern part of the country, the Kwavi Maasai, are nomadic pastoralists.

The settlement of the Maasai in Kenya can be traced to the first millenium A.D., although historians have not been able to ascertain the exact date of their migration and settlement there. Their ancestors have been traced partly to the Hamites, who intermarried with the Nilotes of the Nile River basin north of East Africa. These Nilo–Hamites migrated to the south, down the Nile basin into northern Kenya's Lake Turkana region and into southern Ethiopia. They moved further south, below the equator, to the region of the great lakes Victoria, Tanganyika, and Nyasa, pushing the Bantu from the rich savannah pasture and grazing highlands and confining them to the less–favorable pastoral areas. As they trekked southeast, pushing out the indigenous hunters, they claimed additional savannah country for the increasing number of cattle they had acquired.[41] By the seventeenth century, the Maasai had reached the Kenya Highlands and had spread out to Kinangop, Laikipiak, Nakuru, Naivasha, and other surrounding areas of the Rift Valley.[42] Some groups had spread southward across Loita, Mara,

---

40. VINCENT J. DONOVAN, CHRISTIANITY REDISCOVERED 17, 21 (1978).
41. SOLOMON OLE SAIBULL & RACHEL CARR, HERD AND SPEAR: THE MAASAI OF EAST AFRICA 19 (1981).

and Serengeti into Tanganyika and southeastward to Ngong, across the Athi and Kaputiei plains to the foothills of Mount Kilimanjaro. It is believed that as the Maasai migrated, they either displaced other populations to marginal areas, where they had to abandon their pastoral economy, or they simply assimilated them.[43] A powerful fighting people, the Maasai encountered no resistance because their neighbors lived in endless fear of the Maasai's determination to secure their cattle and capture their women.[44]

The carving up of East Africa in the early 1880s between the British and German colonialists split Maasailand into two different political entities. Those in Kenya came under British control in what was to become the East Africa Protectorate, whereas those in Tanganyika came under German control in what was then German East Africa. In 1904 the *Laibon* (ritual leader) of the Maasai was induced to have the Maasai vacate some of the rich agricultural land traditionally used as their grazing grounds. Instead, they were to be regrouped in two areas on the condition, inter alia, that the agreement "shall be enduring so long as the Maasai as a race shall exist, and that Europeans or other settlers shall not be allowed to take up land in the [Maasai] settlements."[45]

Two Maasai reserves were created by the British: one was in Laikipiak north of the Uganda Railway, which was extended to the south of Rumuruti in 1906; the other was south of the railway between Mount Suswa in the north and the Anglo-German frontier in the south.[46] In 1911, under settler pressure, another agreement was made between the British and the Maasai to move the inhabitants of the Northern Reserve into the Southern Reserve in order to free up more land for the settlers. In order to accomodate all the Maasai, the Southern Reserve was extended on the east as far as the River Kikalewa, a tributary of the Tsavo, and on the west to the River Mara. The move began in June 1911 and was completed by March 1913. The extensions added only a few square miles of less–productive land to the southern reserve—a paltry compensation for what they had given up in the north. The Southern Reserve later became the present–day Kajiado and Narok districts.[47]

---

42. *Id.*

43. *See* J.E.G. Sutton, *Becoming Maasai*, in BEING MAASAI: ETHNICITY AND IDENTITY IN EAST AFRICA 38, (Thomas Spear & Richard Waller eds. 1993); John G. Galaty, *Masaai Expansion and the New East African Pastoralism* in Spear & Waller, *supra* at 61.

44. *See id. generally.*

45. *See* Ol le Njogo & Others v. A.G. of the East Africa Protectorate, 5 E. Africa L. R. 70 at 72 (1914).

46. *See* OLE SAIBULL & CARR, *supra* note 41 at 21–32; GEORGE W.B. HUNTINGFORD, THE SOUTHERN NILO-HAMITES, 103–104 (1969).

When the Maasai brought action in court for the breach of the 1904 agreement, arguing that it still survived as a civil contract after the 1911 agreement was made, the Protectorate government argued that the agreements were not contracts but treaties. Thus, the alleged confiscation of Maasailand was an Act of State and, as an action under the "treaties," was not cognizable in a municipal court. The Court of Appeal for Eastern Africa upheld the government's contentions on the basis that the Maasai were a sovereign entity with whom a treaty could be made by the Protectorate government, although they would not be governed by international law. Instead, they would be governed by "some rules analogous to international law, and [would] have similar force and effect to that held by a treaty, and must be regarded by Municipal Courts in a similar manner."[48] The ruling of the court, reminiscent of how the colonial government manipulated the law to its advantage, marked the end of any hopes that the Maasai might have had of ever getting their lands returned to them, either by the colonial government when Kenya became a colony in 1920 or by the independent Kenya government after 1963.[49]

Although every ethnic community in Kenya qualifies as an indigenous community, the Maasai are regarded as uniquely "indigenous" because of their steadfast adherence to their traditional culture, practices, and way of life in its totality. They are deeply conservative and afraid of change. To date, the Maasai are possibly the only ethnic people in East Africa who have determinedly maintained their traditional way of life and resisted every kind of change to which they have been exposed. While most other ethnic groups such as the Kikuyus, Luhyas, and Luos have adapted to modern ways, including clothing, shelter, education, commerce, and industry, the Maasai have retained their age–old habits, because change is of little value in their eyes. Their antipathy to education, for instance, was well known by the colonial administrators who exerted significant pressure to fill the only two early elementary schools that opened in Narok and Kajiado reserves in 1919 and 1926. The Maasai resisted the schools even though the curriculum emphasized practical and pastoral learning more than book learning.[50] Their strong loyalties and steadfast adherence to tradition and community identity in the face of modern changes make the Maasai a special category of indigenous peoples.[51]

---

47. *Id.*
48. Ol le Njogo & Others v. A.G. of the East Africa Protectorate, *supra* note 45 at 91–92.
49. *See* Y.P. Ghai & J.P.W.B. McAuslan, Public Law And Political Change In Kenya, 23–25 (1970).
50. Robert L. Tignor, The Colonial Transformation Of Kenya: The Kamba, Kikuyu, And Maasai from 1900 to 1939, 279–287 (1976).

The pastoral Maasai are known to be a fearless, warlike, elegant, and proud people. Their way of life is suited to the conditions in which they live: their concept of development is limited to livestock production, from which they earn a living. Their pattern of settlement is dictated both by their view of the land and the environmental conditions. Land was given by God to the entire community, and everyone has equal rights to use it freely for grazing throughout the year in accordance with grazing arrangements mutually agreed upon by the community.[52]

The Maasai attach great importance to livestock, the center of their lives. The cow is sacred in the daily life of the Maasai because it determines one's livelihood. Any danger to Maasai cattle is a danger to the Maasai themselves, and the attraction of neighboring communities' herds is irresistible. The Maasai believe that God gave them all the livestock upon the earth. Hence, the raiding of neighboring communities' cattle simply returns the cattle to their rightful owners.

The pastoral Maasai feel that it is unworthy of their dignity to dig the ground to grow crops. For this reason, they regard their northwestern counterparts as socially inferior, or *olmeg*, a term of opprobrium used for everything that is non–Maasai. Indeed, the purely pastoral Maasai not only despise the agricultural life but also have prohibitions against eating agricultural produce, especially among the young men or warrior age-sets, the *Il Murrani*.[53]

The Maasai perception of the environment, therefore, derives from the importance of land and livestock. The Maasai believe that if pasture and water in one area are exhausted, they can move on to other areas where resources are plentiful. Concepts of individual property boundaries are alien and, therefore, a hindrance to the enjoyment of their God-given right. Degradation of the environment means deterioration of pasture, not soil; soil is important only as long as vegetation for their livestock is present.[54]

---

51. Arvi Hurskainen, *Levels of Identity and National Integrity: The Viewpoint of the Pastoral Maasai and Parakuyo*, 24 NOMADIC PEOPLES 79, 88 (1990).

52. Kenny Matampash, *The Maasai of Kenya*, *in* INDIGENOUS VIEWS OF LAND AND THE ENVIRONMENT 31 (Shelton H. Davis ed.) (1993).

53. OLE SAIBULL & RACHEL CARR, *supra* note 41, at 65–82.

54. Gufu Oba, *Perception of Environment Among Kenyan Pastoralists: Implications for Development*, 19 NOMADIC PEOPLES 33 (1985).

III. ENVIRONMENTAL CHANGES WITHIN THE MAASAI COMMUNITY

Given the attachment to land, environmental changes within the Maasai community can best be understood in terms of changes to and in the community's rights to land. Land is and has always been a very sensitive subject in Kenya's political history. It was the issue that occupied the center stage in the early 1950s and land ownership was the goal of the independence movements of that era. For most Kenyans, ownership of land, whether as outright title holders or as leaseholders, is their dream. This directly conflicts with the beliefs of the Maasai and other pastoralists who, because they do not make their living from cultivating the soil, believe land can only be used; it cannot be owned by an individual.

Since the early colonial period, the Maasai have had their rights to use the land taken away without compensation. As pointed out previously, in 1911 the British colonialists signed a "treaty" with the Maasai *Laibon* Lenana, under which the Maasai ceded to the settlers all lands in the rich areas of Laikipiak and Nairobi and were forced to live in the demarcated reserves of the Narok and Kajiado districts. The reserves were marginal arid and semi-arid areas considered unsuitable for the British settlers' commercial exploitation. The loss of the high–potential areas meant that the Maasai's traditional freedom of movement with their livestock was restricted to the reserves. These reserves remained closed districts until 1967, when the independent Kenyan government declared them open.

The Maasai experienced further restrictions to their own and their livestock's movements in the 1940s, when the colonial government, under the provisions of the 1945 National Parks Ordinance, declared some of their reserves to be national parks and game reserves from which they and their livestock were excluded.[55] These are the present Nairobi, Tsavo West, Amboseli, and the Maasai Mara National parks. The Maasai's sacred cultural ties to the land and the environment have long predisposed them to guard and conserve the flora and fauna of the territories within which they move. They have treated wildlife as creatures that have equal rights and obligations to use the earth, and have learned how to give way to that wildlife in a unique form of coexistence. To them, the relationship between humans, land, and wildlife was very intimate. The wild grazers consumed different food plants from those eaten by cattle and thus do not compete directly with Maasai livestock in areas such as parks and game reserves that, hitherto, were territories available to the Maasai for grazing. Indeed,

---

55. 1945 National Parks Ordinance, *superceded by* Wildlife (Conservation and Management) Act, Laws of Kenya, Revised ed. 1989, ch. 376.

before 1945, when competition for land between the Maasai and wildlife exceeded the community's ability to adapt, the community simply migrated to new territory without any ensuing social instability. Cultural adaptability and resilience to environmental changes were maintained.

Further, the Maasai do not eat wild meat, therefore they do not hunt wildlife and have not been a threat to its survival. They view hunters who destroy animals and farmers who monopolize potential grazing lands as profligate consumers of valuable resources. Hunters who consumed wild animals and lived in the untamed wilderness were viewed as greedy, unrestrained, and uncultured, suitable only for slaughtering cattle, circumcising youth, gathering honey, and performing other tasks pastoralists avoided.[56] Farmers, on the other hand, destroyed grazing lands by planting crops for demeaning agricultural labor, and were seen as fit only for providing food and beer for the pastoralists.[57]

But the lion remains a constant danger and challenge to the Maasai, as it poses a threat to their herds. The Maasai are willing to take on a lion, in groups or singlehandedly, with the aid of their razor–sharp knives or six–foot spears. This is the only wild animal that the Maasai have been known to kill, but only when it attacks their livestock; they do not hunt lions for sport.

Problems of unreliable rainfall and low–fertility soils within their arid and semi–arid lands were solved by adjusting grazing patterns and by various traditional strategies which had to be integrated within the community's socioeconomic framework to suit their modified access to pasture and water. This intuitive response to environmental and ecological variabilities ensured the absence of conflict over land use.[58]

Furthermore, wildlife served to sustain the overall ecosystem. When the national parks and game reserves were created, the state began drawing boundaries to separate the Maasai from the wildlife, an alien concept to them; the conflict between the Maasai and wildlife was imagined on the part of the state.[59] The state paid greater attention to the wildlife industry than to the Maasai's livestock and land. It reserved the best of the Maasai rangelands—with permanent flowing streams and rivers together with dry

---

56. *See* Spear & Waller (eds.), *supra* note 43, at 12.

57. *Id.*

58. David J. Campbell, *Response to Drought Among Farmers and Herders in Southern Kajiado District, Kenya,* 12 HUMAN ECOLOGY 35–64 (1984).

59. S. E. Migot-Adholla and Peter D. Little, *Evolution of Policy Toward the Development of Pastoral Areas in Kenya, in* THE FUTURE OF PASTORAL PEOPLES 144–157 (John G. Galaty, et al. eds. 1984).

season grazing areas, salt licks, and swampy and marshy areas—for the national parks, thereby excluding the Maasai. As a result the Maasai started to experience significant competition and shortages of rangeland for their livestock. This situation has continued even in the independence period, so the ravages of overgrazing and soil deterioration are strikingly evident at the parks' outskirts. Areas within the parks have also been subject to environmental degradation; the growing populations of wild animals deprived of their expansion areas due to confinement within prescribed park boundaries have wreaked havoc on the protected ecosystem. Confined and cut off, elephants, for example, have literally eaten everything, turning verdant countryside into desert as they consume and bulldoze vegetation.[60]

After Kenya achieved political independence in 1963, major financial donors, including the World Bank, offered the government massive funding to develop the country's pastoral areas under the Kenya Livestock Development Project, administered by the Ministry of Agriculture and Animal Husbandry. The aim of the project was to create conditions under which the rangelands, mostly under Maasai occupation, could make a far larger contribution to the national economy through commercial beef farming. As a prerequisite for the loan, the World Bank demanded that legislation be enacted to replace the communal land tenure system with a system that was more responsive to market forces.

At the same time, the Mission on Land Consolidation and Registration in Kenya proposed that it was out of the question, based on social, economic, and practical grounds, to give individual deeds to the Maasai who moved seasonally with their herds across the plains in search of pasture. Instead, it proposed the establishment of group ranches,[61] and the government accepted the proposal. The result was the enactment of the Land (Group Representatives) Act in 1968.[62] This legislation allowed groups of pastoralists to register for large blocks of land with fixed boundaries. Then the groups selected representatives who would be responsible for the day–to–day management of the group ranches. The effect of this was that the traditional communal land tenure system of the Maasai was terminated and replaced by a private land tenure regime regarded as creating more incentives for better utilization of land.[63] Land title holders were

---

60. *See* Edward R. Ricciuti, *The Elephant Wars*, WILDLIFE CONSERVATION, Mar./Apr. 1993, at 14.
    61. *See* Republic of Kenya, *Report of the Mission on Land Consolidation and Registration in Kenya, 1965–66*, para. 106 (1966).
    62. Laws of Kenya, Revised ed. 1978, ch. 287.
    63. *See* David J. Campbell, *Land as Ours, Land as Mine: Economic, Political and Ecological Marginalization in Kajiado District, in* Spear & Waller eds., *supra* note 43, at 258–272.

expected to get loans for agricultural development from the government's Agricultural Finance Corporation, using the titles as collateral security. Apparently no consideration was given to the impact that this would have on the traditional lifestyles of the pastoral communities.

The group ranches turned out to be a fiasco for various reasons.[64] First, the adjudication officials made little effort to ensure the boundaries of group ranches coincided with those of the main traditional unit of cattle management among the pastoral Maasai, namely the *manyatta* (kraal) camp. These traditional camps consisted of several independent polygynous families joined together by a common interest in the economic exploitation of their immediate vicinity.[65] Several *manyatta* camps formed the settlement associations known as *inkutot*, the formal traditional social and political units among the Maasai. These associations tended to shift seasonally, gathering around dry season water supplies. Instead of working with and basing the group ranches on these units, the adjudication officials relied on natural boundaries that had no practical impacts on traditional grazing patterns, particularly in cases where ranches crossed the customary migration routes.[66]

Second, the bodies responsible for managing of the ranches lacked any traditional legitimacy. A board of elected representatives was utterly alien to the Maasai way of life, and even the board members themselves had little sense of collective responsibility.

Third, the concept of the group ranch failed to deal with the problem of outsiders living on the ranches at the invitation of some members. The Maasai custom of inviting relatives, even from across the border in Tanzania, to stay for long periods, was inconsistent with the policy behind the legislation. Such outsiders could not be evicted from the ranches as trespassers.

In short, group ranches were an artificial creation born of an ideology that stressed the importance of what was incorrectly perceived by the government as "development," rather than emerging as a response to the Maasai's self-perceived needs. If the group ranch concept and the resultant policy had been formulated and implemented with the participation of the Maasai, there is no doubt that its effectiveness would have been more laudable.[67]

---

64. *See, e.g.,* Olivia Graham, *A Land Divided: The Impact of Ranching on a Pastoral Society,* 19 THE ECOLOGIST 184 (1989); Matampash, *supra* note 52.

65. Simon F.R. Coldham, *Land-Tenure Reform in Kenya: the Limits of Law,* 17 J. OF MODERN AFRICAN STUDIES, 615–627 (1979).

66. *Id.*

67. *Id.*

Early in 1989, recognizing the inadequacies of group ranches, President Moi directed that group ranches should be subdivided and each member given an individual title deed because "the issue of having group ranches will create problems in the future."[68] However, there was no evidence to back the president's assertion that there would be future problems and no analysis to suggest that subdivision was the proper remedy. The main reason for the directive was probably that the president did not want to openly admit the government's failure in implementing a program based on the assumption that the Maasai had to be directed by governmental authorities in the management of their life.

The old orthodoxy that pastoral communities have too many cattle and that, because of apparently uncontrolled use of the commons, they destroy land, may have reinforced this assumption. However, land degradation comes more from land alienation than from the alleged excessive number of stock and pastoralists' nomadic way of life. It is also probable that the president's directive was due to political pressure from rich politicians and so–called progressive elements among the Maasai who saw subdivision of the ranches as opening up a market in land on the Maasai's land.[69]

Conversion of historically communal property to exclusive private property has had several effects on the Maasai and their environment. First, traditional leaders and elders of the community have been stripped of their customary authority and role in ensuring social cohesion; they have no right of access to, or say in, the exploitation of what is now private property and the resources thereon. This is likely to lead to the disintegration of the Maasai as a sociopolitical unit. Indeed, the formal bureaucratic and judicial processes of policy implementation and adjudication—which do not involve the deliberations of elders, age-grade councils, traditional chiefs, and other specially designated cultural organizations—have wrought a major challenge to the Maasai way of life and have adversely affected the harmony that the Maasai enjoyed with their natural environment. Social values, the common acceptance of which limited conflicts of interests, have been replaced by legal and administrative sanctions in which the elders play no role.

Second, subdivision has led to the total loss of forage regimes critical to the Maasai's own and their livestock's survival. The once sparsely populated areas have been converted to high–density human and animal regimes which are now more intensely used than before. These high intensity regimes do not provide enough rest to enable recovery, resulting

68. See KENYA TIMES, (Nairobi) April 15, 1989; THE NATION, (Nairobi) April 15, 1989.

69. See infra notes 72–74 and accompanying text.

in the destruction of land that is already environmentally fragile. Massive starvation of livestock results, particularly during the dry seasons, due not to overstocking, the popular view, but rather to restricted grazing opportunities. The resulting small parcels in marginal areas cannot support the Maasai's livestock population. The concentration of livestock in the semi-arid zones has created an environment that is highly vulnerable to drought, overgrazing, soil degradation, and loss of biodiversity. The small parcels of land that result from the subdivision are no longer viable for Maasai pastoral use. From an ecological point of view, land holdings in such fragile areas should be kept as large as possible to allow room for environmental adaptation and adjustment. In this respect, the retention of group ranches is not only desirable but also provides much needed room for the Maasai to maneuver as and when environmental changes demand.

According to the government, overgrazing due to improper livestock and range management is one of the principal causes of desertification in Kenya. To combat overstocking and overgrazing, the government proposed that the entire range should be developed, conserved, and managed in accordance with ecological principles of proper land use.[70] Although the proposal may be laudable, the government actually just blames the victim. History shows that the pastoralist Maasai, left to themselves, pursue ecological principles of proper land use. However, the tribe's ability to pursue these principles is increasingly being restricted by outside intervention. This intervention takes the form, for example, of ill–conceived government development policies which encourage population and livestock concentrations in marginal areas. Government development plans have been based on a policy that has consistently emphasized settlement and agriculture (to increase food production and combat desertification) rather than pastoral nomadism.[71] These new government policies have been established and implemented without serious consideration given to the appropriateness of farming or settlement in these marginal areas, nor to the consequences of intervention on the local environment on settlement patterns and on other sectors of the Maasai's pastoral economy.

Furthermore, subdivision of the ranches and issuance of individual title deeds has not only introduced a new and alien concept of land tenure to the Maasai but has also led to the perception of land as a commercial commodity to be bought and sold. Coupled with the fact that parcels

---

70. Republic of Kenya, *Kenya's Experience in Combating Desertification* (a Country Position Paper presented to the UN Conference on Desertification) 5 (1977).

71. *Cf.* Richard Hogg, *Development in Kenya: Drought, Desertification and Food Scarcity*, 82 AFRICAN AFFAIRS 47–58 (1987) (discussion of the impact of this policy in the pastoral areas of Turkana and Isiolo Districts of northern Kenya).

resulting from subdivision of the group ranches are not viable units for Maasai use, this perception has resulted in widespread selling of land to non–Maasai outsiders, for whom land is golden. Currently, there are more Kikuyu, Luo, and Luhya than Maasai land owners in Ngong, Ongata Rongai, Kitengela, and the adjacent areas in the Kajiado District. The Maasai have been forced to move to more arid areas down south. Overcrowding and exacerbated environmental degradation have occurred because the Maasai cannot practice their traditional and cultural conservation methods under such conditions. The majority of the Maasai have experienced a steady decline in their resource base and increased economic and social insecurity. Those who have lost out in the process have either been forced into Nairobi for unskilled employment, contributing to the already serious problems of urban unemployment and squalor, or have been caught in the poverty trap on lands too arid to support them. Some of the non-Maasai landowners have introduced mechanized agriculture to a fragile environment, thereby exacerbating land degradation.

One of the major advantages of the group ranches, assuming that the concept could have been properly designed and implemented, was that Maasai rangeland remained in the hands of the Maasai. Outsiders interested in aquiring land for agricultural and speculative purposes would have been kept out. This is not possible since the subdivision of the ranches. With the influx of outsiders who have acquired most of the Maasai land, there is fear that the traditional Maasai lifestyle and ethnic identity will disappear and with them the Maasai as a people. There are already many cases of intermarriage between the few elite Maasai and the incoming non–Maasai. It remains to be seen whether subdivision and individual title deeds will lead to the cessation of the Maasai living as a pastoral people. To date, it is apparent that subdivision is creating rather than solving problems. The question remains whether the Maasai's rights as an indigenous people—including their rights to control their land, retain their own social, economic, cultural, and political institutions, and develop within Kenya's national goals—can be ensured and protected by the state.

The Maasai community has been forced into relentless social, economic, political, and environmental changes. Subjected to various pressures from wildlife conservation advocates, the Kenyan government has neglected the basic needs of the Maasai and other pastoral farmers and herders who live on the peripheries of the national parks and game reserves.[72] The Maasai lack what the wild animals possess: an active lobby in

---

72. RODGER YEAGER & NORMAN N. MILLER WILDLIFE, WILD DEATH: LAND USE AND SURVIVAL IN EASTERN AFRICA (1986).

and outside Nairobi that effectively speaks on behalf of their interests. The intergovernmental organizations, tour operators, wildlife conservationists and preservationists, game lodge and resort owners, and associated groups are heard more loudly and clearly in Nairobi's corridors of power than the Maasai's political representatives, who are themselves culturally, economically, and physically isolated from their constituents. As the elite among the Maasai, the political representatives have used their political clout to manipulate the land tenure reform to their own benefit, becoming the beneficiaries of the group ranch subdivision. While extensive promotional campaigns are conducted abroad by the government–run Kenya Tourist Development Corporation to sell wildlife for the tourist industry, nothing is done to expose the plight of the Maasai.[73] The Maasai and similar pastoral communities are still regarded as economically noncontributive, difficult to assist, environmentally disruptive, and generally impossible to govern. But it is difficult to see how Kenyan wildlife and land-use situations can improve when the basic needs of those who have been the historic stewards of the land are forced to relocate and are not taken seriously by the government.

The tendency of the government and the international wildlife lobby to be oblivious to the needs of the Maasai who live within the wildlife reserves is, at best, a manifestation of apparent indifferent callousness toward the Maasai. At worst, that ignorance demonstrates a lack of understanding of, or a deliberate refusal to see, the importance of local people to the success of wildlife conservation and environmental protection programs. Following the torching of a $3 million elephant tusk haul in Nairobi by President Moi on July 18, 1989, and the massive global publicity galvanized thereby, the purse strings of Western governments and private philanthropic groups were untied. Donations supporting the conservation of elephants started pouring in to Kenya to an unprecedented degree. Saving the elephant became more important than protecting people whose lives are intertwined with those of protected wild species.[74] Yet, the survival of wildlife is dependent on the survival and welfare of the people who live within the environs of the parks and game reserves, not vice versa.

The appropriation of land from the Maasai, first by European colonialists to make room for white settlers and then by the independent Kenyan government for the creation of national parks and game reserves,

---

73. The sending of a Maasai delegation by the Kenya Government to the 1993 Vienna Conference was more of a symbolic gesture than an expression of a state policy for the protection of the Maasai as an indigenous people.

74. *See* JONATHAN S. ADAMS & THOMAS O. MCSHANE, THE MYTH OF WILD AFRICA: CONSERVATION WITHOUT ILLUSION 59–84 (1992).

raises tremendous issues of social injustice. The injustice comes partly from the misuse of laws and administrative directives to dispossess them as well as from the suffering caused by the loss of access to those resources which the tribe relied upon for its livelihood. The Maasai have been denied access to their traditional rights to grazing, water, and salt licks within the enclosed national parks and game reserves. They have, consequently, suffered sharp declines in their livestock numbers from the stress of reduced forage and a deterioration of their quality of life. Their social and cultural units have disintegrated or been extinguished, and their general welfare has been ignored.

IV. A POSSIBLE WAY AHEAD

To halt future physical and cultural dislocations of the Maasai and to advance their cause as an indigenous people, the government must acknowledge and understand the Maasai way of life, the Maasai's perception of the environment and its conservation, and the Maasai land–use patterns as a means of securing pastoral livelihoods. The government must fashion its approach to development and environmental issues affecting the Maasai based on this acknowledgement and appreciation. Consistent with this appreciation, issues of social justice should be addressed, and Maasai cooperation in development programs should be enhanced. The government condemnation of communal land tenure as being a disincentive to good agriculture and animal husbandry should be replaced. Instead, measures that acknowledge the value and importance of the Maasai traditional land tenure systems, as well as their indigenous knowledge and skills in resource use and environmental management, should be implemented. Development projects and programs should not be imposed on the Maasai in the mistaken belief that they lead backward lives and do not know what is good for them. Rather, projects should be designed with the full participation of the Maasai to ensure better use of their indigenous knowledge and skills in resource management.

Government officials and nongovernmental agencies should integrate and work with the Maasai, tapping their indigenous skills. Integration does not mean, and should not be seen to mean, absorption and assimilation of the Maasai into the mainstream of the larger and dominant ethnic groups. Rather, it should be seen as working together with the Maasai as partners, consulting with them and forging social, economic, and political ties. Such cooperation will enable the Maasai to retain their cultural heritage, identity, and integrity in a spirit of coexistence.

Where this strategy has been applied, there are signs of success. In the Amboseli National Park, the Kenya Wildlife Service, with technical and institutional support from the New York Zoological Society (now the Wildlife Conservation Society) and funding from the World Bank, started an integrated approach to wildlife conservation and economic development. This began in 1977 with the realization that the support of the local Maasai was crucial to sustainable development in the context of elephant protection. The Maasai, who had been forced to give up their grazing lands for the national park and the conservation of the Amboseli ecosystem as a whole, were deeply involved in the planning and execution of the project. The leadership initiative came from the Maasai themselves, with little or no government involvement.[75]

In addition to the full participation of the Maasai in the project, the Kenya Wildlife Service introduced a revenue-sharing plan as an incentive for the Maasai. The Service charges a "bed fee" for each bed used by a tourist in the park lodges, which is passed on to the Maasai, who have had to move out of the elephant watering areas to provide for the park's establishment. This money is intended to be used to open schools and health clinics, and to provide water systems and other infrastructure for the local people. On their part, the Maasai have established their own wildlife committees to complement the efforts of the Service. Poaching levels are very low and attitudes of the Maasai toward wildlife preservation are positive. The wildlife income is steadily becoming a more significant component of Maasai revenue; they view wildlife as their "second cattle."[76] Although a continental catastrophe, the elephant population in the Amboseli National Park has grown so fast that now Richard Leakey, Director of the Kenya Wildlife Service, talks of restricting population increases by regulating their reproduction and fertility.[77]

In the Maasai Mara National Park, the local Maasai have now been given concessions to use open park areas for grazing their livestock.[78] At the same time, the Kenya Wildlife Service has embarked on a program of public education aimed at discouraging the Maasai around Nairobi from selling their land to land speculators. Instead, they are encouraged to use it to support the wildlife conservation measures.[79]

---

75. *See* David Western, *Ecosystem Conservation and Rural Development: The Amboseli Case Study*, Presented to the Claireborne Art Ortenberg Foundation Workshop on Community Based Conservation, held at Airlie, Virginia.

76. *Id.* at 28.

77. Richard E. Leakey, *Elephants Today and Tomorrow: A Perspective from Kenya*, *in* WILDLIFE CONSERVATION Mar./Apr. 1993, at 58.

78. *Interview with Dr. Richard Leakey, the Director of Kenya Wildlife Service*, 4 RESOURCES 24–27 (1993).

79. Louis Kang'ethe & Jimmy Njagi, *Local Community Contribution in Kitengela*, 4 RESOURCES 27–28 (1993).

The National Biodiversity Unit of the National Museums of Kenya, with the financial assistance of the US–based Biodiversity Support Program, has successfully established kitchen gardens for indigenous food species on a Maasai group ranch at Elangata in the Kajiado District.[80] The Biodiversity Support Program is a USAID–funded consortium of the World Wildlife Fund, The Nature Conservancy, and the World Resources Institute. The objectives of the kitchen gardens are, inter alia, to establish a central garden of indigenous vegetable species for research, demonstration, and seed production. Additionally, the seed gardens provide information to women and the community on food values, nutrition, gardening, and conservation of wild food species. The local Maasai women are reported to have shown a lot of interest in the program and have greatly enhanced their appreciation of indigenous vegetables and indigenous food plants.[81]

In these instances, government officials and aid agencies work closely with the Maasai to identify their needs and to use their indigenous knowledge and expertise to facilitate solutions to those needs. Applied on a wider scale, there is no doubt that this participatory process can lead to the alleviation of much human suffering and damage to the environment.

To arrest further environmental degradation and poverty among the Maasai, the Kenyan government needs to rethink the presidential directive to subdivide group ranches. The majority of the Maasai, especially those in the drier areas, do not support the ranch subdivision, because they fear being left with no land at all or with small, economically unviable pieces. In fact, the Maasai were not consulted before the directive was given by the president.[82] Not everybody on the group ranches was registered as an owner. Unregistered members are obviously at a disadvantage when subdivision takes place, as they will find themselves dispossessed. The women will be the hardest hit because under Maasai customary laws they are not allowed to be registered as land owners, even though they are the ones who tend the land.[83] The only hope for unregistered sons of a member receiving a share of the land is to wait until their father subdivides his own share. The inevitable result will be that units will become smaller and smaller with every subdivision. Coupled with population growth and the influx of outsiders, there will to be serious landlessness and poverty among the once-proud Maasai, accompanied by the ensuing social conflicts and unprecedented environmental degradation. The landless and poor Maasai

---

80. Information given to the authors by Dr. Kathryn A. Saterson, the Director of the U.S.A. Biodiversaity Support Program and confirmed by Christine Kabuye, the botanist in charge at the National Museums of Kenya in Nairobi.

81. *Id.*

82. Matampash, *supra* note 52, at 39–40.

83. *See* Telelia Chieni & Paul Spencer, *The World of Telelia: Reflections of a Maasai Woman in Matapato, in* Spear & Waller eds., *supra* note 43; Matapash, *supra* note 52, at 40.

may become squatters and laborers on what was once their traditional land.[84]

Individual land ownership in the Maasai rangeland is likely to lead to a substantial loss of wildlife and biological diversity, as there will no longer be the necessary safety valves from the congested game parks to the rangelands. It is estimated that currently over sixty percent of the wildlife in Kenya roam in the rangeland and national parks in Maasailand. With the loss of forage areas outside the parks, animal numbers are likely to shrink drastically due to overgrazing within park confines. Then the tourism industry and its foreign exchange earnings will be destroyed. Because the Maasai cannot return to lands confiscated during the colonial period, their future survival and that of the wildlife they have been custodians of is in danger if their interests in the lands they still have are not scrupulously protected.

V. CONCLUSION

The Maasai's cultural ties to the land and environment, which for centuries predisposed them to guard and conserve the flora and fauna, have been and continue to be severed through the introduction of various alien programs and policies, including the opening up of their land to outsiders and outside uses. These processes pose serious threats to their survival as a distinct ethnic group. Uprooted from their land and denied access to what were once considered God-given rights to resources for the use of all, their future remains in limbo. More concerted efforts and comprehensive government policies are needed to ensure that the Maasai as an indigenous group survive to conserve wildlife and to enjoy their human rights, including the right to own and use their land and its resources in accordance with their customs and the right to retain their own social, economic, cultural, and political institutions. What is needed is more than the symbolic gesture of sending small groups to international conferences.

Kenya is a party to neither Convention 107 nor Convention 169 of the International Labour Organization, although it is a member of the organization itself. It therefore needs to ratify Convention 169 as soon as possible and enact domestic legislation to implement its provisions. Such action will provide the legal basis and framework for the recognition and protection of the rights of the Maasai and other indigenous peoples in the country. In the absence of such a framework, talk of the rights of indigenous peoples in Kenya is meaningless. The plight of the Maasai is not a unique phenomenon; other indigenous communities throughout the world are and may continue to be subjected to the same problems in the future.

---

84. Matampash, *supra* note 52, at 41.

The Draft Declaration of the Rights of Indigenous peoples has yet to be presented to the UN General Assembly by the Economic and Social Council. Given that the Draft Declaration contains some politically sensitive provisions, it is likely that it will undergo further revision before it is presented to the General Assembly for adoption. However, even if it is adopted as a resolution of the General Assembly, it will have no legally binding effects upon states; only treaties, not declarations, are binding on party states. A treaty on the rights of indigenous peoples is not likely to be negotiated and adopted in the near future. Even if it is adopted, it is likely to take a long time before it enters into force.

In the meantime, nongovernmental organizations such as the Kenya Energy and Environment Organizations, the Legal Education and Aid Program, and the Greenbelt Movement need to work systematically to create awareness and sensitivity among people about environmental protection and conservation issues. Additionally, these groups must advise indigenous peoples of their legal rights and duties.

Organization Summaries

The Indigenous Women's Network[*]

The Indigenous Women's Network (IWN) is a coalition that emerged from a gathering of indigenous women in 1985 in Yelm, Washington, and was formally organized four years later. It is now a nonprofit organization with members and projects scattered throughout the Americas and the Pacific Basin.

I. PURPOSE

The IWN focuses on the many common concerns among indigenous people in the Western Hemisphere, including North, Central, and South America; the Pacific Islands; Aotearoa; New Caledonia; and Australia. These common concerns include severe poverty, loss of subsistence life-styles, homelessness, substance abuse, exploitation and depletion of natural resources, domestic violence, insufficient culturally relevant child care, and ill health. The IWN believes that indigenous people can resolve these problems and create a better future for themselves and coming generations by working within the framework of the visions of their elders.

The purpose of the IWN is "to alleviate poverty and its associated ills through the promotion of economic self-sufficiency and of appropriate environmental and natural resource management practices."[1] It supports "the empowerment of native women through their spiritual and cultural enlightenment and through the practice of their traditional ceremonial rituals," because IWN believes that the promotion of self-esteem and mental well-being among native women is a necessary prerequisite for achieving economic self-sufficiency. More specifically, the IWN's objectives are:

1. To support and strengthen the existing network of women working at a grassroots level, in urban and rural communities, in the Americas

---

* This summary was prepared using information from the Indigenous Women's Network Year End Report for 1992; *Indigenous Woman*, Vol. I, No. III; and other publications of the IWN.
   1. IWN INFORMATIONAL PAMPHLET (on file with the COLO. J. INT'L ENVTL. L. & POL'Y).

and the Pacific Basin; and to reach out to the communities where our network doesn't exist.

2. To gather and share information and resources; co-sponsor skills sharing and problem solving workshops; and work together to develop inter-tribal and international awareness through community education in the areas specific to each community.

3. To facilitate the on-going exchange of skills, experience and knowledge of urban and rural women in the Americas and the Pacific Basin to encourage growth and stimulate individual and community growth.

4. To work together with other Indigenous communities in the Americas and the Pacific Basin to remove the "cloak of invisibility" that covers Indigenous people, and even more so, Indigenous women.

5. To bring the problems, issues, concerns and viewpoints of Indigenous women to our rightful places within the international community.

6. To work within the United Nations Organization to guarantee that the problems, concerns, and issues of Indigenous women and children be voiced and our viewpoints expressed.[2]

II. PROJECTS

IWN publishes *Indigenous Woman*, a magazine that includes articles on current problems and struggles of indigenous women, interviews with elder women in indigenous communities, summaries of important events and meetings involving indigenous women, poetry and artwork by indigenous women, and articles focusing on the situation of indigenous women and their relationships with other peoples, their communities, and their families.

In 1992, the IWN participated in the United Nations Conference on Environment and Development in Brazil by submitting a preparatory briefing document on indigenous environmental issues in North America and by facilitating and promoting the testimony of a number of indigenous women who attended the conference.

Another IWN effort on the environmental front included participation in 1992 in a successful public relations campaign urging Governor Mario

---

2. *Id.*

Cuomo to cancel New York's contract with the James Bay Hydro-Electric Dams.

The IWN is also working to develop the Indigenous Environmental Network, a coalition of approximately fifty native grassroots organizations attempting to secure environmentally sound tribal governance policies. The Network hosts the annual Protecting Mother Earth Conference.

Perhaps IWN's most visible recent effort was to help sponsor and organize the Honor the Earth Concert Tour of the Indigo Girls, which generated $57,000 for IWN and four other environmental organizations. This tour included presentations by Winona LaDuke-Kapashesit and focused on a campaign for the clean-up of radioactive contamination at Point Hope, Alaska. Because this concert tour was so successful, IWN plans an even larger concert series in the near future.

International efforts of the IWN include serving as a North American advocate, raising funds for the development of a Venezuelan women's health clinic, and working closely with the Indigenous People's Alliance.

III. CONTACTS

The IWN Board of Directors includes Winona LaDuke-Kapashesit, Nilak Butler, Lea Foushee, Agnes Williams, Janet McCloud, Mililani Trask, Marsha Gomez, Jane Martin, and Ingrid Washinawatok-El Issa. The IWN National Office is at P.O. Box 174, Lake Elmo, MN 55042, (612) 770-3861.

Cultural Survival, Inc.[*]

Cultural Survival (CS) was founded in 1972 in order to collaborate with and protect indigenous peoples and ethnic minorities in their contacts with industrialized society. David Maybury-Lewis, president and founder of CS, describes the group's philosophy in this way:

> We insist that cultural differences are inherent in humanity, that protecting this human diversity enriches our common earth. Yet in the name of progress, native peoples lose their lands, their natural resources, and control over their lives. The consequences often are disease, destitution, and despair for them—and war and environmental damage for us all. CS believes that this destruction is not inevitable.

I. PURPOSE

Cultural Survival exists to respond to the difficulties that endangered societies face when dealing with dominant societies and the industrialized world. In these encounters, indigenous societies, which inhabit the last remaining wildernesses on earth, are increasingly threatened by outsiders who aggressively exploit their environment for oil, lumber, and other resources, abusing their rights and destroying their resource base in the process. CS believes that a group's culture gives a society its identity, allows it to comprehend its place in the world, and enables it to adapt to changing circumstances. Abuses of human rights, CS argues, generally occur after social erosion and economic marginalization have weakened a group's ability to defend itself. Thus, for the vast majority of peoples, cultural survival is intimately connected to personal survival.

II. PROJECTS

Cultural Survival implements its strategies for defending the group rights of indigenous peoples through field programs which provide funds and technical assistance for projects proposed and run by indigenous and minority groups.

Organization building is one of the issues upon which these projects focus. CS helps indigenous communities influence public policy and pursue effective legal strategies as they develop a unified voice for presenting their concerns in national and international forums.

---

[*] This summary was prepared using various documents submitted by Cultural Survival, Inc.

CS's resource management programs allow endangered peoples to use their natural resources without destroying the resoruce base. By maintaining a visible presence on the land, these efforts keep developers at bay. These small-scale efforts act as models for groups facing common threats and affect the policies of government development agencies.

Other CS programs focus on helping indigenous peoples and ethnic minorities participate in the market economy, thereby giving impoverished communities a source of income and building economic incentives for protecting regions that produce marketable goods. Cultural Survival Enterprises builds markets for products—such as tropical fruits, oils, and essences—that native communities can harvest in a sustainable manner, thereby supporting themselves while preserving natural resources. This branch of CS helped originate Rainforest Crunch™ and supplies the nuts used in the product.

CS is perhaps best known through its award-winning magazine, *Cultural Survival Quarterly*, which includes research gathered from field programs and provides a forum for information about indigenous peoples and ethnic minorities. The *Cultural Survival Quarterly*, however, is only one example of CS's many educational and public policy programs; others include: an action bulletin; information packets; slide shows; and workshops, briefings, and public talks for schools, community groups, and the media. CS also controls the Center for Cultural Survival, which operates two global information services that link indigenous organizations, advocates, and scholars.

III. CONTACTS

Cultural Survival is headquartered at 215 First Street, Cambridge, MA 02142, (617) 621-3818, FAX (617) 621-3814. Legal and public relations information may be obtained from Janet McGowan at that office.